Effective Schools for All

Effective Schools for All

edited by
Mel Ainscow

David Fulton Publishers
London

David Fulton Publishers Ltd
2 Barbon Close, London WC1N 3JX

First published in Great Britain by
David Fulton Publishers 1991

Note: The right of the contributors to be identified as the authors of their work
has been asserted by them in accordance with the Copyright, Designs and Patents
Act 1988.

British Library Cataloguing in Publication Data

Effective schools for all.
  1. Education
  I. Ainscow, Mel
  371

  ISBN 1-85346-164-4

Distributed exclusively in North America by:
Paul H. Brookes Publishing Co. Inc.,
P.O. Box 10624, Baltimore, Maryland 21285-0624

Typeset by Chapterhouse, The Cloisters, Formby, L37 3PX
Printed and bound in Great Britain by
Biddles Ltd, Guildford and King's Lynn

Contents

Contributors

MEL AINSCOW	Tutor in Special Educational Needs, Cambridge Institute of Education
NEVILLE BENNETT	Professor in the School of Education, University of Exeter
JOHN CLARKE	Senior Adviser (Monitoring and Evaluation), Suffolk Local Education Authority
ANN FERGUSSON	National Curriculum Team (Severe Learning Difficulties), Cambridge Institute of Education
BRUCE JOYCE	Director, Booksend Laboratories, Aptos, California
CARLENE MURPHY	Director of Staff Development, Staff Development Center, Augusta, Georgia
JOSEPH MURPHY	Dean of the Faculty of Education, Augusta College, Augusta, Georgia
DAVID REYNOLDS	School of Education, University of Wales
JUDY SEBBA	Coordinator, National Curriculum Development Team (Severe Learning Difficulties), Cambridge Institute of Education
BEVERLY SHOWERS	Director, Booksend Laboratories, Aptos, California
THOMAS M. SKRTIC	Professor of Special Education, University of Kansas

ROGER SLEE	Lecturer in Education and Policy Studies, Queensland University of Technology
LOUISE STOLL	Coordinator of Research and Assessment, Halton Board of Education, Ontario
JACQUELINE S. THOUSAND	Visiting Assistant Professor, Center for Developmental Disabilities, University of Vermont
RICHARD A. VILLA	Director of Instructional Services and Staff Development, Winooski School District, Vermont
MARGARET C. WANG	Professor of Education Psychology and Director, Temple University Center for Research in Human Development and Education, Philadelphia

Preface

The themes and format for this book took shape during the International Special Education Congress held in Cardiff, Wales, at the beginning of August 1990. As part of the congress, I led a two-day symposium around the topic 'Curriculum and Special Educational Needs' during which over 80 papers were presented.

My original idea was to edit a selection of the papers chosen to reflect the diversity of perspectives and approaches outlined during the symposium. However, the idea of special educational needs as a more fundamental aspect of school improvement became so important during the discussions that I came to the decision that this must become the main theme of the book. In particular the excellent keynote presentations made by Neville Bennett, David Reynolds, Tom Skrtic, Louise Stoll and Margaret Wang provided insights from a variety of perspectives as to how attempts to improve the quality of schooling for all pupils may well be the most advantageous way of responding to those who come to be described as having special educational needs.

Consequently, this book is far more than an account of the proceedings of an international symposium. Rather it represents a major resource of findings and ideas presented by educators from around the world that has the potential to inform and inspire a new orientation to educational difficulties. Furthermore this orientation has the capacity to improve the quality of schooling provided for *all* students. The book should, therefore, be of interest to everybody who is interested in improving schools.

Many colleagues and friends have provided help that has contributed to this volume and it is appropriate that I should offer them my thanks. First of all I must pay particular tribute to John

Garrett who coordinated the congress in Cardiff. I hope the book will be some form of reward to him for all his hard work. Similarly I must thank the members of the planning team who worked with me to develop the symposium programme: Lesley Dee, Tony Dessent, John Fish, Martyn Rouse and Judy Sebba. The ideas and inspiration of colleagues at the Cambridge Institute of Education are also present in these pages, particularly Susan Hart, David Hopkins and Mel West. Thanks are also due once again to Ann Sargeant who types my material with care and interest. Finally, of course, I must say a special thanks to all contributors. Each of them has provided an account that is worthy of a very wide audience; together they provide a powerful statement that must not be ignored.

Mel Ainscow
Cambridge
March 1991

Introduction and Overview

Mel Ainscow

The central argument of this book is that the dominant orientation to defining and attempting to meet special needs in education is to the disadvantage of the pupils involved. This represents a paradox. On the one hand, those of us engaged in the field of special education set out to provide positive discrimination to pupils perceived as being vulnerable; on the other hand our activities may have the effect of limiting opportunities for the very pupils whose needs we set out to serve. In other words, as Tony Dessent (1989) puts it, 'helping kids can harm them'.

In considering the implications of this argument in detail, the various authors challenge the basis of much existing special education provision. Indeed, they join others in questioning the continued existence of special education as a separate field of operation (for example, Barton, 1988; Gartner and Lipsky, 1987; Stainback and Stainback, 1984). They also outline a number of different orientations to educational difficulties and pinpoint some actions that need to be taken.

The debate to which this book contributes is not new. Already a number of writers have made significant contributions (for example, Bogdan and Kugelmass, 1984; Dunn, 1968; Dyson, 1990; Heshusius, 1989; Lilly, 1971; Tomlinson, 1982). A significant feature of this volume is the extent to which its contributors draw on ideas and findings from such a wide range of fields. Their use of information from psychology, sociology, political theory and curriculum studies, and the research on effective schools, school improvement, classroom practice and staff development, illustrate the value of studying educational policy and practice from varied perspectives. Indeed this is part of the message of the book – that the traditions of special education have tended to cut its practitioners off from sources of knowledge that are perceived as being outside its boundaries of interest. Thus the perspective has been narrow, leading to limited possibilities for development and, as a result, low expectations for improvement.

The chapters are arranged with reference to a series of interrelated themes. These are:

- the need to critique existing policy and practice
- approaches to school improvement
- classroom processes and effective teaching
- the role of staff development.

The first three chapters are linked by the idea that a critical analysis of existing policies and practice is an essential pre-condition for improvement (Barton, 1988). My introductory chapter examines the traditional assumptions that tend to dominate the special needs field and then presents strategies that are, in my view, central to all the recommendations made throughout the book. This analysis is further developed by Tom Skrtic who presents a detailed explanation as to how the organisation of schools creates students with special needs. Roger Slee then provides a powerful account of the evolution of a policy for integration in Victoria, Australia, showing how, despite good intentions, it led to a series of negative outcomes.

The focus of attention in the next three chapters is the improvement of schools. In Chapter 4 Louise Stoll provides an account of the evidence of research about school effectiveness and describes how this is being used to improve the quality of schooling for all students in one school board in Canada. Whilst maintaining the sense of optimism, David Reynolds includes in his chapter a series of anecdotes that illustrate the difficulties that can arise during attempts at school improvement. John Clarke uses his perspective as a local authority inspector in England to argue that criteria for evaluating school effectiveness should take account of the needs of all pupils.

Chapters 7, 8 and 9 continue the theme of school improvement but adopt a more classroom-focused approach. The contributors each describe outcomes of extensive research in different parts of the world to find ways of making classrooms more responsive to the increased diversity of students faced by teachers. Neville Bennett's work is based upon extensive classroom observation over many years in the United Kingdom. It is interesting to compare his findings with those of another eminent researcher, Margaret Wang. In her chapter she presents a synthesis of an extensive range of studies and explains how this knowledge base can be used to develop forms of teaching that can provide for student diversity in mainstream settings. The work of Jacqueline Thousand and Richard Villa in Vermont provides further illustration of how schools and classrooms can be organised in ways that will promote the learning of all students.

The concluding chapters emphasise the idea of staff development as a means of improving the quality of schooling. Bruce Joyce and his colleagues explain how an intensive staff development initiative has had a significant impact upon the culture of schools in disadvantaged parts of Georgia in the USA. Their approach seems to lead to impressive improvements in both the academic achievements of students *and* their social conduct. Influenced by the work of Bruce Joyce and Beverly Showers (1988), Judy Sebba and Ann Fergusson provide an encouraging account of the ways in which staff development approaches are being used to widen curriculum opportunities for students with severe learning difficulties.

In the final chapter I provide a summary of the main recommendations that emerge as a result of reading the rich accounts presented by the contributors.

References

Barton, L. (1988) 'The politics of special educational needs: An introduction', in Barton, L. (Ed.) *The Politics of Special Educational Needs.* London: Falmer Press.

Bogdan, R. and Kugelmass, J. (1984) 'Case studies of mainstreaming: A symbolic interactionist approach to special schooling', in Barton, L. and Tomlinson, S. (Eds) *Special Education and Social Interests.* London: Croom Helm.

Dessent, T. (1989) 'The paradox of the special school', in Baker, D. and Bovair, K. (Eds) *Making the Special Schools Ordinary?*, Vol. 1. London: Falmer Press.

Dunn, L. M. (1968) 'Special education for the mildly retarded – Is much of it justifiable?', *Exceptional Children,* 35, 1:5–22.

Dyson, A. (1990) 'Special educational needs and the concept of change', *Oxford Review of Education,* 16, 1:55–66.

Gartner, A. and Lipsky, D. K. (1987) 'Beyond special education: Towards a quality system for all students', *Harvard Educational Review,* 54, 2:186–94.

Heshusius, L. (1989) 'The Newtonian mechanistic paradigm, special education, and contours of alternatives: An overview', *Journal of Learning Disabilities,* 22, 7:403–21.

Joyce, B. and Showers, B. (1988) *Student Achievement Through Staff Development.* London: Longman.

Lilly, M. S. (1971) 'A training based model for special education', *Exceptional Children,* **37**, 745–9.

Stainback, W. and Stainback, S. (1984) 'A rationale for the merger of special and regular education', *Exceptional Children,* **51**: 102–11.

Tomlinson, S. (1982) *The Sociology of Special Education.* London: Routledge.

CHAPTER 1

Effective Schools for All: An Alternative Approach to Special Needs in Education

Mel Ainscow

The purposes of this introductory chapter are to outline the case, as I see it, for a reconceptualisation of what we mean by educational difficulty and to make some general proposals as to the actions that need to be taken. The chapter also provides a conceptual framework within which readers will be able to consider the arguments and proposals made in subsequent chapters.

A central theme of this chapter that is current throughout the book is the view that we know more than we use. In other words, as Ron Edmonds (cited in Lezotte, 1989) suggests:

> We can, whenever and wherever we choose, successfully teach all the children whose schooling is of interest to us . . . . Whether we do it or not must finally depend on how we feel about the fact that we haven't done it so far.

Together the chapters in this book provide insights as to why school systems in different parts of the world have so far been unsuccessful in teaching all children. They also provide powerful evidence as to how this situation can be changed.

The dominant perspective

Central to the ways in which educational difficulties have been conceptualised is the view that they arise because of the limitations and/or disabilities of particular pupils. In other words, certain children are perceived as having things wrong with them that make it

1

difficult for them to participate in the normal curriculum of schools (Bogdan and Kugelmass, 1984; Mercer, 1973). Three approaches have resulted from this viewpoint. Current provision tends to consist of an amalgam of these approaches. They are as follows:

(1) *The withdrawal approach*
   Here those pupils who it is felt will not cope with the demands of the mainstream curriculum are withdrawn for at least part of the time to a special class or school. The aim is to provide learning experiences that are more appropriate in that they take account of the limitations of the pupils.

(2) *The remedial approach*
   This term is unfashionable these days but the approach it implies is still evident in many schools. It can take a number of forms and involve a variety of strategies. Essentially it attempts to provide forms of inter-vention that will overcome or compensate deficits within children.

(3) *The maintreaming approach*
   In this approach the main emphasis is on making modifications in the curriculum to allow access for children regarded as being exceptional. It may, for example, involve the provision of an individualised learning programme, the adaption of classroom materials, or additional adult support for the child.

It is important to note that despite the differences between these three approaches they each continue to perceive the problem as being the child's. As a result, they exclude from consideration causal factors that may lie in larger social, political and organisational processes that are external to the individual (Skrtic, 1987). Furthermore, the organis-ation and curriculum of schools remain broadly the same since they are assumed to be appropriate for the great majority of children. The provision of various forms of special education confirms that problems arise because some children are special. In so doing this helps to maintain the status quo of schooling.

There are a number of negative outcomes that can arise from this dominant perspective and these have been well documented (for example, Ainscow, 1989b; Algozzine, 1977; Anderson and Pellicer, 1990; Apter, 1982; Booth, 1988; Hobbs, 1975; Mercer, 1973; Rhodes, 1970; Schrag and Divorky, 1975; Swap, 1978). In summary, the evidence suggests that these traditional approaches work to the dis-advantage of the pupils concerned in the following ways:

(1) The segregation process and inevitable labelling with which it is associated have negative effects upon the attitudes and expectations of pupils, teachers and parents.

(2)   The presence of designated specialists encourages teachers to pass on to others responsibility for children they regard as being special.

(3)   Resources that might otherwise be used to provide more flexible and responsive forms of schooling are channelled into separate provision.

(4)   The nature of the educational experiences provided is often characterised by narrowness of opportunity and low levels of achievement.

An alternative perspective

Since I regard these traditional approaches as limiting opportunities for some children, I believe that school systems must find better ways of conceptualising and responding to educational difficulties. Furthermore this has to be seen first and foremost as an ethical issue that has to be addressed by all those involved in the business of education. We must ask the question, how can we continue to conceptualise educational difficulties in ways that may harm children? What we should be seeking are ways of defining educational difficulties that recognise and respect the complexities of their causes and, in turn, point to more positive forms of intervention.

It seems reasonable to assume that when children experience significant difficulties in schools, they arise as a result of the interaction of a complex range of factors. In practice, however, the problem is a curriculum one. What we are witnessing is the inability of a teacher or group of teachers to provide classroom experiences that are meaningful and relevant given the interests, experiences, and existing skills and knowledge of particular children (Ainscow and Tweddle, 1988). In making this statement it should not be assumed that I am seeking to replace 'child blaming' with 'teacher blaming' (Reynolds, 1988). We have to recognise that the capacity of teachers to provide appropriate learning opportunities for their pupils is constrained by wider school structures and systems (Bottery, 1988; Gitlin, 1987), some of which may be imposed from outside the school (Hartnett and Naish, 1990).

In attempting to conceptualise educational difficulty in a more positive way we can more usefully see pupils experiencing difficulty as indicators of the need for reform. They point to the need to improve schooling in ways that will enable them to achieve success. Furthermore, an observation of their responses and a consideration of their view points may suggest ways in which improvements might be achieved. It is worth adding at this stage that I believe that such reforms would be to the benefit of all pupils. Consequently the aim is *effective schools for all*.

4

Effective schooling

What are the features of such an approach and how might it be achieved? I will start with the features. The now extensive research on effective schools and teaching provides a useful source of ideas as to the sorts of features we should be seeking. For example, Edmonds (1982) has noted the following features that seem to be characteristic of exceptional schools:

(1) The principal's leadership and attention to the quality of instruction.
(2) A pervasive and broadly understood instructional focus.
(3) An orderly, safe climate conducive to teaching and learning.
(4) Teacher behaviours that convey the expectation that all students are expected to obtain at least minimum mastery.
(5) The use of measures of pupil achievement as the basis for programme evaluation.

These rather general features have been confirmed by an impressive range of other studies (for example, Bickel and Bickel, 1986; Lezotte, 1989; Mortimore *et al.*, 1986; Purkey and Smith, 1983; Rutter *et al.*, 1979; Stoll, Chapter 4, this volume). They are perhaps summed up by Rutter who, when commenting on what makes good schools good, noted that it is

> Schools which set good standards, where the teachers provide good models of behaviour, where they (the pupils) are praised and given responsibility, where general conditions are good and where the lessons are well-conducted.

It is interesting to compare these findings from research about effective schools with those of Ainscow and Muncey (1989) who analysed data arising from their project to develop special needs practice in mainstream schools. They noted that the following features seemed to be common to those schools experiencing success within the project:

(1) Effective leadership from a headteacher who is committed to meeting the needs of all pupils.
(2) Confidence amongst staff that they can deal with children's individual needs.
(3) A sense of optimism that all pupils can succeed.
(4) Arrangements for supporting individual members of staff.
(5) A commitment to provide a broad and balanced range of curriculum experiences for all children.
(6) Systematic procedures for monitoring and reviewing progress.

The common strands between these findings and those from the general literature on effective schools provide further justification for the orientation which I am seeking to encourage in this chapter.

Moving on from effective schooling to effective teaching, there again seems to be a general consensus of findings within the research literature (for example, Bennett, Chapter 7, this volume; Bickel and Bickel, 1986; Brophy, 1983; Rosenshine, 1983; Wang, Chapter 8, this volume). A useful synthesis of the findings of this research is provided by Porter and Brophy (1988). They suggest that this provides a picture of effective teachers as semi-autonomous professionals who:

- are clear about their instructional goals
- are knowledgeable about their content and the strategies for teaching it
- communicate to their students what is expected of them – and why
- make expert use of existing instructional materials in order to devote more time to practices that enrich and clarify the content
- are knowledgeable about their students, adapting instruction to their needs and anticipating misconceptions in their existing knowledge
- teach students metacognitive strategies and give them opportunities to master them
- address higher- as well as lower-level cognitive objectives
- monitor students' understanding by offering regular appropriate feedback
- integrate their instruction with that in other subject areas
- accept responsibility for student outcomes
- are thoughtful and reflective about their practice.

Once again it is interesting to compare these findings with those of Ainscow and Muncey (1989) whose concern, it will be recalled, was with policies for meeting special needs in ordinary schools. Within their project the most effective teachers:

- emphasise the importance of meaning
- set tasks that are realistic and challenging
- ensure that there is progression in children's work
- provide a variety of learning experiences
- give pupils opportunities to choose
- have high expectations
- create a positive atmosphere
- provide a consistent approach
- recognise the efforts and achievements of their pupils
- organise resources to facilitate learning
- encourage pupils to work cooperatively
- monitor progress and provide regular feedback.

The evidence seems to support the view that teachers said to be successful in meeting special needs are to a large extent using strategies that help all pupils to experience success. Indeed we are probably referring to the very same teachers. Thus my argument is that what is now needed is not attempts to define special teaching methods for special children, but effective teaching and learning for all children. As Louise Stoll argues in her chapter, 'in an effective school with quality classroom instruction, all children, irrespective of social class differences, can make more progress than all children in an ineffective school with poor teaching methods'.

Improving schools and classrooms

Examining the research findings summarised so far seems to imply that improvements in teaching and learning are relatively straightforward. If we know broadly what good schools and effective teachers are like, doesn't this provide a recipe for improvement? This reminds me of the story of the centipede who, when asked to consider how he walked successfully with so many legs, immediately tripped up and fell over. Schools and classrooms are complex environments involving a range of unpredictable interacting factors. Consequently, bringing about improvements is itself a complex and at times frustrating business. As we know, change, particularly when it involves new ways of thinking and behaving, is difficult and time-consuming. Fullan (1982) argues that for it to be achieved successfully, change has to be understood and accepted by those involved. Understanding and acceptance take time and need encouragement. These problems are made even more complex in educational contexts by what Iano (1986) refers to as 'the inarticulate component of practice', in other words, the practical knowledge that is acquired only through practice and contact with other practitioners. It is developments in this knowledge that form the basis of improvements in classroom practice.

This line of argument leads me to part company with some of the North American writers associated with what has come to be called the 'Regular Education Initiative' (REI) (for example, Reynolds, 1988; Wang and Zollers, 1990; Wang et al., 1986). Their approach shares many of my assumptions and beliefs. For example, Hallahan et al. (1988) suggest that the REI probably has its roots in earlier anti-labelling and deinstitutionalisation movements. They also quote Madeleine C. Will, former Assistant Secretary for the US Office of Special Education and Rehabilitative Services as stating that the 'so-called "pull-out" approach to the educational difficulties of students with learning problems has failed in many instances to meet the educational needs of these students and has created, however unwittingly, barriers to their successful education'.

In an important paper that has influenced the development of the REI, Wang *et al*. (1986) recommended that practices from special and general education be combined into a coordinated system. This 'would combine methods that have a strong research record of effectiveness with comprehensive systems of instruction that have evolved from both general and special education'. Furthermore, they requested that federal government, in cooperation with state and local education systems, should institute experimental trials of 'more integrated forms of education for students who are unjustifiably segregated in separate programmes'.

The idea of the REI continues to be a source of debate in the special education literature. For example, Kauffman *et al*. (1988) question some of its assumptions; McKinney and Hocutt (1988) argue that the initiative is characterised by policy advocacy rather than policy analysis; Hallahan *et al*. (1988) are critical of much of the research evidence that is used to promote the REI, noting that it has so many methodological problems that it is impossible to draw firm conclusions; whilst Bryan *et al*. (1988) and Schumaker and Deshler (1988) feel that the approach does not take account of the organisational and curricular constraints of secondary schools.

My differences with the proponents of the REI are from a different perspective. They can be summarised in terms of the following arguments: (1) Many of those who argue in favour of the REI seem to have a simplistic view of how the practice of teaching can be improved. Their approach is simply to train teachers in techniques validated by empirical research. The task is seen essentially as a technical one. (2) The approach does not take account of wider social, political and organisational factors that influence and constrain the work of teachers. As a result there tends to be a passive acceptance of curriculum and assessment policies which may in themselves contribute to the creation of educational difficulties for some pupils.

The proposals I wish to make, therefore, share many of the assumptions and aspirations of the REI, and acknowledge the value of the research evidence upon which it is founded. They differ in that they seek to take greater account of the complexities involved in changing practice and the wider influences that impact upon the work of teachers. In general terms the approach I wish to promote is based upon two broad strategies. These are to do with the development of:

(1)   schools as problem-solving organisations; and
(2)   teachers as reflective practitioners.

I will look at each of these strategies in turn.

Schools as problem-solving organisations

It is my assumption that problems and problem-solving are a central part of the process of education. Schools should be places where teachers and pupils are engaged in activities that help them to become more successful at understanding and dealing with the problems they meet. In this sense problems that occur in schools can be seen as opportunities for learning. Consequently, the first strategy in seeking to make schools more responsive to the needs of all children is to find ways of gearing them to problem-solving. In other words, I want schools to be organisations within which everybody, both pupils and teachers, is engaged cooperatively in the task of learning.

Unfortunately, too often schools seem to inhibit cooperation and problem-solving. For example, Gitlin (1987) has investigated the impact of organisational and curriculum structures on the work of teachers. His view is that 'common school structures encourage a teacher that emphasises management and technical skills, isolates teachers from one another, and "disconnects" them from their students'. Skrtic (1987) characterises schools as professional bureau-cracies that are unsuited to the creation of divergent thinking. Rather, such organisations tend to use what Mintzberg (1979) has called 'pigeonholing', a process by which problems that occur are matched to one of a series of existing standard responses. Mintzberg suggests that a common problem associated with pigeonholing is that 'the professional confuses the needs of his clients with the skills he has to offer them'.

If we are to find ways of encouraging collaborative problem-solving we will need to be sensitive to the nature of schools as organisations. Most of all we have to remind ourselves that schools are not simply buildings, timetables and curriculum plans. First and foremost they are relationships and interactions between people. Consequently, a successful school is one in which the relationships and interactions are facilitated and coordinated in order that the people involved can achieve their common mission. Commenting on effective schools and school change, Skrtic (1987) argues that 'at bottom, the difference is people. People acting on their values and affecting what the organisation can be'. Or, as Clark *et al.* (1984) suggest, 'The search for excellence in schools is the search for excellence in people'.

Why, then, is the idea of groups of people working collaboratively to solve problems and achieve a common mission so difficult to achieve in schools? The work of Weick (1976; 1985) may help to make sense of this issue. He suggests that schools are 'loosely coupled systems' unlike successful business organisations that tend to be more tightly coupled. The loose coupling within schools occurs because they consist of units, processes, actions and individuals that tend to operate in isolation from one another. It is encouraged by the goal ambiguity that characterises schooling. Despite the rhetoric of curriculum aims and objectives, schools consist of groups of people who may have very different values and, indeed, beliefs about the purposes of schooling. To illustrate this point, Weick uses the metaphor of a soccer game in which players enter and leave the game at will, and attempt to kick the ball towards several goals that are scattered haphazardly around a circular pitch.

Johnson and Johnson (1989) suggest that schools can be constructed in one of three ways: individualistically, competitively or co-operatively. In schools with an individualistic form of organisation teachers work alone to achieve goals unrelated to the goals of their colleagues. Consequently, there is no sense of common purpose, little sharing of expertise and limited support for individuals. Furthermore, such schools often move towards a more competitive form of organisation.

In a competitive system teachers strive to do better than their colleagues, recognising that their fate is negatively linked. The career progress of one teacher is likely to be enhanced by the failure of others within the school. In this win–lose struggle to succeed it is almost inevitable that individuals will celebrate the difficulties experienced by their colleagues since these are likely to increase their own chance of success.

Clearly the organisational approach I wish to encourage is one that emphasises cooperation. The aim should be to create a more tightly coupled system. In such a school staff strive for mutual benefit recognising that they all share a common purpose and, indeed, a common fate. Individuals know that their performance can be influenced positively by the performance of others. This being the case, individuals feel proud when a colleague succeeds and is recognised for professional competence. As Johnson and Johnson argue, 'A clear cooperative structure is the first prerequisite of an effective school'.

A school that is based upon a cooperative structure is likely to make good use of the expertise of all its personnel, provide sources of stimulation and enrichment that will foster their professional development, and encourage positive attitudes to the introduction of new ways of working. In short, it provides the culture necessary for helping teachers to take responsibility for the learning of all their pupils. The chapters by Joyce and his colleagues, Stoll, and Thousand and Villa, in this volume, provide excellent accounts of how such a school culture may be developed.

Having said all that, a word of warning is necessary. Establishing a culture of cooperation within a school is not a simple matter, not least because it is necessary to do so within a format which does not reduce 'teacher discretion' (Skrtic, 1988). Teaching is a complex activity, as I have already argued. Consequently, individual teachers must have sufficient autonomy to make flexible decisions that take account of the individual needs of their pupils and the uniqueness of every encounter that occurs. The aim, therefore, must be to create a more tightly coupled system without losing loose coupling benefits (West and Ainscow, 1991). Skrtic develops this argument in more detail in Chapter 2, this volume.

One significant way in which a culture of collaboration can be developed in schools is through staff development. In this context I am using this term to refer to activities or processes that are intended to improve the skills, attitudes, understandings or performance of teachers (Fullan, 1990). Elsewhere I have described how collaborative approaches to staff development are being used as a central element of an international teacher education project organised by Unesco to help teachers accommodate the diversity of needs within their classes (Ainscow, 1990; 1991). The work of Bruce Joyce and his colleagues (as described in Chapter 10, this volume) in developing the idea of 'peer coaching' as a means of setting up partnerships that can help teachers to implement new ways of working is of particular significance in this respect. My colleague Judy Sebba is also working on a similar basis within a project that is aimed at finding ways of enabling pupils with severe learning difficulties to participate in the National Curriculum (see Chapter 11, this volume).

At this stage in the development of my argument it has to be noted that despite the case that has been made for greater cooperation within schools there is pressure to move in a different direction. Competition between schools and within schools is currently seen as a means of improving educational standards (Sexton, 1988). This rationale is based on a view of education as a means of enhancing life chances, status and employment in the adult world (Hartnett and Naish, 1990). Furthermore, schools are increasingly seen as input–output machines in which children are working units that can service the technology of society, helping it to make a profit. In such a view of schooling, Bottery (1988) argues, children 'are merely means to an end, just as the teachers in an organisation are as well. The children are the future parts for the industrial machine, the teachers are their shapers and oilers'.

An emphasis on competition is consistent with this approach to education. Within it, one child's educational success is achieved at the expense of another's failure. The tension this creates takes us back to the quotation from Edmonds with which I began this chapter. How do we feel about the fact that we are not successfully teaching *all* children?

Teachers as reflective practitioners

One of the key outcomes of schools that are organised to provide stimulation and support for teachers in order that they can collaborate in problem-solving is that they encourage teachers to adopt a reflective attitude towards their own practice. Teachers are encouraged to learn from experience and experiment with new ways of working alongside and with their pupils and colleagues.

This approach to the development of professional practice represents a very different orientation from the traditional pattern of teacher education. Traditionally teacher education, particularly in the special needs field, has been seen as a search for solutions to solve a technical task (Iano, 1986). Consequently, teachers attend courses and workshops to learn about theories and techniques derived from research in order that they can then use these to inform the development of their teaching.

The emphasis within this orientation is on the use of the findings of experimental research studies. Typically these involve the study of the relationship between sets of variables with a view to making generalisations that can be applied across settings (Harre, 1981; House *et al.*, 1989). So, for example, research might consider the impact of teachers' use of praise upon the social conduct of pupils. The aim would be to demonstrate relationships between the two variables, praise and social conduct, in order to prove the existence of laws that would apply in the classrooms of all teachers.

Such investigations are based upon a number of assumptions that are matters of dispute (Barton, 1988; Heshusius, 1989; Iano, 1986; Schindele, 1985; Skrtic, 1986). In particular, they assume that variables such as praise and social conduct can be defined in ways that could be said to apply across settings, times and people. The problems with this are that classrooms are complex environments, and inter-actions between teachers and pupils are unique, so that the idea of such generalised interpretations are always subject to doubt (Bassey, 1980).

Whilst special education was framed as a series of technical tasks concerned with finding solutions to the problems of children perceived as sharing similar difficulties, this approach to the improvement of practice seemed to provide a reasonable fit. Although issues of research methodology, not least to do with rigour, continued to encourage argument, the idea of seeking to establish laws of cause and effect that could be used to make generalisations about classroom life seemed appropriate.

However, the perspective on educational difficulties taken in this chapter points to the need for a very different approach to the improvement of practice. My concern is to find approaches that encourage teachers to learn from their own experience, taking note of evidence from elsewhere certainly, but recognising the importance of the inarticulate component of practice that is developed through a more intuitive form of learning (Iano, 1986). Consequently, I want teachers to analyse and reflect upon their own classrooms. Their concern should be with particular children as they interact with particular tasks and processes. The idea of establishing research-based predictions across people, time and contexts is, therefore, to say the least inappropriate. Rather, what is needed is for each teacher to seek deeper understandings of the nature and outcomes of particular educational events and situations. In this sense the reality of classroom encounters is seen as something that is created in the minds of the people involved rather than something that can be defined objectively, observed systematically and measured accurately (Lincoln and Guba, 1985).

In the light of this argument I wish to promote forms of teacher education that encourage teachers to take responsibility for their own professional learning. Such approaches, as well as having a resonance with teaching as an activity, are also a means of helping teachers to recognise and respond to the wider pressures within which they have to operate. As Heron (1981) suggests, 'persons, as autonomous beings, have a moral right to participate in decisions that claim to generate knowledge about them. Such a right . . . protects them . . . from being managed and manipulated'.

In my own work recently I have been seeking to introduce teachers involved in various forms of inservice education to approaches that are derived from and based upon the analysis presented in this chapter (for example, Ainscow, 1989a; 1989b; 1990; 1991). In particular, course participants are introduced to approaches that will be useful in their everyday work, encouraging them to see themselves as 'reflective practitioners', skilled in learning from their own experience (Schon, 1983; 1987). Consequently, the work they undertake tends to take the form of investigations into aspects of their own practice.

This work has been influenced by a number of groups of writers including those concerned with the idea of the teacher as researcher (for example, Hopkins, 1985; Stenhouse, 1975; Walker, 1985); the action research movement (for example, Elliott, 1981; Kemmis and McTaggart, 1981); those who argue for cooperative inquiry (for example, Heron, 1981; Lather, 1986; Reason, 1988); and evaluators and researchers who base their work on the notion of naturalistic inquiry (for example, Lincoln and Guba, 1985; Merriam, 1988; Skrtic, 1985; Woods, 1986). Across this diverse literature a number of common strands emerge which have influenced my work. They include:

(1) Forms of inquiry are used that encourage teachers to examine particular events or processes as a whole and in their natural settings.

(2) The design of the inquiry is seen as being emergent; that is to say, the directions and forms of an investigation are decided upon as information is collected.

(3) The teacher is seen as the primary 'instrument' for gathering information, using natural methods of information-gathering such as observation and discussion.

(4) Wherever possible inquiry is seen as a collaborative process involving colleagues and pupils.

(5) Through processes of data analysis and interpretation, theories emerge from information that is collected. This is usually referred to as 'grounded theory' in that it is seen as being grounded in the data (Glaser and Strauss, 1967).

(6) Accounts are usually presented as case studies with, where possible, some attempt to suggest tentative applications of the findings to other settings.

Some accounts of work carried out by teachers based on these ideas are provided in Ainscow (1989a). It is also worth adding that the idea of teachers working collaboratively to investigate and develop their own practice is an increasing emphasis in the teacher education field (for example, Berlak and Berlak, 1987; Day, 1987; Smyth, 1989).

My colleague David Tweddle and I have provided a framework that may be useful to teachers as they review their practice (Ainscow and Tweddle, 1988). The focus of it is the question which is implicit in the argument that is presented throughout this chapter. It is, *how can we help all pupils to succeed in the classroom*? We choose to call the approach 'classroom evaluation' in order to emphasise the importance of gathering information about how pupils respond to the curriculum as it is enacted. The suggested focus for classroom evaluation is areas of decision making over which teachers have a significant influence. Broadly speaking these areas are:

> *Objectives*, i.e., are objectives being achieved?
> *Tasks and activities*, i.e., are tasks and activities being completed?
> *Classroom arrangements*, i.e., do classroom arrangements make effective use of available resources?

Also, since unintended outcomes are important, a further question is added:

> What else is happening?

Given the aim of making classroom evaluation a continuous process and the recognition that pupils have a significant role to play in assessing and recording their own progress, the intention is that these four questions should provide a broad agenda within which teachers and pupils can reflect upon the encounters in which they are engaged and the difficulties they experience. The emphasis is on collaboration and negotiation as a means of taking account of the individuality of pupils. This helps to ensure that the pupils have a greater understanding of the nature and purpose of their classroom tasks.

This approach therefore represents a new broader orientation to assessment and recording, which attempts to gather information about the development of individual pupils within a given context. Furthermore, it assumes that it is sensible to monitor all aspects of that context with a view to making and amending decisions in an attempt to help all pupils experience success. In particular, the aim is to ensure that the curriculum, as it is planned and enacted, takes account of individual pupils, their interests, skills, knowledge and previous experience, and is understood by all those involved.

Proposing this wide perspective has major implications for the way in which the education service provides support to youngsters experiencing difficulties in learning. It requires that the focus of assessment and recording should be the child in his or her normal classroom environment; that information should be collected on a continuous basis; that pupils should have a key role in reflecting upon their own learning; and that the overall aim should be to improve the quality of teaching and learning provided for *all* pupils.

Conclusion

In this chapter I have provided a critique of the predominant perspective on special needs in education, suggesting that despite good intentions it is often to the disadvantage of the pupils it sets out to help. My support is for the new, wider perspectives that have emerged in recent years but which have, so far, had limited impact upon the organisation of provision and practice. In particular I have argued that this new perspective is more likely to be achieved in schools that create a collaborative context for problem-solving and encourage teachers to take responsibility for the development of their practice. The chapters in this book provide a rich source of ideas as to how the culture of schools can be helped to develop along these lines.

As I write, the situation in my own country is such that as a result of recent legislation (the 1988 Education Act) the prospects for the proposals I am making are not good. Despite encouraging statements about curriculum entitlement for all children, the more specific proposals related to the introduction of the National Curriculum and procedures for assessment seem likely to reinforce the idea of schools as 'sorting offices', preparing young people for particular roles in what is still a class-based society. The question remains, therefore, how do we feel about the fact that we are not successfully teaching *all* children?

Note

I would like to acknowledge the influence of my colleagues and friends Susan Hart, David Hopkins, Jim Muncey, Tom Skrtic and David Tweddle in the writing of this chapter.

16

References

Ainscow, M. (1989a) (Ed.) *Special Education in Change*. London: David Fulton Publishers.

Ainscow, M. (1989b) 'Developing the special school curriculum: where next?', in Baker, D. and Bovair, K. (Eds) *Making the Special School Ordinary?* London: Falmer Press.

Ainscow, M. (1990) 'Special needs in the classroom: the development of a teacher education resource pack', *International Journal of Special Education*, **5**, 1:13–20.

Ainscow, M. (1991) 'Towards effective schools for all: an account of the rationale of the Unesco teacher education project, "Special Needs in the Classroom"', in Upton, G. (Ed.) *Staff Training and Special Educational Needs: Innovatory Strategies and Models of Delivery*. London: David Fulton Publishers.

Ainscow, M. and Muncy, J. (1989) *Meeting Individual Needs in the Primary School*. London: David Fulton Publishers.

Ainscow, M. and Tweddle, D. A. (1988) *Encouraging Classroom Success*. London: David Fulton Publishers.

Algozzine, M. (1977) 'The emotionally disturbed child: disturbed or disturbing?' *Journal of Abnormal Child Psychology*, **5**, 2:205–11.

Anderson, L. W. and Pellicer, L. O. (1990) 'Synthesis of research on compensatory and remedial education', *Educational Leadership*, **48**, 1:10–16.

Apter, S. J. (1982) *Troubled Children, Troubled Systems*. New York: Pergamon.

Barton, L. (1988) 'Research and practice: the need for alternative perspectives', in Barton, L. (Ed.) *The Politics of Special Educational Needs*. London: Falmer Press.

Bassey, M. (1980) 'Crocodiles eat children', *CARN Bulletin No. 4*. Cambridge, Cambridge Institute of Education.

Berlak, A. and Berlak, H. (1987) 'Teachers working with teachers to transform schools', in Smyth, J. (Ed.) *Educating Teachers: Changing the Nature of Pedagogical Knowledge*. London: Falmer Press.

Bickel, W. E. and Bickel, D. D. (1986) 'Effective schools, classrooms and instruction: implications for special education', *Exceptional Children*, **52**, 6:489–500.

Bogdan, R. and Kugelmass, J. (1984) 'Case studies of mainstreaming: a symbolic interactionist approach to special schooling', in Barton, L. and Tomlinson, S. (Eds) *Special Education and Social Interests*. London: Croom Helm.

Booth, T. (1988) 'Challenging conceptions of integration', in Barton, L. (Ed.) *The Politics of Special Educational Needs*. London: Falmer Press.

Bottery, M. P. (1988) 'Educational management: an ethical critique', *Oxford Review of Education*, **14**, 3:341–51.

Brophy, J. E. (1983) 'Classroom organisation and management', *The Elementary School Journal'*, **82**:266–85.

Bryan, T. *et al.* (1988) 'Implications of the learning disabilities definition for the Regular Education Initiative', *Journal of Learning Disabilities*, **21**, 1:23–8.

Clark, D. L., Lotto, L. S. and Astuto, T. A. (1984) 'Effective schools and school improvement: a comparative analysis of two lines of inquiry', *Educational Administration Quarterly*, **20**, 3:41–68.

Day, C. (1987) 'Professional learning through collaborative in-service activity', in Smyth, J. (Ed.) *Educating Teachers: Changing the Nature of Pedagogical Knowledge*. London: Falmer Press.

Dessent, T. (1989) 'The paradox of the special school', in Baker, D. and Bovair, K. (Eds) *Making the Special School Ordinary?* (Volume 1). London: Falmer Press.

Edmonds, R. (1982) 'Programs of school improvement: an overview', *Educational Leadership*, **40**, 3:4–11.

Elliott, J. (1981) *Action Research: A Framework for Self Evaluation in Schools*. Cambridge Institute of Education, mimeo.

Fullan, M. (1982) *The Meaning of Educational Change*. New York: Teachers College Press.

Fullan, M. (1990) 'Staff development, innovation and institutional development', in Joyce, B. (Ed.) *Changing School Culture Through Staff Development*. Association for Supervision and Curriculum Development Yearbook.

Gitlin, A. D. (1987) 'Common school structures and teacher behaviour', in Smyth, J. (Ed.) *Educating Teachers: Changing the Nature of Pedagogical Knowledge*. London: Falmer Press.

Glaser, B. G. and Strauss, A. L. (1967) *The Discovery of Grounded Theory*. Chicago: Aldine.

Hallahan, D. P., Keller, C. E., McKinney, J. D., Lloyd, J. W. and Bryan, T. (1988) 'Examining the research base of the Regular Education Initiative', *Journal of Learning Disabilities*, **21**, 1:29–35.

Harre, R. (1981) 'The positivist-empiricist approach and its alternative', in Reason, P. and Rowan, J. (Eds) *Human Inquiry*. Chichester: Wiley.

Hartnett, A. and Naish, M. (1990) 'The sleep of reason breeds monsters: the birth of a statutory curriculum in England and Wales', *Journal of Curriculum Studies*, **22**, 1:1–16.

Heron, R. (1981) 'Philosophical basis for a new paradigm', in Reason, P. and Rowan, J. (Eds) *Human Inquiry*. Chichester: Wiley.

Heshusius, L. (1989) 'The Newtonian mechanistic paradigm, special education, and contours of alternatives: an overview', *Journal of Learning Disabilities*, **22**, 7:403–21.

Hobbs, N. (1975) *The Futures of Children: Categories and Their Consequences*. San Francisco: Jossey-Bass.

Hopkins, D. (1985) *A Teacher's Guide to Classroom Research*. Milton Keynes: Open University.

House, E., Lapan, S. and Mathison, S. (1989) 'Teacher inference', *Cambridge Journal of Education*, **19**, 1:53–8.

Iano, R. P. (1986) 'The study and development of teaching: with implications for the advancement of special education', *Remedial and Special Education*, **7**, 5:50–61.

Johnson, D. W. and Johnson, R. T. (1989) *Leading the Cooperative School*. Edina: Interaction Book Co.

18

Kauffman, J. M. *et al.* (1988) 'Arguable assumptions underlying the Regular Education Initiative', *Journal of Learning Disabilities*, **21**, 1:6–11.

Kemmis, S. and McTaggart, R. (1981) *The Action Research Planner*. Victoria: Deakin University Press.

Lather, P. (1986) 'Research as praxis', *Harvard Educational Review*, **56**, 3:257–77.

Lezotte, L. W. (1989) 'School improvement based on the effective schools research', in Lipsky, D. K. and Gartner, A. (Eds) *Beyond Separate Education: Quality Education for All*. Baltimore: Paul H. Brookes.

Lilly, M. S. (1971) 'A training based model for special education', *Exceptional Children*, **37**:745–9.

Lincoln, Y. S. and Guba, E. G. (1985) *Naturalistic Inquiry*. Beverly Hills: Sage.

McKinney, J. D. and Hocutt, A. M. (1988) 'The need for policy analysis in evaluating the Regular Education Initiative', *Journal of Learning Disabilities*, **21**, 1:12–18.

Mercer, J. (1973) *Labeling the Mentally Retarded*. Berkeley: University of California Press.

Merriam, S. B. (1988) *Case Study Research in Education*. London: Jossey-Bass.

Mintzberg, H. (1979) *The Structuring of Organisations*. Englewood Cliffs: Prentice Hall.

Mortimore, P. *et al.* (1988) *School Matters – The Junior Years*. Exeter: Open Books.

Porter, A. C. and Brophy, J. E. (1988) 'Synthesis of research on good teaching: insights from the work of the Institute of Research on Teaching', *Educational Leadership*, **48**, 8:74–85.

Purkey, S. and Smith, M. (1983) 'Effective schools: a review', *The Elementary School Journal*, **83**, 4:427–52.

Reason, P. (1988) (Ed.) *Human Inquiry in Action*. Beverly Hills: Sage.

Reynolds, M. C. (1988) 'A reaction to the JLD special series on the Regular Education Initiative', *Journal of Learning Disabilities*, **21**, 6:352–6.

Rhodes, W. C. (1970) 'A community participation analysis of emotional disturbance', *Exceptional Children*, **36**:306–14.

Rosenshine, B. (1983) 'Teaching functions in instructional programs', *The Elementary School Journal*, **83**, 4:335–51.

Rutter, M. *et al.* (1979) *Fifteen Thousand Hours*. London: Open Books.

Schindele, R. A. (1985) 'Research methodology in special education: a framework approach to special problems and solutions', in Hegarty, S. and Evans, P. (Eds) *Research and Evaluation Methods in Special Education*. Windsor: NFER Nelson.

Schon, D. A. (1983) *The Reflective Practitioner*. New York: Basic Books.

Schon, D. A. (1987) *Educating the Reflective Practitioner*. San Francisco: Jossey-Bass.

Schrag, P. and Divorky, D. (1975) *The Myth of the Hyperactive Child*. New York: Pantheon.

Schumaker, J. B. and Deshler, D. D. (1988) 'Implementing the Regular Education Initiative in secondary schools: a different ball game', *Journal of Learning Disabilities*, **21**, 1:36–42.

Sexton, S. (1988) *Our Schools: A Radical Policy*. London: IEA (Education Unit).

Skrtic, T. M. (1985) 'Doing naturalistic research into educational organisation', in Lincoln, Y. S. (Ed.), *Organisational Theory and Inquiry*. Beverly Hills: Sage.

Skrtic, T. M. (1986) 'The crisis in special education knowledge: a perspective on perspective', *Focus on Exceptional Children*, **18**, 7:1–15.

Skrtic, T. M. (1987) 'An organisational analysis of special education reform', *Counterpoint*, **8**, 2:15–19.

Skrtic, T. M. (1988) 'The organisational context of special education', in Meyen, E. L. and Skrtic, T. M. (Eds) *Exceptional Children and Youth: An Introduction*. Denver: Love.

Smyth, J. (1989) 'A critical pedagogy of classroom practice', *Journal of Curriculum Studies*, **21**, 6:483–502.

Stainback, W. and Stainback, S. (1984) 'A rationale for the merger of special and regular education', *Exceptional Children,* 51:102–11.

Stenhouse, L. (1975) *An Introduction to Curriculum Research and Development*. London: Heinemann.

Swap, S. (1978) 'The ecological model of emotional disturbance in children: a status report and proposed synthesis', *Behavioural Disorders*, **3**, 3:156–86.

Walker, R. (1985) *Doing Research: A Handbook for Teachers*. London: Methuen.

Wang, M. C. and Zollers, J. Z. (1990) 'Adaptive instruction: an alternative service delivery approach', *Remedial and Special Education*, **11**, 1:7–21.

Wang, M. C., Reynolds, M. C. and Walberg, H. J. (1986) 'Rethinking special education', *Educational Leadership*, **44**: 26–31.

Weick, K. E. (1976) 'Educational organisations as loosely coupled systems', *Administrative Science Quarterly*, **21**: 1–19.

Weick, K. E. (1985) 'Sources of order in underorganised systems: themes in recent organisational theory', in Lincoln, Y. S. (Ed.) *Organisational Theory and Inquiry*. Beverly Hills: Sage.

West, M. and Ainscow, M. (1991) *Managing School Development: A Practical Guide*. London: David Fulton Publishers.

Woods, P. (1986) *Inside Schools*. London: Routledge and Kegan Paul.

CHAPTER 2

Students with Special Educational Needs: Artifacts of the Traditional Curriculum

Thomas M. Skrtic

> The first right of any disabled person is not to be disabled, never to have been disabled.
>
> Federico Mayor Zargoza[1]

Although Zargoza's statement refers to persons with visual impairments, a small fraction of all people with disabilities, my primary aim in this chapter is to extend his idea of 'the right not to be disabled' to every student who has a special educational need in school. I am not denying that some students have special needs, nor that meeting these needs can be a formidable challenge to educators. I am questioning whether there are any good reasons for thinking of students with special educational needs as disabled or handicapped, regardless of the cause or extent of their particular needs.

I will make my case for extending the right not to be disabled to every student with a special educational need by considering the grounding assumptions of 20th-century special education from an organizational perspective. These assumptions are that:

(1) Disabilities are objective, pathological conditions that students have.
(2) Special education is a rationally conceived and coordinated system of services that benefits students with disabilities.
(3) Progress in the field of special education results from rational, technological improvements in diagnosis and intervention.[2]

The first assumption stems from special education's disciplinary

20

grounding in psychology and biology (medicine). By their very nature, of course, these disciplines tend to locate the cause of deviance within the person and thus to exclude from consideration causal factors that lie in the larger social context in which deviance occurs (Mercer, 1973; Skrtic, 1986). The second and third assumptions derive from the notion of organizational rationality (Skrtic, 1987; 1988b) which, as we will see below, assumes that organizations are (or can be, if managed efficiently) as rational as machines and that changing them is a rational-technical process of fine tuning an existing machine (rather than replacing it with a new one).

By considering these grounding assumptions from an organizational perspective, I want to question the sense of objectivity and rationality that they imply and make three counter-arguments about the nature of student disability, special education, and progress. As suggested by my title, the first of these counter-arguments is that students who are thought of in school as having objective disabilities or handicaps are, in fact, handicapped *by* the experience of schooling. That is, students who are identified as educationally handicapped in school – students who, as a result, tend to become psychologically, socially, economically, and politically handicapped in life – are artifacts of the traditional curriculum, construed broadly as the bureaucratically-organized experience of schooling.

My second counter-argument is that the institutional practice of special education itself is an artifact of the bureaucratic organization of schools. In this regard, I will argue that special education is a non-rational and uncoordinated practice that emerged in 20th-century industrialized democracies to contain the inherent contradiction between the democratic goal of universal public education and the bureaucratic school organizations that were used to address it. Finally, I want to argue that there is little that can be done to make bureaucratic school organizations more adaptable and inclusive. Here, I will argue that neither the goals of reform measures like mainstreaming and integration, nor the more radical goals associated with the post-mainstreaming, or Regular Education Initiative (see below) reform movement in the United States, can be realized in bureaucratically-organized schools. Moreover, I will argue that reform efforts such as these, although well meaning and politically and ethically correct, actually make school bureaucracies less adaptable and inclusive, which makes schooling less effective for students who have special educational needs and, ultimately, creates even more students with such needs who, as a result, must be identified as handicapped.

Another of my aims in the chapter is to demonstrate that, although the phenomenon of creating students with disabilities is inherent to bureaucratic school organizations, it is not inherent to the process of schooling *per se*. In this regard, I will argue that there is an alternative, non-bureaucratic configuration for schooling that eliminates the need to identify students as disabled and, at the same time, makes possible the kind of educational excellence that is needed in the 21st century. Finally, then, my third aim is to persuade the international special education community to work hard toward extending the right not to be disabled to all students by shifting its focus from reforming traditional school organizations to replacing them with this alternative organizational form, an undertaking, I will argue, that should emphasize organizational arguments for educational excellence over the customary moral arguments for educational equity.

School organization and adaptability[3]

The normative view of organizations is that they are merely social tools, mechanisms that societies use to achieve goals that are beyond the reach of individuals (Parsons, 1960). But organizations do more than achieve social goals; the nature and needs of organizations shape the very goals that societies use to achieve them (Scott, 1981). Education is a social goal that is shaped by the medium of an organization; society wants education, but what it gets is a particular kind of schooling, one that is shaped by the school organizations that are used to provide it.

Understanding the organizational context of schooling has been complicated by the fact that, for most of this century, the question of school organization has been left almost exclusively to educational administrators. This has been a problem because the field of educational administration has been dominated by the extremely narrow perspective of organizational rationality contained in the notion of scientific management (Callahan, 1962; Spring, 1980). Scientific management is an approach to managing the mass production process in industrial organizations or what I will refer to below as machine bureaucracies. The problem with scientific management and the machine bureaucracy is that, because of their great success in industry, they became social norms, standards for what was assumed to be the most efficient way to organize and manage all organizations, including schools (Callahan, 1962; Haber, 1964).

Although educational administration continues to be dominated by

scientific management and the machine bureaucracy conceptualization of school organizations (see Bates, 1980; Sirotnik and Oakes,
1986; Weick, 1982), recent developments in the social sciences have
produced a number of new theories of organization and change
(Burrell and Morgan, 1979; Pffefer, 1982; Scott, 1981), many of which
are directly applicable to school organization (see Skrtic, 1987; 1988b;
1991). In the remainder of this section I use two of these newer theories
to address the question of school organization and change.[4] In
subsequent sections I draw insights from this analysis to make my
counter-arguments about the nature of disability, special education,
and reform, as well as to an alternative organizational form for
schools.

The first theoretical perspective that I will use is configuration theory
(Miller and Mintzberg, 1983; Mintzberg, 1979). It is an important
vantage point because, among other things, it characterizes the nature
and functioning of two organizational configurations – the *machine
bureaucracy* and the *professional bureaucracy* – that are essential for
understanding traditional school organization and the problem of
change, as well as a third configuration, the *adhocracy*, which is the
organizational form that I will recommend as an alternative to the
traditional bureaucratic configuration of schooling. The second
theoretical perspective is institutional theory (Meyer and Rowan,
1977; 1978; Meyer and Scott, 1983). It is useful because, in conjunction
with configuration theory, it provides a way to understand school
organization as a two-structure arrangement, a combined machine
bureaucracy-professional bureaucracy configuration that is inherently
non-adaptable at both the micro level of the professional and the
macro level of the organization.

Differences between machine and professional bureaucracies[5]

The central idea in configuration theory is that organizations structure
themselves into somewhat naturally occurring configurations
according to the nature of their work, their means of coordination,
and a variety of situational factors. Given the nature of their work, coordination, and situational conditions, school organizations structure
themselves as professional bureaucracies. This is so even though in this
century schools have been managed and governed as if they were
machine bureaucracies (Callahan, 1962; Clark, 1985). According to
the logic of institutional theory, school organizations deal with this
contradiction by maintaining two structures: an inner professional

bureaucracy structure that conforms to the technical demands of their work, and an outer machine bureaucracy structure that conforms to the social norm of scientific management.

At bottom, the differences between the two configurations stem from the nature of their work, which is a key factor because it influences the two most fundamental aspects of any organized activity: division of labor and coordination of work. Organizations configure themselves as machine bureaucracies when their work is simple enough to permit them to divide their labor through *rationalization* (or task analysis), a process in which the total work activity is divided into a sequence of separate subtasks, each of which can be assigned to a separate worker. The completion of this type of work is coordinated through *formalization*, a process in which the procedures for doing each subtask in the sequence are standardized by specifying precise rules for each worker to follow in completing his or her assigned work activity. The best example of a machine bureaucracy is an organization that builds automobiles on an assembly line.

When their work is too complex to be rationalized, and thus too ambiguous to be formalized, organizations configure themselves as professional bureaucracies. The best examples of this configuration are organizations that do client-centered work such as hospitals, legal firms, universities, and public schools. In these organizations, division of labor is achieved through *specialization*, which distributes the clients among the workers, each of whom does all aspects of the work with his or her assigned client cohort. Specialization is premised on the assumption that each worker has the specialized skills necessary to meet the needs of his or her assigned clients. This type of work is coordinated by standardizing the skills of the worker, which is accomplished through *professionalization*, or intensive skill training and socialization carried out in professional schools.

An organization's division of labor and means of coordination shape the nature of the interdependency, or coupling, among its workers (Thompson, 1967; Weick, 1976; 1982). Because machine bureaucracies divide and coordinate their work through rationalization and formalization, their workers are *tightly coupled*, a situation in which workers, like links in a chain, are highly dependent on one another. In a professional bureaucracy, however, specialization and professionalization create a *loosely coupled* form of interdependency, a situation in which each professional works closely with his or her clients but only loosely with other professionals. Specialization and professionalization virtually eliminate the need for coordination among professionals because each does all aspects of the work with his or her assigned clients. What little coordination is needed is achieved by each professional knowing roughly what every other professional (within a given specialization) is doing by way of their common training and socialization.

Managing professional bureaucracies like machines

The logic of formalization in the machine bureacracy is premised on separating theory from practice and minimizing worker discretion. The theory behind the work in these organizations rests with the managers and engineers who rationalize and formalize it; they do the thinking and the workers simply follow the rules. Conversely, professionalization is premised on uniting theory and practice in the professional and maximizing his or her discretion in completing the work. This is necessary because the ambiguity of complex work requires the workers to adapt the theory to their clients' particular needs. In schools, teachers must know the theory behind their work and have enough discretion to be able to adapt it to the unique and changing needs of their clients.

From the configuration perspective, however, professionalization circumscribes professional practice because it only provides professionals with a finite repertoire of preconceived standard programs that are matched to a finite set of presumed client needs. In schools, the logic of specialization means that students whose needs fall outside their teacher's repertoire of standard programs must be sent to a different teacher, one who presumably has a repertoire that contains the appropriate standard programs. Moreover, professionalization tends to circumscribe professional practice even further because, ultimately, it results in convergent thinking and deductive reasoning, a situation in which 'the professional confuses the needs of his clients with the skills he has to offer them' (Mintzberg, 1979, p. 374). A fully open-ended process – one that seeks a truly creative solution to each unique need – requires a problem-solving orientation premised on innovation rather than standardization. But professionals are performers. They do not invent new programs; they perfect the standard programs in their repertoires by practicing them over and over again (Simon, 1977; Weick, 1976). Instead of accommodating heterogeneity, they screen it out, either by forcing the client's needs into one of their standard programs, or by forcing the client out of the professional-client relationship altogether (Perrow, 1970; Segal, 1974).

Given the dominance of scientific management in the field of educational administration, schools are managed as if they were machine bureaucracies (Clark, 1985; Weick, 1982), even though rationalization and formalization are ill-suited to the technical demands of doing complex work. In principle, this drives the professional bureaucracy toward the machine bureacracy configuration because, given the logic behind rationalization and formalization, it separates theory and practice and reduces professional discretion. This reduces further the degree to which teachers can personalize their standard programs, which results in fewer students whose need can be met by these programs and thus fewer students who can be retained in their classrooms.

Fortunately, however, rationalization and formalization do not work completely in school organizations. From the institutional perspective, the machine bureacracy structure, where the rationalization and formulation are inscribed, is decoupled from the professional bureaucracy structure, where the work is done. That is, the outer machine bureaucracy structure of schools acts largely as a myth, an assortment of symbols and ceremonies that protect the organization's legitimacy by giving it the appearance of the machine bureaucracy that the public expects, while at the same time permitting it to do its work according to the localized judgements of its professionals. Although this decoupled, two-structure arrangement protects teachers' discretion somewhat, it does not work completely either because, regardless of how contradictory they may be, rationalization and formalization require at least overt conformity to their precepts (Dalton, 1959). Thus, decoupled structures notwithstanding, the misplaced rationalization and formalization contained in the scientific management approach to educational administration further circumscribe professional discretion, which ultimately forces more students out of the regular classroom and into the special needs programs.

Bureaucracies and change

From the configuration perspective, both the machine bureaucracy and the professional bureaucracy are premised on the principle of standardization, which means that, in principle, both are inherently non-adaptable structures. Although change is resisted in both configurations, it can be forced on a machine bureaucracy through a rational-technical process of re-rationalizing the work and re-formalizing worker behavior. However, when a professional bureaucracy is required to change, it cannot respond by making rational-technical adjustments in the way its work is done because its coordination rests within each professional, not in its work processes. Nevertheless, because schools are managed and governed as if they were machine bureaucracies, attempts to change them typically follow the rational-technical approach (House, 1979), which assumes that changes in, or additions to, the existing rationalization and formalization will result in changes in the way the work gets done. But, because the existing rationalization and formalization are decoupled from the actual work in schools, rational-technical reforms are largely absorbed into the mythical machine bureaucracy structure, where they serve the purpose of signalling the public that a change has occurred. Of course, because they are decoupled from the actual work, such reforms fail to bring about the desired changes (Cuban, 1979; Elmore and McLaughlin, 1988). Nevertheless, rational-technical reforms do extend the existing rationalization and formalization which, because they require at least overt conformity, drives the organization further toward the machine bureaucracy configuration (Skrtic, 1987; Wise, 1988). This, of course, circumscribes professional discretion further still, which ultimately forces even more students out of regular classrooms.

Even though schools are non-adaptable structures, their status as public organizations means that they must respond to public demands for change. As we know, one way that schools deal with this problem is by using their outer machine bureaucracy structure to signal the public that a change has occurred. Another way that school organizations relieve pressure for change is by creating decoupled subunits, that is, separate programs or specialists to deal with the change demand. This is possible, of course, because of the loosely coupled interdependency within the organization. As such, schools can respond to pressure for change by simply adding on separate subunits to deal with the change demand and subsequently decoupling these units from their basic operation. This buffers the organization from the change demand because it gives the appearance of responding to it while, at the same time, makes any substantial reorganization of activity unnecessary (Meyer and Rowan, 1977; Zucker, 1981).

The adhocracy configuration

Professional bureaucracies are non-adaptable because they are premised on the principle of standardization, which configures them as performance organizations for perfecting their existing standard programs. However, the adhocracy configuration is premised on the principle of innovation rather than standardization; it is a problem-solving organization configured to invent new programs. Adhocracies emerge in dynamic, uncertain environments where innovation and adaptation through divergent thinking and inductive reasoning are necessary for organizational survival (see Pugh *et al.*, 1963). As such, an adhocracy is the inverse of the bureaucratic form (Burns and Stalker, 1966; Woodward, 1965), an organizational configuration that emerges around work that is so ambiguous that neither the standard programs nor the knowledge and skills for doing it are known. The key difference between the two configurations is that, faced with a problem, the adhocracy 'engages in creative effort to find a novel solution; then professional bureaucracy pigeonholes it into a known contingency to which it can apply a standard program. One engages in divergent thinking aimed at innovation; the other in convergent thinking aimed at perfection' (Mintzberg, 1979, p. 436).

Perhaps the best example of this configuration in the United States is the National Aeronautics and Space Administration (NASA) in the 1960s when, during its Apollo phase, its mission was a manned lunar landing. It configured itself as an adhocracy because at that time there were no standard programs for landing people on the moon and returning them safely to earth. At that point in its history, NASA had to rely on its workers to invent and reinvent these programs on an *ad hoc* basis, on the way to the moon, as it were. Moreover, although NASA employed professional workers, it could not use specialization and professionalization to distribute and coordinate its work because there were no professional specialties that had perfected the standard programs for doing the type of work that was required. Thus, its division of labor and coordination of work were premised on *collaboration* and *mutual adjustment*, respectively.

Under such an arrangement, division of labor is achieved by deploying professionals from various specializations on multi-disciplinary project teams, a situation in which team members work collaboratively on the teams' project of innovation and assume joint responsibility for its completion. Under mutual adjustment, co-ordination is achieved though informal communication among team members as they invent and reinvent novel problem solutions on an *ad hoc* basis, a process that requires them to adapt their conventional theories and practices relative to those of their colleagues and the teams' progress on the tasks at hand (Chandler and Sayles, 1971; Mintzberg, 1979). Together, the structural contingencies of collaboration and mutual adjustment give rise to a *discursive coupling* arrangement that is premised on reflective thought and thus on the unification of theory and practice in the team of professionals (see Burns and Stalker, 1966). By contrast, during its current Space Shuttle phase, NASA has reconfigured itself as a professional bureaucracy (see Romzek and Dubnik, 1987), as a performance organization that perfects a repertoire of standard launch and recovery programs, most of which were invented during its Apollo phase.

School organization and special education's grounding assumptions[6]

In this section I make my counter-arguments about student disability, special education, and progress by considering special education's grounding assumptions from the perspective of school organization and adaptability. The section is organized according to the three traditional assumptions, which are recast below in the form of questions.

Are disabilities objective pathologies?

As we know, the professional bureaucracy is a performance organization that perfects its existing programs, an organizational context in which professional practice is premised on matching a preconceived standard program to a presumed client need. We also know that professionalization, the means of coordination in these organizations, results in convergent thinking and deductive reasoning, a situation in which professionals tend to confuse the needs of their clients with the skills they have to offer them. Moreover, although the assumption is that professionals have the discretion to adapt their standard programs to fit the particular needs of their clients, professional bureaucracies are not problem-solving organizations that seek a creative solution to each unique need. A client cannot have just any need, he or she must have a need that the organization and its professionals have been standardized to meet.

Given a finite repertoire of standard programs and an inherently diverse and changing set of student needs, the professional bureaucracy configuration can do nothing but create students who do not fit the system. Students are identified as handicapped in this context simply because they have needs that cannot be accommodated within the standard programs contained in particular teachers' repertoires. Moreover, the situation is compounded by both the scientific management approach to educational administration and the rational-technical approach to school change, which, by introducing unwarranted rationalization and formalization, reduce professional thought and discretion and thus the degree to which teachers can personalize their standard programs. From an organizational perspective, student disability is neither a pathological condition nor an objective distinction; it is an organizational artifact, a matter of not fitting the conventional practices in an organization that is not configured to accommodate diversity and so must screen it out.

Is special education a rational system?

We can ask whether special education is a rational system by considering the non-adaptability of school organizations in conjunction with their status as public organizations. As we know, as public organizations schools depend on the public for their support and legitimacy and, as such, they must respond to public demands for change. We have seen, for example, that school organizations had to adopt the machine bureaucracy structure earlier in the century, not because it conformed to its technical needs or added to its effectiveness, but because it is what the public thought all legitimate organizations should look like. Although the public is a constant source of pressure on school organizations in this respect, on occasion it makes additional change demands, ones that require the organization and its teachers to do something other than what they were standardized to do.

From the institutional perspective, we have seen how school organizations deal with such demands. We know, for example, that school organizations live with the contradiction of maintaining an inappropriate machine bureaucracy structure by mythologizing it through symbols and ceremonies and then decoupling it from their day-to-day activities. We know, too, that the loosely coupled internal structure of schools allows them to respond to change demands by simply adding separate, decoupled programs or specialists to the existing operation. The segregated special classroom – the dominant model for special education in the 20th century – is the extreme case of this process at work. At the start of this century, when schools in the United States were required to start serving a broader range of students in the interest of the democratic goal of universal public education, the 'ungraded' or special classroom emerged to deal with students that could not be squeezed into the available standard programs (Bogdan and Knoll, 1988; Lazerson, 1983; Sarason and Doris, 1979). From an organizational perspective, the segregated special classroom served as a legitimating device, a mechanism that signalled the public that schools had complied with the demand for universal public education, while at the same time allowing public education to maintain its traditional organizations and conventional practices. Once special classrooms were created, they were decoupled from the internal workings of the school. Indeed, this lack of connection between the special classroom and the rest of the school enterprise was one of the major criticisms in the United States that lead to a passage of the Education for All Handicapped Children Act of 1975 (EHA) and the introduction of the mainstreaming model of special education (see Christophos and Renz, 1969; Dunn, 1968; Johnson, 1962).

Considering the function of special education within public education from an organizational perspective, one can hardly claim that it is a rationally conceived and coordinated system of services. Special education is not rationally conceived because, historically, it has served as a myth, a legitimating device that school organizations used to cope with shifting value demands in society. Special education is not rationally coordinated because, by design, it is decoupled from the basic operation of the school. Recall that the unintended consequence of using organizations to achieve social goals is that the goals are shaped by the nature and needs of the organizations themselves. From an organizational perspective, special education is an unintended consequence of the particular kind of schooling that traditional school organizations provide. It is an organizational artifact that emerged to protect the legitimacy of a non-adaptable bureaucratic structure faced with the changing value demands of a dynamic democratic environment.

Is progress a rational-technical matter?

We can address the question by considering the EHA, the most comprehensive special education reform ever undertaken in the United States. From an organizational perspective, the problem with the EHA is that it attempts to change a professional bureaucracy into an adhocracy by treating it as if it were a machine bureaucracy. Implicitly, the goal of the EHA is an adhocratic school organization in which educational problems are solved by interdisciplinary teams of professionals and parents who collaborate to invent personalized programs for students with special educational needs (see Turnbull, 1986). This, of course, contradicts the logic of the inner professional bureaucracy configuration of schools in every way, given that it is a performance organization in which individual professionals work alone to perfect standard programs. As we will see below, the result has been that the EHA has produced virtually the opposite results.

Moreover, although it seeks an adhocratic school organization, the EHA's approach to change assumes that schools are machine bureaucracies, organizations in which worker behavior is controlled by procedural rules that are subject to modification through revision and extension of rationalization and formalization (see Elmore and McLaughlin, 1982). Thus, because the EHA's means are completely consistent with their outer machine bureaucracy structure of schools, it extends and elaborates the existing rationalization and formalization. Structurally, this both deflects the adhocratic ends of the EHA from the actual work and further reduces professional thought and discretion, thus intensifying professionalization and reducing personalization (see Skrtic, Guba and Knowlton, 1985; Weatherley, 1979). This results in even more students who fall outside the standard programs, many of whom must be identified as handicapped. Moreover, because there is a legal limit on the number of students that can be identified as handicapped under the EHA, as well as a political limit on the amount of school failure society will tolerate, the EHA, in conjunction with other rational-technical reforms associated with the so-called excellence movement in general education, created a new class of student casualties called 'at-risk', which, at this point, is decoupled from both general education and special education (see Cuban, 1989; Skrtic, 1991).

Because the EHA requires at least overt conformity, an array of symbols and ceremonies of compliance have emerged. One of the primary symbols of compliance with the law's requirement of education in the least restrictive setting is a new type of decoupled subunit – the resource room.[7] From an organizational perspective, the resource room is even more problematic than the traditional special classroom because it violates both the division of labor and means of coordination in the professional bureaucracy configuration. Under the logic of mainstreaming, the responsibility for the student's instructional program is divided among one or more regular classroom teachers and a special education resource teacher. This contradicts the division of labor in schools because it requires that the student's instructional program be rationalized and assigned to more than one professional, which is justified implicitly on the assumption that the professionals will work collaboratively to integrate the program. However, the collaboration required to integrate the student's instructional program contradicts the logic of professionalization and thus the form of interdependency among workers. In principle, teachers working collaboratively in the interest of a single student for whom they share responsibility violates the logic of loose coupling. That is, because professionalization locates virtually all of the necessary coordination within the individual professional, there is little need for teachers to collaborate or even communicate in schools (see Bishop, 1977; Lortie, 1975; 1978; Skrtic et al., 1985; Tye and Tye, 1984).

Moreover, although regular classroom placement (to the maximum extent possible) is required for these students under the EHA, they are identified as handicapped precisely because they cannot be accommodated within existing standard programs in particular regular classrooms (see Skrtic et al., 1985; Walker, 1987). As such, mainstreaming for these students largely represents symbolic integration in non-academic subjects (Biklen, 1985; Skrtic et al., 1985; Wright et al., 1982). Given the adhocratic goals of the EHA, it was intended to decrease the effects of student disability by increasing personalized instruction and regular classroom integration. However, given the professionalized and formalized character of school organizations and the rationalized and formalized nature of the law itself, the result has been an increase in the number of students classified as disabled, disintegration of instruction, and a decrease in personalization in regular and special education classrooms (see Bryan et al., 1988; Carlberg and Kavale, 1980; Gartner and Lipsky, 1987; Gerber and Levine-Donnerstein, 1989; Keogh, 1988; Skrtic et al., 1985; USDE, 1988; Walker, 1987; Wang et al., 1986; 1987).

Although the adhocratic ends of the EHA are distorted because of the bureaucratic nature of the law and its implementation context, schools appear to be complying with its procedural requirements because they adopt practices which, although they may be well-intended and in some respects may actually result in positive outcomes, serve largely to symbolize and ceremonialize compliance with the letter of the law rather than conform to its spirit (see for example, Carlberg and Kavale, 1980; Gerardi et al., 1984; Schenk, 1980; Skrtic et al., 1985). From a policy perspective, symbolic compliance with procedural requirements is problematic because it can lead advocates, monitors, and implementation researchers to faulty conclusions. For example, Singer and Butler (1987) reported in their study of the implementation of the EHA that 'federal demands have equilibrated rapidly with local capacity to respond', and thus concluded that the EHA demonstrates that 'a federal initiative *can* result in significant social reforms at the local level' (p. 151). Although they are correct in asserting that such equilibration has resulted in 'a basically workable system' (p. 151), they fail to recognize that equilibration is largely a process of institutionalizing the necessary symbols and ceremonies of compliance. Given the limited capacity of bureaucratic school organizations to respond to the adhocratic requirements of the EHA, such equilibration renders the system workable for school organizations, but not necessarily for the intended beneficiaries of the federal initiative.

The special classroom model of special education was criticized in the 1960s for being racially biased, instructionally ineffective, and psychologically and socially damaging (Dunn, 1968; Johnson, 1962), problems for which the EHA and the mainstreaming model were presumed to be solutions. Rather than resolving these problems, however, the EHA and mainstreaming merely reproduced them in the 1980s (see Heller *et al.*, 1982; Skrtic, 1987; Wang *et al.*, 1987), which gave rise to the new Regular Education Initiative (REI) reform movement. The REI is premised on the argument that the elaborate classification procedures of the EHA and the pull-out logic of mainstreaming are fundamentally flawed (see for example, Gartner and Lipsky, 1987; Reynolds *et al.*, 1987). For the REI proponents, the solution is to restructure the separate special education and general education systems into a single adaptable system, one in which virtually all students with special educational needs are retained in regular classrooms and provided with in-class support services. Although space does not permit consideration of the four REI proposals that have surfaced to this point (Gartner and Lipsky, 1987; Lipsky and Gartner, 1989; Pugach and Lilly, 1984; Reynolds and Wang, 1983; Reynolds *et al.*, 1987; Stainback and Stainback, 1984; Stainback *et al.*, 1989), I have argued elsewhere (Skrtic, 1991) that, from an organizational perspective, each of them replicates the means-ends contradictions of the EHA. That is, each proposal implicitly calls for an adhocratic school organization but retains the professional bureaucracy inner configuration of schools and extends their outer machine bureaucracy configuration. As such, if these proposals are implemented, they will reproduce the inadequacies of the current system of special education in the 1990s and beyond. Nevertheless, although the actual REI reform proposals do not resolve the inadequacies of the special education system in the United States, the REI reform movement is important because of its relationship to the most recent phase of the excellence movement in general education.

Equity, excellence and adhocracy

Historically, the relationship between general education and special education reform movements in the United States has been strained by the inability to reconcile the goals of educational excellence and educational equity. Recently, however, there has been a convergence of interests between the REI proponents in special education and advocates of the new 'school restructuring' approach to educational excellence in general education (see for example, Boyer, 1983; Cuban, 1983; 1989; Goodlad, 1984; Oakes, 1985; Sizer 1984; Wise, 1988). The point of convergence is that both groups of reformers are calling for a system of education that provides virtually all students with personalized instruction in heterogeneous classrooms. In both cases, such a system is to be achieved through structural reforms that increase professional discretion and promote collaborative problem-solving among professionals and between professionals and parents at local school sites. Although there are differences between the REI and school restructuring reform proposals, they are differences in degree, not in kind. Implicitly, both groups of reformers are calling for the elimination of specialization, professionalization, and loose coupling, the structural contingencies of the professional bureaucracy configuration of schools, and the introduction of collaboration, mutual adjustment, and discursive coupling, the structural contingencies of the adhocratic configuration (see Skrtic, 1991). In organizational terms, achieving excellence and equity in public education will require that school organization be reconfigurated as adhocracies.

As we know, adhocracies are premised on the principle of innovation; they are problem-solving organizations that configure themselves around uncertain work – work that requires the invention of new programs for unfamiliar contingencies through divergent thinking and inductive reasoning on the part of multidisciplinary teams of professionals engaged in a reflective discourse. Thus, because an organization's configuration is shaped by the nature of its work, re-configuring school organizations as adhocracies will require an enduring source of instructional uncertainty. In organizational terms, schooling cannot be excellent and equitable unless school organizations are adhocratic. In structural terms, school organizations cannot become and remain adhocratic without the uncertainty of student diversity. As such, educational equity is the precondition for educational excellence in the 21st century.

As we have seen, the traditional bureaucratic configuration of schools is a performance organization, an inherently non-adaptable organizational form that must screen out diversity by forcing students with special educational needs out of the system. But student diversity is not an inherent problem for school organizations; it is only a problem when they are configured as performance organizations. Regardless of its cause and its extent, student diversity is not a liability in a problem-solving organization; in the adhocratic school organization it is an asset, an enduring source of uncertainty and thus the driving force behind innovation, growth of knowledge, and progress. Although the moral argument for educational equity for students with special educational needs has always been right, the international special education community is now in a position to strengthen its argument for equity by arguing that, from an organizational perspective, equity is the way to excellence. And, of course, the first step toward extending the right not to be disabled to all students is for special educators to stop thinking of special educational needs as human pathologies, and to start thinking of disabilities and handicaps as organizational pathologies, as artifacts of the traditional curriculum.

Endnotes

1. Federico Mayor Zargoza is the Secretary General of UNESCO. This quote was taken from an exhibit at the United Nations complex in New York on March 3, 1990.
2. See Bogdan and Kugelmass (1984), Mercer (1973), Skrtic (1986, 1988a), and Tomlinson (1982).
3. In the remaining sections of this chapter, when I refer to specific cases and historical events, I am referring to public education in the United States. Beyond the fact that it is the system of education with which I am most familiar, I will use schooling in America as my examplar because it represents the extreme case of the organizational phenomenon of creating students with disabilities. This is so because, if Alexis de Tocqueville (1966), Max Weber (1958; 1978), and Thomas Jefferson (see Ford, 1904; Greer, 1972) were right about the relationship among capitalism, bureaucracy, democracy, and education, and the particular manifestation of this relationship in America, schooling in the United States is the extreme case

of the contradiction between the democratic ends and bureaucratic means of universal public education (see Skrtic, 1991). As an extreme case, such an analysis has utility for special educators in other industrialized democracies because, although the specifics may vary, it provides them with an analytic device for reappraising student disability, special education, and progress in the context of their particular national experience. Such an analysis has utility for special educators in non-industrialized and industrializing countries through providing insights into how some of the problems that are noted might be avoided or minimized.

4. The organizational analysis to follow is a largely structural interpretation of school organization and change. This is an admittedly narrow interpretation because it does not consider in any substantive way the culture of school organizations or the cultural implications for change. For a combined structural-cultural interpretation that makes the same arguments and reaches the same conclusion as the present analysis, see Skrtic (1991, in press a, in press b).

5. All of the material on configuration theory (division of labor, co-ordination of work, and internal coupling) and institutional theory (decoupled structures and units, and myth, symbol, and ceremony) is drawn from Mintzberg (1979) and Miller and Mintzberg (1983) and Meyer and Rowan (1977, 1978) and Meyer and Scott (1983), respectively, except where noted otherwise.

6. The authors cited in this section are not making the theoretical claims that are presented. I am making the theoretical claims based on the analysis presented in the previous section. The citations appearing in this section are references to empirical and interpretive research evidence that supports my theoretical claims.

7. The symbol of compliance for programs that serve students with severe and profound disabilities is the traditional decoupled subunit, the segregated special classroom. These programs are simply added to the existing school organization and, to one degree or another, decoupled from the basic operation. The degree of decoupling depends in large measure on the local history of special education services, which reflects values embedded in political cultures at the state, local, and school organization levels (see Biklen, 1985; McDonnel and McLaughlin, 1982; Noel and Fuller, 1985; Skrtic et al., 1985). Although I will not consider these programs here, I argue elsewhere (Skrtic, 1991) that they are important because, given the nature of the needs of the students in these programs and the interdisciplinary approach that is employed, they are prototypical of the adhocratic organizational form.

References

Bates, R. J. (1980) 'Educational administration, the sociology of science, and the management of knowledge', *Educational Administration Quarterly*, **16**,2:1–20.
Biklen, D. (1985) *Achieving the Complete School: Strategies for Effective Mainstreaming*. New York: Columbia University.

38

Bishop, J.M. (1977) 'Organizational influences on the work orientations of elementary teachers', *Sociology of Work and Occupation*, 4:171-208.

Bogdan, R. and Knoll, J. (1988) 'The sociology of disability', in Meyen, E.L. and Skrtic, T.M. (Eds), *Exceptional Children and Youth: An Introduction*, pp. 449-77. Denver: Love Publishing.

Bogdan, R. and Kugelmass, J. (1984) 'Case studies of mainstreaming: A symbolic interactionist approach to special schooling', in Barton, L. and Tomlinson, S. (Eds), *Special Education and Social Interests*, pp. 173-91. New York: Nichols Publishing.

Boyer, E.L. (1983) *High School*. New York: Harper & Row.

Burns, T. and Stalker, G.M. (1966) *The Management of Innovation* (2nd edn.). London: Tavistock Publications.

Burrell, G. and Morgan, G. (1979) *Sociological Paradigms and Organizational Analysis*. London: Heinemann.

Callahan, R. (1962) *Education and the Cult of Efficiency*. Chicago: University of Chicago Press.

Carlberg, C. and Kavale, K. (1980) 'The efficacy of special versus regular class placement for exceptional children: A meta-analysis,' *Journal of Special Education*, 14:295-309.

Chandler, M.D. and Sayles, L.R. (1971) *Managing Large Systems*. New York: Harper & Row.

Christophos, F. and Renz, P. (1969) 'A critical examination of special education programs', *Journal of Special Education*, 3,4:371-80.

Clark, D.L. (1985) 'Emerging paradigms in organizational theory and research', in Lincoln, Y.S. (Ed.), *Organizational Theory and Inquiry: The Paradigm Revolution*, pp. 43-78. Beverly Hills, CA: Sage Publications.

Cuban, L. (1979) 'Determinants of curriculum change and stability, 1870-1970', in Schaffarzick, J. and Sykes, G. (Eds), *Value Conflicts and Curriculum Issues*. Berkeley, CA: McCutchan.

Cuban, L. (1983) 'Effective schools: A friendly but cautionary note', *Phi Delta Kappan*, 64,10:695-6.

Cuban, L. (1989) 'The "at-risk" label and the problem of urban school reform', *Phi Delta Kappan*, 70,10:780-84 and 799-801.

Dalton, M. (1959) *Men who Manage*. New York: Wiley.

Deno, E. (1970) 'Special education as developmental capital', *Exceptional Children*, 37,3:229-37.

Dunn, L.M. (1968) 'Special education for the mildly retarded – Is much of it justifiable?', *Exceptional Children*, 35,1:5-22.

Elmore, R.F. and McLaughlin, M.W. (1982) 'Strategic choice in federal education policy: The compliance-assistance trade-off', in Lieberman, A. and McLaughlin, M.W. (Eds), *Policy Making in Education: Eighty-first Yearbook of the National Society for the Study of Education*, pp. 159-94. Chicago: University of Chicago Press.

Elmore, R.F. and McLaughlin, M.W. (1988) *Steady Work: Policy, Practice, and the Reform of American Education*. Santa Monica, CA: The Rand Corporation.

Ford, P.L. (1904) (Ed.) *Thomas Jefferson Works*. New York: Knickerbocker Press.

Gartner, A. and Lipsky, D. K. (1987) 'Beyond special education: Toward a quality system for all students', *Harvard Educational Review*, **57**,4:367–90.

Gartner, A. and Lipsky, D. K. (1989) 'New conceptualizations for special education', *European Journal of Special Needs Education*, **4**,1:16.

Gerardi, R. J., Grohe, B., Benedict, G. C. and Coolidge, P. G. (1984) 'I.E.P. – More paperwork and wasted time', *Contemporary Education*, **56**,1:39–42.

Gerber, M. M. and Levine-Donnerstein (1989) 'Educating all children: Ten years later', *Exceptional Children*, **56**,1:17–27.

Goodlad, J. I. (1984) *A Place called School: Prospects for the Future*. New York: McGraw-Hill.

Greer, C. (1972) *The Great School Legend: A Revisionist Interpretation of American Public Education*. New York: Basic Books.

Haber, S. (1964) *Efficiency and Uplight: Scientific Management in the Progressive Era, 1890–1920*. Chicago: University of Chicago Press.

Hallahan, D. P., Kauffman, J. M., Lloyd, J. W. and McKinney, J. D. (1988) 'Introduction to the series: Questions about the regular education initiative', *Journal of Learning Disabilities*, **21**,1:3–5.

Heller, K., Holtzman, W. and Messick, S. (1982) *Placing Children in Special Education: A Strategy for Equity*. Washington, DC: National Academy of Sciences Press.

House, E. R. (1979) 'Technology versus craft: A ten year perspective on innovation', *Journal of Curriculum Studies*, **11**, 1:1–15.

Johnson, G. O. (1962) 'Special education for the mentally handicapped – A paradox', *Exceptional Children*, October, 62–9.

Kauffman, J. M., Gerber, M. M. and Semmel, M. I. (1988) 'Arguable assumptions underlying the regular education initiative', *Journal of Learning Disabilities*, **21**, 1:6–11.

Lazerson, M. (1983) 'The origins of special education', in Chambers, J. G. and Hartman, W. T. (Eds) *Special Education Policies: Their History, Implementation and Finance*. Philadelphia: Temple University Press.

Lipsky, D. K. and Gartner, A. (1989) *Beyond Separate Education: Quality Education for All*. Baltimore: Paul H. Brookes.

Lortie, D. C. (1975) *Schoolteacher: A Sociological Study*. Chicago: University of Chicago Press.

Lortie, D. C. (1978) 'Some reflections on renegotiation', in Reynolds, M. C. (Ed.) *Futures of Education for Exceptional Students: Emerging Structures*, pp. 235–43. Reston, VA: Council for Exceptional Children.

Mercer, J. (1973) *Labeling the Mentally Retarded: Clinical and Social System Perspectives on Mental Retardation*. Berkeley, CA: University of California Press.

Meyer, J. W. and Rowan, B. (1977) 'Institutionalized organizations: Formal structure as myth and ceremony', *American Journal of Sociology*, **83**:340–63.

Meyer, J. W. and Rowan, B. (1978) 'The structure of educational organizations', in Meyer, M. W. (Ed.), *Environments and Organizations*, pp. 78–109. San Francisco: Jossey-Bass.

Meyer, J. W. and Scott, W. R. (1983) *Organizational Environments: Ritual and Rationality*. Beverly Hills, CA: Sage Publications.

Miller, D. and Mintzberg, H. (1983) 'The case for configuration', in Morgan, G. (Ed.), *Beyond Method: Strategies for Social Research*, pp. 57–73. Beverly Hills, CA: Sage Publications.

Mintzberg, H. (1979) *The Structuring of Organizations*. Englewood Cliffs, NJ: Prentice-Hall.

Noel, M. M. and Fuller, B. C. (1985) 'The social policy construction of special education: The impact of state characteristics on identification and integration of handicapped children', *Remedial and Special Education*, **63**,3:27–35.

Oakes, J. (1985) *Keeping Track: How Schools Structure Inequality*. New Haven, CT: Yale University Press.

Parsons, T. (1960) *Structure and Process in Modern Societies*. Glencoe, IL: Free Press.

Perrow, C. (1970) *Organizational Analysis: A Sociological Review*. Belmont, CA: Wadsworth.

Pfeffer, J. (1982) *Organizations amd Organization Theory*. Marshfield, MA: Pitman Publishing.

Pugach, M. and Lilly, M. S. (1984) 'Reconceptualizing support services for classroom teachers: Implications for teacher education', *Journal of Teacher Education*, **35**,5:48–55.

Pugh, D. S., Hickson, D. J., Hinnings, C. R., MacDonald, K. M., Turner, C. and Lupton, T. (1963) 'A conceptual scheme for organizational analysis', *Administrative Science Quarterly*, **8**, 4:289–315.

Reynolds, M. C. and Wang, M. C. (1983) 'Restructuring "special" school programs: A position paper', *Policy Studies Review'*, **2**,1:189–212.

Reynolds, M. C., Wang, M. C. and Walberg, H. J. (1987) 'The necessary restructuring of special and general education', *Exceptional Children*, **53**, 1:391–8.

Romzek, B. S. and Dubnick, M. J. (1987) 'Accountability in the public sector: Lessons from the Challenger tragedy', *Public Administration Review*, **47**, 3:227–38.

Sarason, S. B. and Doris, J. (1979) *Educational Handicap, Public Policy, and Social History*. New York: The Free Press.

Schenck, S. J. (1980) 'The diagnostic/instructional link in individualized education programs', *Journal of Special Education*, **14**, 3:337–45.

Scott, R. W. (1981) *Organizations: Rational, Natural, and Open Systems*. Englewood Cliffs, NJ: Prentice-Hall.

Segal, M. (1974) 'Organization and environment: A typology of adaptability and structure', *Public Administration Review*, **34**,3:212–20.

Simon, H. A. (1977) *The New Science of Management Decision*. Englewood Cliffs, NJ: Prentice-Hall.

Singer, J. D. and Butler, J. A. (1987) 'The Education for All Handicapped Children Act: Schools as agents of social reform', *Harvard Educational Review*, **57**:125–52.

Sirotnik, K. A. and Oakes, J. (1986) *Critical Perspectives on the Organization and Improvement of Schooling*. Boston: Kluwer-Nijhoff.

Sizer, T. R. (1984) *Horace's Compromise: The Dilemma of the American High School*. Boston: Houghton Mifflin.

Skrtic, T. M. (1986) 'The crisis in special education knowledge: A perspective on perspective', *Focus on Exceptional Children*, **18**,7:1-16.

Skrtic, T. M. (1987) 'An organizational analysis of special education reform', *Counterpoint*, **8**,2:15-19.

Skrtic, T. M. (1988a) 'The crisis in special education knowledge', in Meyen, E. L. and Skrtic, T. M. (Eds), *Exceptional Children and Youth: An Introduction*. Denver, CO: Love Publishing.

Skrtic, T. M. (1988b) 'The organizational context of special education', in Meyen, E. L. and Skrtic, T. M. (Eds), *Exceptional Children and Youth: An Introduction*. Denver, CO: Love Publishing.

Skrtic, T. M. (1991) *Behind Special Education: A Critical Analysis of Professional Culture and School Organization*. Denver, CO: Love Publishing.

Skrtic, T. M. (in press a) *Exploring the Theory/Practice Link in Special Education: A Critical Perspective*. Reston, VA: Council for Exceptional Children.

Skrtic, T. M. (in press b) 'The special education paradox: Equity as the way to excellence', *Harvard Educational Review*.

Skrtic, T. M., Guba, E. G. and Knowlton, H. E. (1985) *Interorganizational Special Education Programming in Rural Areas: Technical Report on the Multisite Naturalistic Field Study*. Washington: National Institute of Education.

Spring, J. (1980) *Educating the Worker-Citizen: The Social, Economic, and Political Foundations of Education*. New York: Longman.

Stainback, S. and Stainback, W. (1984) 'A rationale for the merger of special and regular education', *Exceptional Children*, **51**:102-11.

Stainback, S., Stainback, W. and Forest, M. (1989) *Educating All Students in the Mainstream of Regular Education*. Baltimore: Paul H. Brookes.

Thompson, J. D. (1967) *Organizations in Action*. New York: McGraw-Hill.

Tocqueville, A. (1966) *Democracy in America* (J. P. Mayer, Ed.; G. Lawrence, trans), Vol. 1. New York: Harper & Row.

Tomlinson, S. (1982) *A Sociology of Special Education*. Boston: Routledge and Kegan Paul.

Turnbull, H. R. (1986) *Free Appropriate Public Education: The Law and Children with Disabilities*. Denver, CO: Love Publishing.

Tye, K. A. and Tye, B. B. (1984) 'Teacher isolation and school reform', *Phi Delta Kappan*, **65**, 5:319-22.

US Department of Education (USDE), Office of Special Education and Rehabilitative Services (1988) *Annual Report to Congress on the Implementation of the Education for All Handicapped Children Act*. Washington, DC: Author.

Walker, L. J. (1987) 'Procedural rights in the wrong system: Special education is not enough', in Gartner, A. and Joe, T. (Eds) *Images of the Disabled/Disabling Images*. New York: Praeger.

Wang, M. C., Reynolds, M. C. and Walberg, H. J. (1986) 'Rethinking special education', *Educational Leadership*, **44**, 1:26-31.

Wang, M. C., Reynolds, M. C. and Walberg, H. J. (1987) *Handbook of Special Education: Research and Practice (Vol. 1: Learner Characteristics and Adaptive Education)*. Oxford: Pergamon Press.

42

Weatherley, R. (1979) *Reforming Special Education: Policy Implementation from State Level to Street Level*. Cambridge, MA: MIT Press.

Weber, M. (1958) *The Protestant Ethic and the Spirit of Capitalism*. New York: Charles Scribner's Sons; (Original work published 1904–5).

Weber, M. (1978) *Economy and Society*. (G. Roth and C. Wittich, Eds., E. Fischoll *et al.*, trans.) 2 vols. Berkeley: University of California Press. (Original work published 1922).

Weick, K. E. (1976) 'Educational organizations as loosely coupled systems', *Administrative Science Quarterly*, **21**,1:1–19.

Weick, K. E. (1982) 'Administering education in loosely coupled schools', *Phi Delta Kappan*, **63**, 10:673–6.

Wise, A. E. (1988) 'The two conflicting trends in school reform: Legislated learning revisited', *Phi Delta Kappan*, **69**, 5:328–33.

Woodward, J. (1965) *Industrial Organizations: Theory and Practice*. Oxford: Oxford University Press.

Wright, A. R., Cooperstein, R. A., Reneker, E. G. and Padilla, C. (1982) *Local Implementation of PL94–142: Final Report of a Longitudinal Study*. Menlo Park, CA: SRI International.

Zucker, L. G. (1981) 'Institutional structure and organizational processes: The role of evaluation units in schools', in Bank, A. and Williams, R. C. (Eds), *Evaluation and Decision Making*, (CSE Monograph Series, No. 10). Los Angeles: UCLA Center for the Study of Evaluation.

CHAPTER 3

Learning Initiatives to Include All Students in Regular Schools

Roger Slee

Learning the language

Geographical isolation has not distanced the Australian education and special education communities from the integration debate. State education authorities in this country have gradually had to consider their positions with regard to the integration of students 'with special educational needs' into regular schools. As one moves around the continent, it is evident that there are similarities and differences in how integration or 'mainstreaming' is perceived, translated into policy and, in turn, implemented and practised.

Released in 1984, *Integration in Victorian Education* (Ministry of Education – Victoria, 1984b) contrasts with documents from the other Australian states in its unconditional acceptance of the right of all children to an education in the regular classroom. This departs from the American precedent, Public Law 94–142, The Education for All Handicapped Children's Act, 1975, where the decision to integrate rests with the discretionary authority of professionals and experts.

Not surprisingly the report and consequent policy guidelines generated much contest and acrimony about the philosophy and process of integration. For change in education is not simply an issue of redrafting legislation. The complexity of schooling requires a more systematic and considered approach to the process of implementing changes which target both the culture and processes of the organisation (Ball, 1987; Fullan, 1990). What the research suggests is that to effect organisational change at all levels, and which is enduring, the constituents of that organisation should be included in the process of setting and enacting the agenda for change themselves (Evans *et al.*, 1989).

This chapter seeks to address a number of issues arising from the competing interests of special education and unconditional integration (Biklen, 1985a) as they were played out on the Victorian stage. Some rehearsal of the growing sociology of special education (Barton and Tomlinson, 1981; Ford, Mongon and Whelan, 1982; Fulcher, 1989; Skrtic, 1986; Tomlinson, 1982) will be pursued to assist in the dressing of that stage. This research highlights what Ainscow (Chapter 1, this volume) identifies as the fundamental paradox of the contradictory intent and effect of special education.

The final section of this chapter describes how the Victorian Education Ministry attempted to transform the debate so that the focus shifted from the disabilities and deficits of individuals to a consideration of the contribution of the curriculum, pedagogy and organisation of schooling to the inclusion, or exclusion, of students.

Seconded to the Ministry of Education's Portfolio Policy Co-ordination Division, it was my task to coordinate the 'Learning Initiatives To Include All Learners In Regular Schools' project. Our task embraced:

(1) identifying key issues in the implementation of integration policy;
(2) identifying learning initiatives and school practices which had contributed to the inclusion of all students, and to the improvement of their educational outcomes; and
(3) to advise on school organisation, programmes and pedagogy to extend these achievements to other schools and their communities.

At the outset it is necessary to acknowledge the complex matrix of issues which accompanies any discussion of integration. Complex because it strikes at the heart of the purpose of schooling, and concomitantly, at the nature of the society served by those schools. This is compounded by problems of linguistics or discourse. Observing the application of integration policy reveals divergence between the stated and the actual function of integration. Indeed, 'integration' has generated what Barthes contends is a discourse of concealment (1972:143). While all employ an integration discourse, practices reveal contradictions between extensions of control of difference and the movement towards the establishment of an authentic place for all in the regular classroom. Put simply, special educators excise old vocabulary, insert epithets of integration and continue traditional practice with new explanations for what they have traditionally done. This educational surgery is merely cosmetic.

Failure to recognize such contradictions depoliticizes language, conforming to the functionalist imperative of fixing kids to minimize disruption to the schooling process. As Fulcher contends, 'how language is used matters' (1989:4). Special educators have donned the discourse of integration devoid of an appropriate paradigmatic shift (Skrtic, 1986) and consequent transformation of practice.

Setting the stage

Identifying *The Politics of Special Educational Needs*, Barton (1988) employs a broad brush to map the political and economic context within which educational decisions are currently made. The monetarist perspective of the Conservative British government, he argues, 'has heralded a commitment to competition, privatization and extensive legislative powers' (Barton, 1988:1). As a result the democratic rites of passage are denied to a significant sector of the population. In this way special education allows itself to serve the function of containment for those deemed unfit, a rapidly expanding throng, for schooling in the 'mainstream'.

One is mindful of Warnock's own conceding to the conceptual ambiguity of 'special educational needs', a term she legitimized in the 1978 report of that name:

> Perhaps the main reason for the newly apparent poverty of special needs is in its definition . . . or rather its lack of definition . . . the concept of 'special need' carries a fake objectivity. For one of the main, indeed almost overwhelming, difficulties is to decide whose needs are special, or what 'special' means (Warnock, 1982:372).

Gartner and Lipsky support such doubt about the objectivity of definition. Ascertainment of 'special needs' is not simply a function of the characteristics of the student, but also of:

> . . . the number of programs, availability of space, incentives for identification, range and kind of competing programs and services, number of professionals . . . (Gartner and Lipsky, 1987:372).

Galloway (1985), Ford *et al.* (1982), and Tomlinson (1982) had previously explored this correspondence between service provision and the incidence of disability in the United Kingdom. Moreover, the processes and apparatus for acertainment of 'special educational needs' have attracted much critical scrutiny:

... when test results do not produce the desired outcome, evaluators often change the yardstick: 'If the test scores indicate the child is ineligible, but the teacher really feels the child needs help, we try to select other tests that might make the child eligible ... '. The tests then become 'a means of corroborating referral decisions. Testing, therefore, does not drive decisions but is driven by decisions' (Gartner and Lipsky, 1987:372).

Studies by Gould (1981), Blum (1978), Kamin (1974) and Henriques, Holloway, Urwin, Venn and Walkerdine (1984) would suggest that the accounts documented in Gartner and Lipsky's survey of school psychologists and teachers leave little room for astonishment.

The challenge, recently offered by Biklen, is that of how schools perceive integration:

Is integration understood as an outsider coming in, or as creating a school culture so that it accepts all comers? (Fulcher et al., 1990:4).

Integration is thus the proper concern for all students rather than a policy initiative which focuses upon those ascertained in various ways as having differences which separate them from their peers. Difference, and in turn integration, is not simply a question of how we respond to disability. More precisely, the central issue is how we extend education and social justice to all students. This becomes a more pressing concern when we acknowledge that deviance is socially constructed (Becker, 1963; Cohen, 1985; DeSwaan, 1990; Gilman, 1988; Goode, 1984; Schur, 1971; Suchar, 1978). Schools apply similar processes to transform difference into deviance (Barton, 1988; Ford et al., 1982; Polk and Schafer, 1972).

What does all this mean for 'special needs'?

Reflecting upon his work as an Integration Teacher in a Victorian secondary school, Semmens distinguishes between 'comprehensive schooling' and 'apprehensive schooling'. The responsibility for schools with respect to comprehensive education is enunciated by the Ministry for Education in *The School Curriculum and Organisation Framework: P-12* (Ministry of Education – Victoria, 1988:8-9):

Existing statewide policies require each school to provide a comprehensive curriculum for each of its students, to have high expectations of all students and to involve them in challenging courses and tasks.

The policies also commit the education system to the provision of the highest quality for all students, regardless of location, ethnic origin, gender, socio-economic background or **level of ability**. All schools are expected to seek to redress educational disadvantage, and **improve learning for all students, by making a firm commitment to the objectives of social justice**.

While the language and intent of policy is apparently unambiguous, the practice of schooling has shown divergent trends. The political and economic contingencies previously described have precipitated a rush to the private schools as parents seek to purchase successful academic and vocational credentials for their children (Ashenden, 1989). It has also created a press upon public schools to compete with the private sector and to emulate their perceived curriculum and pedagogy. This trend is not unique to Australia (Ball, 1988:134).

On the one hand there is a rhetorical commitment to comprehensive curriculum which takes *all comers*, provides quality learning, exhibits high expectations and promises that students will emerge to take up effective roles in the wider community. This stands in stark contrast to a reality, on the other hand, where some schools are decidedly apprehensive about some of the students who present at their doors to be enrolled. School administrators are all too aware of the widespread community belief that integration leads inexorably to a diminution in standards. Commitment to traditional academic profiles eclipses notions of democratic schooling, of a principled educational theory which redresses disadvantage (Guttman, 1988).

The imperative for apprehensive schooling is to predict students' potential for success in the final year of secondary education and to lead them to that success. For those who clearly will not succeed, the schooling process serves to separate them into alternative or terminal programmes. The implications of this process of culling and selection are indeed dire.

As Polk (1988) and Sweet (1988) have demonstrated, structural changes in the youth labour market have had a significant impact on schooling. The evaporation of unskilled and semi-skilled work in manufacturing industry, together with disproportionate employment of older applicants in the service sector and the emergence of new skill and knowledge requirements in the emerging growth areas translates as severe disadvantage for those who leave, or who are forced out, of school prematurely (Polk, 1988:116–20). As the turnstile which regulates the conditions and flow of youth towards scarce employment opportunities, success at school is vital. To be unsuccessful is to risk being vocationally gelded as you try to negotiate the aforementioned turnstile without the appropriate credentials.

A recent action-research project undertaken by secondary school students in Victoria demonstrates that students are desperately aware of this state of affairs (Slee, 1988a). They realize early in their academic careers whether they are in the *sponsored* or *marginal* tracks (Knight, 1985; Polk, 1984). We provide some students with reasons for commitment to their schooling. Others search, but find little reason for application, conformity or attendance. In short, they have nothing to lose. With a rather savage twist of the knife, we then explain their disillusionment, resistance and failure to learn as a consequence of their own deficits (Henriques *et al.*, 1984). They have a learning difficulty, a personality problem, come from a defective family or social context, or they are pathologically maladjusted. This list of causation is not exhaustive. Ryan (1976) has observed this process of victim blaming in the American urban context. Coulby and Harper (1985) are amongst researchers who have considered the application of victim blaming theory to schooling and special educational ascertainment and labelling.

As competition becomes more intense, increasing numbers of students will be moved into trajectories that steer them to the margins of school life. Whether it takes the form of an alternative or special needs annexe, a life skills programme or pastoral care, the result is the same. Foucault's elegant analysis of the history of the surveillance and containment of the insane is poignant in this context (Foucault, 1987:35). Teachers need to resist the temptation of expanding the provision for students discarded by the mainstream, of proliferating educational ships of fools (Slee, 1989).

Make no mistake, the process is not benign. This is not a random selection which seizes upon those who have no ability and who, therefore, do not deserve to succeed because they have flouted equal opportunities fairly dispensed. The weight of evidence from the work of the Commonwealth Schools Commission (Karmel, 1973) to the findings of Connell *et al.* (1982) demonstrates the relative disadvantage and vulnerability of particular groups of students within our schools. This is congruent with findings elsewhere. Tomlinson (1978), Galloway and Barrett (1984) and Morrisette and Koshiyama (1976) each demonstrate the disproportionate assignment of students from ethnic minority groups to off-site educational centres.

Ball (1986), Henderson (1976) and Willis (1978) plot similar patterns in the marginalization of students according to socioeconomic class. Gender, as has been prodigiously argued, represents another factor to the exclusion equation: Kenway (1990), Porter (1986), Spender (1982) and Wolpe (1988) are indicative.

Genuine redress of disadvantage does require a commitment to comprehensive education and to a rethinking of credentialling. Such a commitment must move beyond rhetoric. There is a need to enlist teachers, parents and students in the transformation of schools into enabling or inclusive institutions. *Successful Schooling* (Fulcher *et al.*, 1990), the report of the 'learning initiatives' project, goes part of the way in documenting attempts within some Australian schools to include all students and effect the paradigmatic shift from defective individuals to improving schools.

Integration in Victoria – a policy backdrop

The preceding discussion reconstructs the notions of *disability* and *integration*. Clearly, some students are enabled by the apprehensive school. Others are disabled. Disability is not simply a characteristic of the learner, it is a reflection of the interaction between the learner and the organisation, curriculum, pedagogy and culture of the school. While the organisation, pedagogy, curriculum and culture of some schools pushes some children to the margins and beyond, others are included and assisted. This chapter argues that this process of social selection is not changed by acting on the students placed at risk, but by addressing the process of schooling. This represents the conceptual core of *Integration in Victorian Education* (Ministry of Education – Victoria, 1984b), the report which established the foundations for government policy.

The principal author of that report has subsequently provided a rigorous analysis of policy development and implementation, and, significantly, of the contests that policy has generated (Fulcher, 1989). Particularly interesting is her assertion that 'policy is made at all levels' (pp. 5–7). In 'an educational system too rooted in a philosophy of selection' it is folly to imagine that broad policy statements, nor even changes in bureaucratic procedures, is sufficient to produce 'a consensus shift in education practice' (Booth and Potts, 1983:56–7). Vested interests remain, and conventional attitudes, practices and discourse can be adjusted to occlude the original intent of policy. In this way policies enunciated at different levels become distractive noise (Ball, 1988:132) or, as Mannheim (1946) depicted it some time ago, a functional rationality.

What this means is that while state policy manifests commitment to unconditional integration (Biklen, 1985a), the classroom teacher may decide in his or her domain that it is appropriate that the child be separated for a language lesson. It may even mean that school councils draft caveats in their integration policies and school operating manuals that protect the rights of the majority of students against minority interests. Clearly both contradict the spirit of integration in Victorian Education Ministry policy, yet both are proposed and defended by an untheorized language of integration. As Fulcher contends, integration suffers from conceptual chaos (Ministry of Education – Victoria, 1984b:10).

Policy, therefore, needs to recognize the presence of lateral as well as vertical relationships of power and competition (Ball, 1987; 1989). How policy is developed and implemented must account for these relationships. Victorian integration policy did not.

Issues in Victorian integration – a selective summary
Integration was considered a part of the Labor Government's commitment to social justice. The Integration Report (*Integration in Victorian Education*, Ministry of Education – Victoria, 1984b) thus advanced a rights model, assuming a systems approach to understanding impairment, disability and handicap (WHO, 1980). Integration was indentified as:

> (1) a process of **increasing** the participation of children with impairments, disabilities and problems with schooling in the education and social life of regular schools in which their peers without disabilities participate;
> (2) a process of **maintaining** the participation of all children in the educational programmes and social life of regular schools (Ministry of Education – Victoria, 1984b:6).

The focus of the report writers included not only students with conspicuous disability outside the regular school, but sought also to ensure that students be maintained in a school system which did not create disabled and deviant students.

The report recommended the deployment of resources to the regular school and redeployment of some specialist and support staff. All the hallmarks for controversy were contained within the report, and as Fulcher records, were played out in its drafting (1989:189–91). Professional interest is an extremely sensitive variable when commissioning architects to reassemble job descriptions.

Contests over professional interest, resources and, implicitly, over attitudes towards the disabled emerged. An interesting late inclusion in the report's focus was the designation: students with problems in schooling. The increasingly populous group of so-called 'socially/emotionally disturbed' seemed to fit this label very neatly. The equation became disarmingly simple. Disruptive students must be socially/emotionally disturbed and therefore require the specialist support and resources which the classroom teacher is unable to provide. Discipline problems could now be administratively transferred to the integration processes. Albeit inadvertently, schools were thereby offered further mechanisms for control and containment as the effectiveness of traditional punitive measures became less effective (Slee, 1988b). The effects of the application of this new deviant status to yesterday's naughty children warrants further investigation.

Predictably, resources became a major point for dispute between schools and the Education Ministry. Schools largely perceived the challenge of integration being the successful application for additional school resources. Where resources were not forthcoming, schools argued their inability to accept these additional children. In order to extinguish the frequent spot fires the Minister intervened to decree that while all children would be enrolled in their local school, their admission would be delayed until such time as the school had secured the resources required for the integration of that student.

What this legal sleight of hand concedes is that integration is merely contingent upon the provision of personnel and physical resources. It constructs integration as a technical issue denying the implications for curriculum or social justice. To be sure integration is not dumping (Biklen, 1985b) and we cannot expect children to pursue their education in the absence of resources necessary for their effective participation. However, the deployment of resources is not in itself a guarantee for successful integration.

What 'The Integration Report' did not pursue was the way in which school curriculum, teaching methodologies and school organisation may be the disabling factors in a child's education. It is disturbing that in another Australian state, Queensland, the teachers' union has placed an embargo on integration until appropriate resources are supplied. What constitutes appropriate resources? When the cargo arrives to satiate the cult, the school may still experience failure to include all of its students if we consider successful integration to be synonymous with effective teaching.

Two disturbing trends emerged in the way in which some schools respond to integration funding procedures: (1) wanting to maintain solid academic profiles, some schools made outlandish submissions for resources in order to deter parents from pursuing the rights of passage for their children; (2) the promise of additional resources led some enterprising schools to the discovery of new integration students. It was simply a matter of ascertainment and furnishing the submission with the endorsement of Student Services (Educational Psychologists and Social Workers Branch). Formerly withdrawn, low-achieving or disruptive students became the targets of funding as socially/emotionally disturbed, maladjusted, learning disabled, developmentally delayed...time and space prevents us from exhausting the lexicon of exclusion.

Another major arena for integration scrutiny has been pre-service education and professional development. Here too, interests clashed and political agendas unfolded. For many the appropriate response was to move special education academics into undergraduate and postgraduate courses. These courses could then be topped up with traditional approaches to the diagnosis of special needs and introduce a range of remedial and palliative responses that the new breed of teachers could offer these additional students in their classrooms. This certainly appeared to be the popular manifestation of the tertiary reaction to state policy. Moreover, thus construed, it presents a further windfall to special education establishments to maintain and expand traditional practice.

A more interesting response was a proposal for a school-based graduate diploma in special education. The course developers negotiated with a local school to place graduate students (i.e., trained teachers) in that school and collaborate with classroom teachers to identify the issues which beset students and teachers in order to develop curriculum and teaching strategies to improve the educational programme for all students. Educational theory would be related to the practice of teaching and administration of school programmes. Tertiary educators would move into the school to supervise and teach. In this way the programme provides a sound instructional model and additional resources for the pilot school. Though the school, the Education Ministry and teachers wishing to enrol were fulsome in their support, the College's Department of Special Education was able to mobilize support to counter innovation and sustain traditional postures impervious to changing contexts. A great deal more consideration has to be given to the implications of the paradigmatic shift required if we are to effectively train teachers in inclusive curriculum and practice.

This summary needs also to acknowledge the plight of parents in the implementation of policy. Many schools would claim that their commitment to collaborative decision-making was more than rhetorical. Indeed, this tenet is considered axiomatic by the Ministry. There have been numerous considerations of the relationship between stated and enacted policy in this regard (Rizvi, 1985; Rizvi *et al.*, 1987). Marks (1989) considers the institutional disadvantage of parents in the integration enrolment processes. Her work provides further testimony to similar findings (Galloway, 1985).

Amidst official commitment to integration in Victoria a curious development has been noted. Segregated special educational provision continues to grow (Fulcher, 1988). Not only was the segregated provision attracting increased funding, but there was also the discovery of a new clientele in the regular setting: the paradoxically entitled integration student. This reflects surveillance and control in the area of decarceration policy in general (Cohen, 1985; Edwards, 1988; Scull, 1984).

Learning Initiatives To Include All Students in Regular Schools – the successful schooling report

Commencing as an initiative of the Ministerial Standing Committee to Advise on the Education of Pupils with Impairments and Disabilities (SCAEPID), *Learning Initiatives To Include All Students In Regular Schools* sought to identify these critical issues and successful learning initiatives which enabled more students to be successful in regular classrooms.

In 1987, a discussion paper drew together all of the significant Ministry of Education and State Board of Education documents pertaining to school curriculum, organisation and policy. This paper was used to establish the parameters for a representative steering committee which was to consider issues pursuant to the implementation of integration policy.

One of the first tasks confronting the group was to come to terms with the issue of focus. The challenge seemed to be that of moving the glare of scrutiny from those who were having problems in schooling or who were impaired or disabled, to all students, and to identify the ways in which schools were including and enabling them. We were attempting to effect a shift from disability as an individual issue to a systems issue. It was necessary to wrest integration from the mono-dimensional debates over resources and to consider the contribution of curriculum, pedagogy and school organisation to the success or failure of integration.

Bringing in the players

The committee then designed a strategy to incorporate schools which were systems focused within the project. Education Ministry regional officers were requested to identify three schools they considered to be successfully integrating their students. The schools represented both the primary and secondary sectors. Time was spent discussing our expectations for the project with the regions to assist them with their choices.

There remained an element of interpretation, regions having differing perceptions concerning integration. Each of the schools were sent a survey instrument which invited them to describe and evaluate the 'learning initiatives to include all students in regular schools' that they had created in their programmes. The proforma was open in its design so as to encourage diversity in response.

Following the completion of the survey, the schools were invited to send representatives to a meeting where they could discuss the integration issues that concerned them, their learning initiatives, and the next phase of the project. This was in itself an excellent exercise in professional development. Participants attested to the benefits accrued from talking to each other about integration issues and the strategies developed at school level to meet these challenges. Significantly, the sessions were positive in tone as participants felt that they had been recognised for achievement and were keen to share their success and learn from others.

The list of participating schools was then culled to seven for further observation and research. The data collected from the other schools formed a continuing bank of information to be incorporated in the report.

Members of the steering committee visited each of the seven schools to spend time with administrators, school council representatives, teachers, students, parents and support personnel. School programmes were observed during these visits. The selection of schools was a difficult and strategic task. The schools chosen were representative of the range of schools within the state so that there was greater potential for connection between the case studies in the final report and the reader.

The schools selected exhibited a variety of approaches to including all students, but were consistent in a number of important features. The schools, to varying extents, had perceived integration as extending beyond opening their doors to a student with a conspicuous disability. Their understanding embraced consideration of how they were supporting all students to continue successfully within the school. This was clearly stated by one of the post-primary schools that had become the destination for many students who were squeezed, or who opted, out of the local academic high schools. Faced with the task of framing their integration funding submissions, their choice seemed to be that of deciding whether to name three-quarters of their students who, in another school, may be designated integration students. The issue to them was one of developing a school culture and curriculum that enabled the students at the school to be successful, rather than an idealized notion of the successful students. Lidsay Connors, one of the Counsellors on the Australian National Board of Employment, Education and Training (NBEET), relates a conversation with a principal who was proud of his school, but extremely disappointed that they were getting the wrong kinds of students!

Rather than precipitating a diminution in standards, the school we observed has delivered results according to a range of indicators. It has done so without ascribing students to integration or special needs status. It boasts greater success in enabling students to progress to higher education than other local high schools specifically aiming at that goal and discarding those who threaten success. It has documented better articulation to the workforce than many other schools because of its initiatives in enlisting the support of the business community in its school programmes. It demonstrates greater levels of commitment within its student body as reflected in lower levels of absenteeism, suspension and premature leaving.

One of the students we spoke to at this school was referred to the school having been labelled 'school phobic' and 'chronic truant' by the school guidance branch. His explanation is compelling in its candour: 'I can't stay away from here because I've got too much responsibility to stay away'. Indeed he has. As chairperson of the student representative council, member of the debating team, leading performer in the school production and successful year-eleven student, he is more than busy. A range of curriculum options and teaching strategies and a share in the governance of his school have contributed in this transformation.

Teachers and parents described the ways in which they had traversed and eliminated what Knight refers to as the false dichotomy between academic development and social skills development (1988:322). Traditionally, difficulties which arise in the classroom are referred to experts outside of the classroom. Student problems, as they are described, are treated and the student returns. The issues are expunged from the classroom agenda. This removes responsibility for resolution from the students. Moreover, students are frequently unable to articulate the issues arising in their classrooms. It also limits the range of that with which the teacher feels willing or capable to deal (Grunsell, 1980).

By discussing difference and the unique issues confronting some of their peers, teachers assist their students to appreciate difference and the adjustments required to enable all students to enjoy a regular education. Moreover, we were able to observe how students were empowered to contribute to each others' success. Cooperative learning programmes, peer and cross-age tutoring, and flexible timetabling are indicative.

Effective schools and integration

Believing successful integration to be akin to successful schooling, the committee considered the effective schools research in the light of its own observations and data. Such consideration was underwritten by the belief that:

> ... successful schools are concerned, first, with reducing inequalities between students, both now and in their later life chances (Fulcher *et al*, 1990:19).

We also had to come to terms with the often cited conviction that integration could usually be a successful social exercise, but one should not expect similar results in the children's learning. In his work on the 'complete school', Biklen establishes integration and learning as correlated goals (1985a:61). Integration is thus not simply a means for appeasing our collective conscience. It is founded upon a commitment to improving life chances through improved learning programmes.

Approaching the effective schooling literature was undertaken with an element of caution. Ball points to the way in which such research can be mobilized against schools within conservative political discourse. Lists are constructed against which schools can be measured and manipulated (Ball, 1988:132). Pink (1988) observes similar trends in American educational politics.

In his 'search for effective schools', Reynolds (1982) notes his early concerns about abuses of the research. Schools would do better, he asserted, to look at school culture and the social relations of school life rather than structures in their quest for reform (p. 234). Some years later Reynolds and his colleagues call for extensions of effective schooling initiatives beyond 'simplistic five, seven, or nine factor theories derived from school effectiveness research that is itself now over a decade in age' (Creemers *et al.*, 1989:382). Research into effective curriculum and pedagogy lags.

The report argues that while effective schooling has the capacity to be hijacked by those seeking to instil corporate practice and values in schools, effective schools have as their central concern the achievement of broader educational objectives: developing talent, tolerance and participation (Ball, 1988:150), critical literacy and civic courage (Giroux, 1984). Moreover, schools which are effective aim to produce a culture to improve the credentials of all students. These objectives are congruent with the educational, political and social aims of integration.

The committee was impressed by the commonality of certain features of the schools within our cohort. Of particular interest was that these features were certainly identified within the school effectiveness data. The New Zealand studies of Ramsay *et al.* (1983) concluded that while the schools that were generally regarded as 'successful' varied from each other in a number of respects, they also had a number of shared characteristics which distinguished them from the unsuccessful schools within their cohort. These characteristics included:

(1) a clearly articulated philosophy or statement of goals;
(2) clear patterns of formal and informal communications;
(3) democratic decision-making processes;
(4) systematic attention to student records (to enhance performance rather than as a surveillance mechanism);
(5) parents involved as helpers, teachers and in decision-making, and students working in projects outside of the school;
(6) school resources were available *and used*;
(7) students and teachers worked together to improve the school environment; and
(8) senior staff took responsibility for ensuring that teachers' morale was high.

Successful Schooling (Fulcher *et al.*, 1990) documents consistency between Ramsay *et al*'s findings and the schools identified within the Victorian cohort. The New Zealand research findings were augmented by the findings of others such as Pink (1988) and Reynolds (1982; 1985). The importance of educational and administrative leadership, of school-based curriculum development and evaluation, of high expectations for staff and student performance, and of staff collegiality may be added to the previous list.

The State Board of Education – Victoria, having previously warned against simplistic recipes for school reform (1986), cited the following as fundamental to the process of school improvement:

> educationally effective administration
> positive school climate
> goal-focused curriculum
> participatory structures
> school evaluation based on problem-solving practices.

Although not used in this project, Mortimore *et al.*'s work (1988) with the headteachers, teachers, parents and pupils of 50 inner London schools led them to the conclusion that school does matter in the determination of educational outcomes. Significantly they structure their findings in a way that suggests strategies, or points of entry, in the various constituent parts of the educational complex (pp. 263–90). The study suggests that the school is more than the sum total of the constituent parts which militates against the recipe approach to this research.

Successful schooling
The descriptions within the report are linked to actual school practices and action-research within school communities. In this way the intention is not prescription, rather it provides indications of processes which resulted in significant achievements for those school communities participating in this project.

In early discussions it was clear that the committee had the capacity to inflame debate by announcing to schools that many of them had got it wrong, and then blithely reiterating policy. Conversely we attempted to include the constituents in the processes of the review. In so doing, the processes of school-based curriculum development which had included and maintained more students in regular classrooms could be demonstrated to other schools in order to clarify the practical implications of policy and provide some indications of how they might become less apprehensive about integration. The clear links to documented school practice lend added credibility to the report.

This is not to say that the report fails to address controversy. From the outset, the report attests to the increasing propensity of schools to fail increasing numbers of students who remain at school through lack of viable options. Implicitly acknowledged is the need for the continued evaluation of credentialling processes. The expansion of special needs is considered in this context. The debate over integration is intensely political. The rights of all children remains the central philosophical and educational issue.

While it is difficult to comprehensively deal with our findings some of the significant issues addressed comprise:

1. Curriculum as a central concern

The successful schools in the cohort approached the task of including all of their students by addressing curriculum. Curriculum was understood as the formal and informal learnings determined by what is and what is not taught; how it is taught; and the school organisation, ethos, routines and rituals. The focus was clearly placed on the role of the school systematically sponsoring change. This stands in contrast to the traditional special educational gaze upon the perceived pathology and capacity of the individual.

To this end, vertical modular grouping, where students were able to plot, in concert with their teachers, their academic paths, with an emphasis on success, represents a way in which flexibility to meet all students' needs may be achieved. Where students required more time in particular disciplines because they experienced difficulty, there was no stigma attached because the variety of units within strands afforded this opportunity devoid of the imputation of failure.

Peer tutoring, cross-age tutoring and cooperative learning programmes ensured variety in learning and teaching so as to enable more students to progress than were enabled in the more restrictive didactic models. The successful schools encouraged a problem-solving approach to learning and to the organisation of the classroom. Students participated in classroom and school decision-making. They were responsible for individual conduct and, collectively, for that of the organisation.

2. Reframing the resources debate

That schools had largely assumed a cargo cult approach to integration is witnessed through the many disputes over unmet resources submissions. In these cases students were frequently denied access to the classroom. The intercession of the department to defuse the debate effectively supported the view that integration was essentially about the allocation of resources. In the light of our preceding discussion of the role of schools in regulating the flow of kids into special needs categories, scrutiny on resources is only part of the issue. We need to consider how they are deployed.

The maintenance of resources in segregated centres and the search for additional resources to facilitate integration becomes significant.

The other dimension here is how we decide what resources are in fact needed. Observation suggests that integration aides stood as obstacles to integration, often increasing the learned helplessness of students.

Where resources were not plentiful and schools still pursued the provision of schooling for all children, they collaboratively considered their needs and then deployed resources, rearranged teaching organisation and called on community support pursuant to successful integration. A case in point was where one integration aide stated that her aim was to make herself redundant as rapidly as possible. Her strategy was to consult with the various specialists to whom the child was referred, learn how to supervise the child in the exercises applied at the specialist centre, and then return to the school and have the teachers and the child's peers learn how to assist the child in their own physiotherapy. The expert's role was then transformed to visiting the school to evaluate progress. The child no longer had extended absences from the classroom.

One aspect of the resources conundrum is how we can deploy resources so that they can move with the children requiring assistance. Presently there is a reluctance to challenge the separation of resources into specialist centres, to which children must be allocated.

3. Shifting the focus from experts to expertise

An inspiring anecdote discovered during discussions with parents from one of our successful schools best explains our concern here. In a large regional township in the north of Victoria we met a group of parents whose children were being integrated into a primary school we visited. We learnt a great deal from this group of people about parents' perceptions of integration in general and the role of teachers and experts in particular. Particularly moving was the account of a child whose parents were told soon after birth that the most appropriate education would be found in a special developmental school. It was expert opinion that the child would never be able to communicate with anyone throughout her life. Other parents spoke of similar prognostications given to them by the town's paediatrician.

Fortunately the parents resisted the expert's scenario and struggled to have their child placed in an environment where regular communication could be observed and mimicked. The children in this girl's class decided, upon hearing their friend's first attempts at speech, to hold a class 'five word sentence party' when she put five words together in a sensible sentence. The party had taken place before we arrived at the school. One can only speculate about the level of progress she may have made if all she had to mimic was the unintelligible monosyllables of a speech therapist in a room removed from social dialogue. The expertise of parents is an important variable to be utilized by schools in the education of all children.

Expertise is important but it should be derived from context in working with the particular child, parents and teachers. Schools were able to demonstrate how they had sought to expand their own competencies in a range of areas to meet the needs of their students, rather than send the kids away to experts. In this way the teachers, students and parents all learnt about the function of physiotherapy in maintaining Michael in the classroom. More than this they learnt how to help Michael with particular exercises so that he could remain in the room. Expertise was consulted and utilized pursuant to enabling all to maintain a range of differences in their proper place in the classroom.

4. Reducing bureaucratic procedures to increase communication
Predictably, we observed the continued struggle parents experience in dealing with teachers, school administrators, medics, psychologists and the host of other professionals who move in and out of the life of the integrated child. Equally, the procedures designed to regulate the communication between the school and the parents of these children presented numerous difficulties to parents and teachers alike. Assertive parents assuming the proper role as advocates for their children are met with hostility. Parents lacking confidence or who are less articulate experience manipulation and describe ways in which their children are actually or symbolically removed from their control. Teachers and other professionals confidently make prognoses which are speculative rather than authoritative, displaying little regard for the deterministic power of such forecasting.

Equally, teachers lacking knowledge about the implications of specific impairments or conditions for students' learning, feel vulnerable. Their vulnerability is actually maintained through the bureaucratic processes which retain expert control for the itinerant special consultants who work with the child, and who use jargon in meetings that teachers feel reluctant to seek clarification on, let alone challenge.

A variety of strategies were observed that were locally created and locally effective. One such strategy was the keeping of a daily journal where parents and teachers made entries to keep each other informed of progress, events and significant issues. This augmented the valuable informal interchanges between teachers and parents. Other schools had established tea and coffee sessions where those involved could sit in a relaxed way to reflect on issues pertinent to including the child in the school.

Where schools had moved away from the formal integration procedures to meet with their community, there appeared to be greater evidence of progress for all involved. Teachers and parents welcomed formal and informal access to each other so that progress could be monitored and extended. An often-stated concern was that teachers felt it was difficult to measure success with the integrated child. The parents of these same children would speak with great animation and excitement about their child's progress. What seemed less significant to the teachers was monumental for parents. Where this information was shared, both the parents and the teachers felt better able to continue as partners.

5. Inclusive school organisation

These schools made sure that organisation, curriculum options and teaching strategies made all feel competent, challenged and valued within the school community. Involvement in school governance for the children and the parents was an important characteristic of successful schooling.

The practice of streaming students was avoided in preference to having high expectations for all students. Where students felt they were valued because of the organisation, curriculum and pedagogy of the school, resistance decreased and commitment increased. Participatory rather than hierarchical organisation proved more inclusive.

6. Re-educating the teacher educators

A fundamental blockage to integration is the conviction, held by many teachers, that because they have not had special educational training, they will not be able to teach the 'disabled'. The corollary has been that if they must have integration children, then they must either have a specially trained aide or teacher in their room to manage the needs of these different children. Alternatively they themselves must enrol in a post-graduate course in special education.

Teacher education, pre- and post-service, should be reformed so that it addresses questions about inclusive teaching rather than managing individual problems through exclusive special teaching practices. The difficulty here is not simply teacher-driven. Resistance to reforming special education remains the prerogative of the special education fraternity itself. Persuading this group to jettison individual deficit paradigms to consider alternative ways of understanding the construction of disability in education is a significant challenge.

The report recommends the development of school-based professional development initiatives for teachers to consider inclusive pedagogy and curriculum. Bound to its sociological analysis of the production of disability within the schooling process, integration is synonymous with democratic schooling. Consequently, the role of professional development and pre-service education for teachers is pivotal, given the historical foundations of schooling upon hierarchy and exclusion.

Conclusion

By its nature the 'Learning Initiatives' project is ongoing. The report, upon its release, seeks to further inform school administrators, teachers, parents, students, and teacher educators about inclusive schooling. It remains a working document with a number of functions to perform in various education arenas. No doubt it will be contested as it threatens vested interests. Others may embrace it as it provides confirmation, by similar example, for their perception of and response to the demand for provision of quality education for all students.

What it effectively chronicles is the way in which a number of schools have taken up the challenge of educating all comers, and arranging their teaching, programmes and resources to that end. Recognizing the paradoxically deleterious effects of special education upon students, they have generated inclusive teaching and curriculum to maximize the educational achievement for all students in the regular classroom.

This chapter has attempted to reconceptualize integration as an issue of democratic citizenship as well as an educational issue. Because it challenges the traditional understandings of disability and special education, a number of questions are raised, but not directly answered within the chapter. I need not apologize for leaving us suspended in a state where questions outnumber answers.

Brecht invites the audience of *The Good Person of Szechwan* to write their own conclusions to the play if dissatisfied with the playwright's. His challenge is one of critical reflection and action for social justice. This it seems is the challenge collectively presented within this book: how do we reconceptualize the practice of special and regular schooling to improve the educational experience and outcomes for all students? Effective schooling is predicated by the questioning of all of the 'givens' in this educational production, and the collective writing

64

of just endings for all students through the collaborative research and action of all of the players.

Practically, as this chapter indicates, a number of theatres of action exist for local and comprehensive policy development, implementation and evaluation. This project in Victoria provides a process rather than a prescription for such research and action.

References

Ashenden, D. (1989) *State Aid and the Division of Schooling in Australia*. Geelong: Deakin University Press.

Ball, S. J. (1987) *The Micro-Politics of the School*. London: Methuen.

Ball, S. J. (1988) 'Comprehensive schooling, effectiveness and control: an analysis of educational discourses', in Slee, R. (Ed.) *Discipline and Schools: A Curriculum Perspective*, pp. 132–52. Melbourne: Macmillan.

Ball, S. J. (1989) 'Micro-politics versus management: towards a sociology of school organisation', in Walker, S. and Barton, L. (Eds) *Politics and the Processes of Schooling*. Milton Keynes: Open University Press.

Barthes, R. (1972) *Mythologies*. New York: Hill and Wang.

Barton, L. (1988) *The Politics of Special Educational Needs*. London: Falmer Press.

Barton, L. and Tomlinson, S. (1981) *Special Education – Policy, Practices and Social Issues*. London: Harper and Row.

Becker, H. (1963) *Outsiders – Studies in the Sociology of Deviance*. New York: The Free Press.

Becker, H. (1964) *The Other Side – Perspectives on Deviance*. New York: The Free Press.

Biklen, D. (1985a) *Achieving the Complete School*. New York: Teachers College Press.

Biklen, D. (1985b) 'Mainstreaming: from compliance to quality', *Journal of Learning Disabilities*, **18**,1:58–61.

Blum, J. (1978) *Pseudoscience and Mental Ability: The Origins and Fallacies of the IQ Controversy*. New York: Monthly Review Press.

Booth, T. and Potts, P. (1983) *Integrating Special Education*. London: Basil Blackwell.

Burdekin, B. (1989) *Our Homeless Children: Report of the National Enquiry into Homeless Children*. Canberra: Human Rights and Equal Opportunity Commission.

Cohen, S. (1985) *Visions of Social Control*. Cambridge: Polity Press.

Connell, R., Ashenden, D., Kessler, S. and Dowsett, G. (1982) *Making the Difference*. Sydney: Allen and Unwin.

Cooper, H. M. and Good, T. L. (1983) *Pygmalion Grows Up*. New York: Longman.

Coulby, D. and Harper, T. (1985) *Preventing Classroom Disruption*. London: Croom Helm.

Creemers, B., Peters, T. and Reynolds, D. (1989) (Eds) *School Effectiveness and School Improvement*. Amsterdam: Swets and Zeitlinger.

Dawkins, J. and Holding, C. (1987) *Skills for Australia*. Canberra: Australian Government Printer.
DeSwann, A. (1990) *The Management of Normality*. London: Routledge.
Eder, D. (1981) 'Micro-analysis of teacher–student interaction', *Sociology of Education*, **54**:151–61.
Edwards, A. (1988) *Regulation and Repression*. Sydney: Allen and Unwin.
Entwistle, D. R. and Hayduk, L. A. (1981) 'Academic expectations and the school attainment of young children', *Sociology of Education*, **54**.
Evans, B., Cook, A., Slee, R. and Bates, R. (1989) *Changing the Culture of Queensland University of Technology*. Brisbane: Leadership Centre.
Ford, J., Mongon, D. and Whelan, M. (1982) *Invisible Disasters: Special Education and Social Control*. London: Routledge and Kegan Paul.
Foucault, M. (1987) *Madness and Civilization*. London: Tavistock.
Fulcher, G. (1988) 'Integration: inclusion or exclusion?', in Slee, R. (Ed.) *Discipline and Schools: A Curriculum Perspective*. Melbourne: Macmillan.
Fulcher, G. (1989) *Disabling Policies? A Comparative Approach to Education Policy and Disability*. London: Falmer Press.
Fulcher, G., Semmens, R. and Slee, R. (1990) *Successful Schooling*. Melbourne: Ministry of Education – Victoria.
Fullan, M. (1990) *Implementation and Change*. Milton Keynes: Open University Press.
Galloway, D. (1985) *Schools, Pupils and Special Educational Needs*. London: Croom Helm.
Galloway, D. and Barrett, C. (1984) 'Factors associated with suspension from New Zealand secondary schools', *Educational Review*, **36**,3:277–85.
Gartner, A. and Lipsky, D. K. (1987) 'Beyond special education: toward a quality system for all students', *Harvard Educational Review*, **57**,43:367–95.
Gilman, S. L. (1988) *Disease and Representation: Images of Illness from Madness to Aids*. Ithaca: Cornell University Press.
Giroux, H. (1984) 'Public philosophy and the crisis in education', *Harvard Educational Review*, **54**,2:186–94.
Good, T. and Brophy, J. (1984) *Looking in Classrooms*. New York: Harper and Row.
Goode, E. (1984) *Deviant Behaviour*. Englewood Cliffs: Prentice Hall.
Gould, S. J. (1981) *The Mismeasure of Man*. Harmondsworth: Penguin.
Grunsell, R. (1980) *Beyond Control: Schools and Suspension*. London: Writers and Readers.
Guttmann, A. (1988) *Democratic Education*. Princeton: Princeton University Press.
Henriques, J., Holloway, W., Urwin, C., Venn, C. and Walkerdine, V. (1984) *Changing the Subject: Psychology, Social Regulation and Subjectivity*. London: Methuen.
Kamin, L. J. (1974) *The Science and Politics of IQ*. Harmondsworth: Penguin.
Karmel, P. (1973) *Schools in Australia Report of the Interim Committee for the Australian Schools Commission*. Canberra: Australian Government Printing Service.

Kenway, J. (1990) *Gender and Education Policy: A Call for New Directions*. Geelong: Deakin University Press.

Knight, T. (1985) 'Schools and delinquency', in Murray, J. M. and Borowski, A. (Eds) *Juvenile Delinquency in Australia*. Sydney: Methuen.

Knight, T. (1988) 'Student discipline as a curriculum concern', in Slee, R. (Ed.) *Discipline and Schools: A Curriculum Perspective*. Melbourne: Macmillan.

Lewis, J. (1987) 'So much grit in the hub of the educational machine – schools, society and the invention of measurable intelligence', in Bessant, R. (Ed.) *Mother State and Her Little Ones*. Bundoora: LaTrobe University Press.

Mannheim, K. (1946) *Ideology and Utopia*. London: Harcourt, Brace and World.

Marks, G. (1989) *Each an Individual*. Geelong: Deakin University Press.

Ministry of Education – Victoria (1984a) *Curriculum Development and Planning in Victoria*. Melbourne: Victorian Government Printer.

Ministry of Education – Victoria (1984b) *Integration in Victorian Education – Report of the Ministerial Review of Educational Services for the Disabled*. Melbourne: Victorian Government Printer.

Ministry of Education – Victoria (1986) *Taking Schools into the 1990s. A Proposal from the Ministry Structures Project Team*. Melbourne: Victorian Government Printer.

Ministry of Education – Victoria (1988) *The School Curriculum and Organisation Framework: P-12*. Melbourne: Victorian Government Printer.

Morrisette, M. and Koshiyama, A. N. (1976) 'Student advocacy in school discipline: a look at suspensions', *Thrust for Educational Leadership*, 6,2:16–18.

Mortimore, P., Sammons, P., Stoll, L., Lewis, D. and Ecob, R. (1988) *School Matters: The Junior Years*. Wells: Open Books.

Pink, W. T. (1988) 'School climate and effective school programmes in America', in Slee, R. (Ed.) *Discipline and Schools: A Curriculum Perspective*. Melbourne: Macmillan.

Polk, K. (1984) 'The new marginal youth', *Crime and Delinquency*, 30:462–80.

Polk, K. (1988) 'Education, youth unemployment and student resistance', in Slee, R. (Ed.) *Discipline and Schools: A Curriculum Perspective*. Melbourne: Macmillan.

Polk, K. and Schafer, W. (1972) *Schools and Delinquency*. Englewood Cliffs: Prentice Hall.

Porter, P. (1986) *Gender and Education*. Geelong: Deakin University Press.

Ramsay, P., Sneddon, D., Grenfell, J. and Ford, I. (1983) 'Successful and unsuccessful schools: a study in Southern Auckland', *Australian and New Zealand Journal of Sociology*, 19,2:272–303.

Reynolds, D. (1982) 'The search for effective schools', *School Organisation*, 2,3:215–37.

Reynolds, D. (1985) (Ed.) *Studying School Effectiveness*. London: Falmer Press.

Rizvi, F. (1984) 'Problems of devolution in Victorian education', *Regional Journal of Social Issues*, 15:24–31.

Rizvi, F., Kemmis, S., Walker, R., Fisher, J. and Parker, Y. (1987) *Dilemmas of Reform*. Geelong: Deakin University Press.

Ryan, W. (1976) *Blaming the Victim*. New York: Random House.

Schur, E. (1971) *Labelling Deviant Behaviour*. New York: Harper and Row.

Scull, A. (1984) *Decarceration – Community Treatment and the Deviant: A Radical View*. Cambridge: Polity Press.

Semmens, R. (1990) 'Quality education for all? Reflections on a year in the life of Hobson's Bay Secondary College'. Unpublished paper.

Skrtic, T. (1986) 'The crisis in special education knowledge: a perspective on perspective', *Focus on Exceptional Children*, **18**,7:1–16.

Slee, R. (1988a) *Education Action Research Report*. Collingwood: Good Shepherd Youth and Family Service.

Slee, R. (1988b) *Discipline and Schools: A Curriculum Perspective*. Melbourne: Macmillan.

Slee, R. (1989) 'How young people see school: this is no ship of fools'. Paper prepared for the Australian Institute of Criminology – Preventing Juvenile Crime, Melbourne.

Spender, D. (1982) *Invisible Women: The Schooling Scandal*. London: Writers and Readers.

Suchar, C. S. (1978) *Social Deviance: Perspectives and Prospects*. New York: Holt, Rinehart and Winston.

Sweet, R. (1988) 'What do developments in the labour market imply for post-compulsory education in Australia?', *Australian Journal of Education*, **32**, 3:331–56.

Tomlinson, S. (1978) 'West Indian children and ESN-M schooling', *New Community*, **6**,3.

Tomlinson, S. (1981) *Educational Subnormality – A Study in Decision-Making*. London: Routledge and Kegan Paul.

Tomlinson, S. (1982) *A Sociology of Special Education*. London: Routledge and Kegan Paul.

Warnock, M. (1978) *Special Educational Needs*. London: HMSO.

Warnock, M. (1982) 'Children with special needs in ordinary schools: integration revisited', *Education Today*, **32**,3:56–61.

Willis, P. (1978) *Learning to Labour*. Farnborough: Saxon House.

Wolpe, A. (1988) *Within School Walls*. London: Routledge.

World Health Organisation (1980) *International Classifications of Impairments, Disabilities and Handicaps*. Geneva: WHO.

CHAPTER 4

School Effectiveness in Action: Supporting Growth in Schools and Classrooms

Louise Stoll

In the last 20 years, educational researchers have been fascinated by the questions: 'Do schools make a difference?', 'Are some schools and classes more effective than others?'; and, if so: 'Does an effective school have a positive impact on *all* of its pupils?'. These are also questions of interest to all educators and parents, for if schools have little or no impact on the students who attend them, this would be a depressing message for all who care about the future of children.

That, however, was the impression given by social scientists in the United States in the late 1960s and early 1970s. Their studies indicated that a child's home background had a much greater influence than school upon her or his development (Coleman *et al.*, 1966; Jencks *et al.*, 1972). Many interpreted this to mean that what happened in schools was of little consequence to pupils' educational outcomes, which posed a challenge for subsequent researchers. Within the school effectiveness research movement, two groups began to look at the different issues. In Great Britain, in particular, researchers concerned with school differences worked to find a way to separate the impact of family background from that of the school (Reynolds, 1985). They also strived to ascertain whether, indeed, some schools were more effective than others and, if so, what factors contributed to the positive effects (Rutter *et al.*, 1979; Reynolds, 1982).

Other researchers, by contrast, have concentrated more attention on the issue of equity; that is, to quote the late Ron Edmonds (1979),

'Specifically, I require that an effective school bring the children of the poor to those minimal masteries of basic school skills that now describe minimally successful pupil performance for the children of the middle class' (p. 16). Since the work of Edmonds, many researchers have focused on the issue of effective schools for disadvantaged students (see, for example, Bashi and Sass, 1989; Chrispeels and Pollack, 1990; Hallinger and Murphy, 1986; Scheerens, 1987; Teddlie and Stringfield, 1985).

The dichotomy between the two approaches may appear to cause a philosophical tension (Reynolds and Creemers, 1989), and yet it has ensured the examination of school effectiveness from a variety of perspectives and in many different contexts. Both sets of questions are important. We do need to know whether some schools are more effective than others and to ensure equality of opportunity for children from disadvantaged backgrounds. Equally, however, we must not forget that all children are important. Every child needs to be challenged to her or his fullest potential.

In this chapter, I will describe one study of school effectiveness and its application in a school board through a school growth planning process. The system support and reorganisation to sustain such a process will then be examined, along with the implications for special education.

The Junior School Project

One study that has examined many of the school effectiveness issues cited earlier took place in Inner London, with a focus on 50 primary schools (Mortimore *et al.*, 1988). The Junior School Project followed 2000 pupils throughout their junior schooling and examined their progress over this period, taking into account individual children's social class and ethnic background, gender and age.

Broadly, we wanted to answer three key questions:

(1) Are some schools or classes more effective for pupils' educational outcomes, both academic and social, when their initial attainment and background characteristics have been taken into account?
(2) Are some schools or classes more effective for different groups; that is, girls or boys, older or younger pupils, or children of different social class or ethnic backgrounds?
(3) If some schools and classes are more effective, what factors are responsible for their effectiveness?

The range of pupil outcomes on which school effects were examined was broad. Pupils' progress and attainment were followed in reading, written and practical mathematics and writing, and their attainment was also assessed in speaking skills. It was interesting to note that several students who performed less well on the traditional reading assessments, gave competent performances in the speaking skills assessment. This should be a caution to those who judge students solely upon what they can read or write. Students have many intelligences (Gardner, 1983), and account of these should also be taken when assessments are made. This is particularly pertinent for students with special education needs and those for whom English is not their first language.

The Project also monitored pupils' development in terms of attitude, behaviour, self-concept and attendance. Our belief was that a good school is one in which a wide range of student outcomes are positive. Consequently, through an examination of a broad selection of outcomes, a fairer assessment of the general effectiveness of schools could be obtained.

Because the study was longitudinal, it was possible to examine progress as well as attainment. Only through the study of progress was it possible to take adequate account of the widely differing skill levels of children at the start of their junior schooling.

Extensive observations were carried out in classrooms, as well as use of interviews of teachers, administrators, special educators and second language teachers, questionnaires, inventories and checklists. Thus, classroom and teaching effectiveness was as much a focus of this study as school organisational effectiveness. Multi-level statistical models were used to explain differences between schools in terms of data measured at the different levels, such as the individual child, the class and the school.

Information was also collected for each child on a range of background factors, including parental occupation, sex, ethnic background and one-parent family status. Full account of these was taken before examining schools' effects on their pupils. Even when this was done, however, it was found that the school made a very important contribution to pupils' progress and development. In fact, the school was much more important than background in determining the progress of pupils. For reading it was four times more important than background characteristics, and for mathematics and writing, ten times more important. These findings demonstrate conclusively that schools *do* make a difference. Furthermore, there was a considerable difference between the most and least effective schools on each of the range of outcomes we examined. For example, in the reading assessment, there was a 25 point difference between students' average raw scores in the most and least effective schools, out of a possible total of 100 and with an overall average score of 54. This was after all the background effects and initial attainment had been taken into consideration. That was the impact of the school, and the effect of the school was similar for many of the other outcomes.

In terms of the second question – are some schools or classes more effective for different groups of students? – the answer was 'no'. When the effects of schools on the progress of different groups of pupils, by age, race, gender and social class were compared, generally schools which were effective in promoting the progress of one group were also effective for other groups, and those which were less effective for one group were also less effective for others. An effective school tended to be effective for all of its pupils, irrespective of their gender, social class or race. This is an important finding, because certain groups have been found to be more 'at risk' of educational difficulties (Essen and Wedge, 1982; Sammons *et al.*, 1983) and of being placed in special education classes (Wang *et al.*, 1986).

What is it then, that distinguished the more effective schools and classes from those which were less effective?

What makes a school effective?

Certain 'given' features provided an enabling environment in which to create an effective school. These were aspects over which schools and teachers have little direct control, such as class size and school size. These 'given' characteristics, however, only contribute to effectiveness. They do not, by themselves, ensure it. It is the characteristics within the control of the headteacher (principal) and teachers that are vital. These are the characteristics that can be changed and which can provide a framework for school improvement efforts.

Key characteristics of effective schools
We identified 12 key factors of effectiveness. They are outlined below.

(1) Purposeful leadership of the staff by the headteacher – heads in effective schools were actively involved in the school's work, without exerting total control. For example, the head took part in curriculum discussions and influenced guideline content, without completely determining curriculum policies.

(2) Involvement of the deputy head – deputies can play a major role in school effectiveness. Where heads shared and delegated responsibilities, benefits to pupils occurred. Frequent absence of the deputy, in contrast, was detrimental to pupil progress.

(3) Involvement of teachers – better effects were seen in schools where teachers were involved in curriculum planning, guideline development and various aspects of decision-making.

(4) Consistency amongst teachers – where all teachers were consistent in their use of guidelines, the impact on pupil progress was positive.

(5) Structured sessions – positive effects were found when teachers had planned adequate amounts of work and were well organised. Once work had been allocated, the more effective teachers encouraged pupils to work fairly independently.

(6) Intellectually challenging teaching – 'higher order' questions and statements which encouraged pupils to be creative and to solve problems, promoted pupil progress.

(7) Work-centred environment – effective classrooms were busy and purposeful. Teacher time spent discussing the content of work, rather than classroom management issues, had a positive effect on progress. In effective classrooms, pupils appeared to enjoy work and were keen to commence new tasks.

(8) Limited focus within sessions – learning was facilitated when teachers concentrated on one or two subject areas within a session. When three or more activities took place, teachers' attention was more likely to be fragmented and more time was spent on classroom management, and less on the work itself.

A focus on one curriculum area, however, does not imply that all the pupils were doing the same work. On the contrary, different approaches were effective at different times. Effects were most positive when the teacher geared the level of work to the pupils' needs.

(9) Maximum communication between teachers and pupils – pupils gained from having a lot of communications with the teacher. The majority of teachers devoted most of their attention to speaking with individuals. During the course of the day, however, each pupil only received an average of 11 contacts with the teacher. By speaking to the whole class or to groups, teachers increased the overall number of contacts with children. In particular, 'higher-order' communications occurred more frequently when the teacher talked to the whole class.

This does not, however, advocate traditional 'class teaching'. The findings did not show this approach to be beneficial. In fact, from the research, there was no evidence of identifiable 'teaching styles.' We felt that teaching is far too complex to categorise teachers in this way. Nonetheless, the results point to a flexible approach, utilising a blend of individual, class and group communications, as appropriate.

(10) Record keeping – this valuable aspect of teachers' planning and assessment had a positive effect on the pupils. Records included those concerning pupils' personal and social development as well as those relating to work progress.

(11) Parental involvement – an informal 'open-door' policy, parental help in the classrooms and on visits, and the organisation of meetings with parents to discuss their children's progress all promoted school effectiveness. Parental involvement in pupils' educational development within the home was also beneficial.

(12) Positive climate – the Junior School Project provided confirmation that an effective school has a positive atmosphere. Both around the school and within the classroom, less emphasis on criticism and punishment and more on praise and rewarding pupils, had a positive impact. The research pointed to the effectiveness of firm but fair classroom management.

   Teachers with a positive attitude to their classes and an interest in the children as individuals and not just learners fostered progress. The organisation of trips, visits and lunchtime or after-school clubs also contributed to a positive 'ethos'.

   It is important to note that the climate in effective schools was not only positive for the pupils. Teachers' working conditions were important. Where they had timetabled non-teaching periods, positive effects occurred in pupils' progress and development.

The 12 key factors point to effective schools as being inviting, supportive environments, led by headteachers who are not afraid to assert their views and yet are able to share management and decision-making with the staff. Class teachers within effective schools provide a structured learning situation for their pupils, within which freedom and personal responsibility are encouraged. Through the flexible use of whole class and individual contacts, they maximise communication with each pupil. Furthermore, by limiting their focus within a session, teachers' attention is less fragmented, and the opportunities for presenting challenging work to pupils are increased.

Although one or two of these characteristics are specific to the context within which they were studied, it is remarkable how closely the majority resemble the findings of school effectiveness studies undertaken in other countries and under different circumstances. Nonetheless, it is the translation of these findings into practice that makes the difference. This is not straightforward. As Lezotte (1989a) reflects, 'the effective schools research provided a vision of a more desirable place for schools to be, but gave little insight as to how best to make the journey to that place'.

School effectiveness and school improvement

Through the linkage of school effectiveness research with what is known about school improvement, planned change and staff development, schools can be supported in their journey towards effectiveness. The traditional top-down change model, whereby districts mandate 'effectiveness', has seen poor results due to lack of staff involvement and therefore, commitment (Lezotte, 1989a). In the diffusion or 'trainer of trainers' model, one person from each school receives inservice on the topic of school effectiveness and then is responsible for 'spreading the word' back at their school. This may work well if the receiving culture of the school is positive. But if there is little interest on the part of other staff members, the impetus is often lost. What has proved to be more effective is when the whole school is seen as the unit for change and the responsibility for school and classroom improvement lies with those who work in the school, rather than being imposed from outside (Fullan, 1982; Goodlad, 1984; Joyce *et al.*, 1983). This is the model adopted by the Halton Board of Education in its School Effectiveness Project.

The School Effectiveness Project

When I came to the Halton Board of Education in Ontario, I was offered the opportunity to work with a Canadian school system to help implement some of the findings of our British research. The school district, located near Toronto on the north shore of Lake Ontario, Canada, serves 44,000 students in 65 elementary schools and 16 secondary schools. In 1986, a Task Force was set up with the mandate to enhance the quality of the system's performance through the application of the characteristics of effective schools. Over a four-year period a comprehensive model and plan have been developed and many implementation activities have commenced (Stoll and Fink, 1988; 1989; 1990), although there is still a long way to go. The remainder of this chapter examines three key features of Halton's project: a comprehensive model of school effectiveness characteristics; a school growth planning process; and the development of strategic directions and reorganisation of the system to support school-based planning for effectiveness. It also focuses on the implications of the project for meeting the needs of all students within regular classrooms.

Halton's characteristics of effectiveness

As the characteristics of effectiveness had been demonstrated in research to enhance student achievement and self-concept, it was felt that they could form the basis for discussions on the present state of education in Halton.

A detailed examination was made of the findings of international school effectiveness studies in order to isolate the characteristics most commonly defined in a variety of contexts and at elementary and secondary levels. The composite list of characteristics developed by the Task Force was based on a model developed by Sackney (1986) (see Figure 4.1). It can be seen that there is significant overlap between these characteristics and those quoted in the British research outlined previously.

Figure 4.1   The characteristics of effective schools

There are twelve key characteristics in Halton's model. These fall within three broader areas:

- A common mission
- Emphasis on learning
- A climate conducive to learning

The three areas and twelve characteristics are summarised below in brief.

A common mission

Bennis and Nanus (1985) describe a common mission as the articulation of 'a view of a realistic credible future...a condition that is better in some important ways than what now exists'. The mission reflects the shared vision of teachers, students and parents.

Clear goals
Clearly stated and agreed-upon goals give the school a sense of purpose, and enhance its planning and implementation.

Instructional leadership
The principal's leadership is critical to improving the workplace for teachers (Smith and Andrews, 1989). The principal of an effective school has a clear vision for the school and is acknowledged to be the leader of the instructional program.

Shared values and beliefs
Effective schools are characterised by a culture of collaboration in which all of the partners within the school, that is principals, teachers, students, parents and community, share a commitment to work together to develop the schools' learning environment.

Emphasis on learning

'Learning is seen as the primary purpose of schools', state Lezotte and Bancroft (1985). This is demonstrated in effective schools in a variety of ways, as outlined below.

Frequent monitoring of students' behaviours
Regular and systematic monitoring of students' progress helps to identify strengths and weaknesses in learning and instruction. This is achieved through a variety of formal and informal assessments.

High expectations
Teachers in effective schools believe all students can learn (Purkey and Novak, 1984) and set high but achievable learning standards. The principal also communicates high expectations for staff in the promotion of student achievement.

Teacher collegiality and development
Students benefit academically when their teachers share ideas, cooperate in activities and assist one another's intellectual growth. In more effective schools, the emphasis is on teachers as learners, as well as students as learners. Staff exhibit cohesiveness, identify problems and take action, and have a shared approach to planning.

Focus on instruction and curriculum
Intellectually challenging teaching is characterised by: appropriate curriculum and materials; planning; problem-solving; high academic learning time; frequent monitored homework; maximum communication, and use of a variety of instructional skills and strategies. Student needs are determined. A plan is then developed to meet these needs, and is implemented with appropriate strategies and resources.

A climate conducive to learning

'Pupils behaved better and achieved more when teachers treated them in ways which emphasised their success and good potential rather than those that focused on their failings and short-comings', noted Rutter *et al.* (1979). A positive school climate is one where affective development is facilitated; where students see themselves as able and responsible; and where students choose to learn and are invited to learn.

Student involvement and responsibility
In effective schools, many students hold positions of responsibility. They are also encouraged to take responsibility for their learning and, through involvement, to learn organisation, planning, discussion, decision-making and leadership skills.

Physical environment
Pictures, plants and student work are more in evidence in effective schools, and attention is paid to both staff and student comfort and safety.

78

Recognition and incentives
All forms of reward, praise or appreciation have a positive impact on students. Effective schools have multiple opportunities for recognition.

Positive student behaviour
In more effective schools, there is less emphasis on punishment and behaviour management. All teachers and students are involved in problem-solving, which focuses on causes rather than symptoms, and student self-control is encouraged.

Parent and community involvement and support
Parental involvement has a positive influence upon pupils' progress and development. There is regular communication between the school and the home as to how parents can support their child's achievement as well as the school's academic goals. There are also a wide variety of opportunities for parents and the community to become constructively involved in the school.

School growth plan

To enable schools to look at these characteristics within their own context, a School Growth Planning process was developed, drawing upon models of other researchers and school districts (see, for example, ILEA, 1986; McMahon *et al.*, 1984). A School Growth Plan is a systematic means by which a school can achieve sustained growth (Halton Board of Education, 1988). By taking into account external initiatives as well as the views of its own students, parents and teachers, a school can plan its own development over time. The choice of the word 'growth' was deliberate. Elsewhere in this book, David Reynolds discusses the 'pathology' of a staff as an inhibition to school planning. When we developed our planning process, we did not want to focus on a model of improvement, which has negative connotations, and is more likely to encourage a pathological response. Rather, as we saw many excellent activities already occurring in Halton schools, we preferred to focus upon growth. This has a more positive emphasis and, we believed, would be more likely to encourage an enthusiastic response from staff.

The development of a school growth plan

The process for developing a School Growth Plan is cyclical. There are four stages, however, that broadly correspond to four key questions:

(1)   Assessment – where are we now?
(2)   Planning – where would we like to be in three years' time?
(3)   Implementation – how best can we move in that direction?
(4)   Evaluation – how do we evaluate the changes we are making?

Assessment

The assessment stage is the time where all the necessary information is gathered together to provide an objective picture of the school. Assessment includes an examination of the school effectiveness characteristics in the context of the school as perceived by teachers, students and parents. After the information has been collected, it is analyzed so that the school can check its own understanding of its situation with this additional data.

Disaggregation of data (Lezotte, 1989b), that is the examination of information for separate groups of pupils, allows the school to see whether the needs of all children are being met. Schools are, therefore, advised to compare the assessment results of females and males, students from different backgrounds and those placed in classes that cater to different levels of difficulty (Ontario Ministry of Education, 1984).

Although improvement efforts should involve all of a school's staff, the initial data collection and analysis are done more easily by a small team. The number of people on the team depends on the size of the school, but the team usually includes both administrators and teachers, representing various perspectives. Schools are also encouraged to involve parents, students, school support staff, elected members and community members, because these people can have useful and different perspectives on issues being addressed. The rest of the school staff are consulted as part of the assessment process, and feedback of the results is given to them before the planning phase when they participate more actively.

Planning

At the planning stage, the assessment information is used to develop the School Growth Plan. Specific goals or objectives are set through detailed discussion of the results among the staff. A maximum of three areas that require emphasis over the next three years are translated by groups of people into goal statements which capture a description of what success would look like when the Growth Plan is completed; in other words, what the school needs to change, and what will be acceptable as a measure of success. Once areas of emphasis have been set, teachers select an area that interests them and work in groups to brainstorm activities and actions to enhance that particular goal.

An action plan is then compiled, including responsibilities of staff members for specific activities, timelines by which they should be completed, and resources necessary to carry out the activities. Included under resources are requests for help from people both within and outside the school to meet staff development needs. The action plan also includes a space for evaluation of each goal. Staff decide what criteria they will use to assess the effectiveness of the goal, and agree how and when the goal will be assessed.

Implementation

During the implementation process, the school follows through with the Growth Plan, and includes all of the actions necessary to carry it out. This is a long-range process, and requires review and monitoring to see whether activities have taken place and whether they appear to be having the intended impact.

As the implementation progresses, schools are encouraged to focus on support strategies to help staff who are involved in the initiation and implementation of change and development. These include monitoring and meeting in-service needs, dealing with problems effectively, and building an environment of trust and support in which teachers feel able to take risks.

Evaluation

The final stage of the School Growth Plan is its evaluation. This is fundamental to the Growth Plan because it is essential to devise ways of knowing whether the changes lead to improvement in students' learning and self-concept. Not only, however, is it important to know the degree to which objectives have been achieved, but also whether the activities have been completed and if the plan itself has been useful.

Two sets of assessments may be used, one which is formative (Scriven, 1967) or ongoing to find out if arrangements are working satisfactorily and whether people are fairly content; and a summative, final evaluation to assess the success of the Plan and whether objectives have been met.

The key feature of the evaluation assessment is that it is for internal school use, and its prime purpose is to give teachers information about what has been achieved. It is important that the evaluation is not perceived by teachers to be a means of external accountability in terms of

individuals' performance. Otherwise, this could lead to the pathological response described by Reynolds.

Implementation profile for school growth planning

Not all schools are at the same stage of the School Growth Planning
process, nor should they be expected to be. Just as the Concerns-Based
Adoption Model (Loucks and Hall, 1979) demonstrates that
individual teachers may be at different stages of readiness concerning a
school initiative, so are whole schools and their principals.

An implementation profile has been developed for principals' use to
examine the progress of their school in school growth planning.
Implementation profiles are based upon the Concerns-Based
Adoption Model and have been used in the past in Halton to look at
the implementation of different curriculum areas.

This particular profile incorporates what we have learned from pilot
schools where successful school growth planning already occurs. The
first four stages of the profile are prerequisites to planning. These
involve the development of vision, climate, collegiality and mission. In
these stages, the principal moves the school from a vision of a more
attractive future to total staff commitment to a mission, which in turn
drives the Growth Plan. Successful principals spend a considerable
amount of time establishing a climate of trust and openness with staff,
students and the community before they embark on substantive
changes. Our pilot school principals invariably attended to issues like
improvements to the physical plant, the development of a behaviour
code, establishment of lines of communication and decision-making
procedures before they moved into the growth planning cycle.

A challenge is to ensure that principals attend to these essentials in
order to create a basis for a successful growth planning experience.
Considerable attention also has to be paid to the application of
collegial relationships in schools (Rosenholtz, 1989). Among Halton's
more successful schools in the development of school-based initiatives
are those that have spent time to facilitate staff planning together.
Many schools have moved from self-reliance to collaborative cultures
(Hargreaves, 1989a). The principals in the most successful schools had
clear visions of what kind of communities they wanted their schools to
be, and worked hard on minor details to bring that view to fruition.
They found that the planning process is not straightforward, but more
evolutionary in nature (Louis and Miles, 1990).They also realised that
the process was slow, but had faith in the outcome even though this
required periods of high tolerance of uncertainty and ambiguity.

System reorganisation to support school growth plans

Bollen and Robin (1985) maintain that a school's capacity to effect significant changes 'depends not only on the school's internal organization and its readiness for change, but also on the availability of external resources, (and) the nature of the relevant school improvement policy' (p. 71).

In July 1989, the Halton Board of Education gave its approval to a strategic plan which highlighted three areas of emphasis. The first focused upon the promotion of, and support for, the School Growth Planning process:

● We must empower our schools to make their own decisions . . . direct our energies and resources through cooperative planning to support and encourage school-based planning . . . . The staff within each school will create a professional learning community where members share and learn together.

Planned support for this area of emphasis includes: training for school teams in the skills of planning, consultation, collaboration and decision-making; specific training for leaders; provision of relevant data for school-based decision-making; and the organisation and co-ordination of support staff teams to help schools.

The second strategic direction was related to an expressed need for expansion and growth of teaching methods, as highlighted in the school effectiveness characteristics:

● We must direct our energies and resources to support the teaching-learning process, by assisting our teachers to develop expertise in the four areas of instruction:

  ● Implementation of curriculum
  ● Classroom management
  ● Instructional skills
  ● Instructional strategies.

As a result of the Halton Board's involvement in the Learning Consortium, a cooperative venture with three other local school boards, the University of Toronto's Faculty of Education and the Ontario Institute for Studies in Education (Fullan *et al.*, 1990), a consultant, Barrie Bennett, offered workshops throughout the system on teaching skills and strategies, and classroom management. The Consortium also held a two-week Summer Institute, attended by teams of teachers and administrators from schools, and consultants, and gave further training to a smaller group of educators. Gradually, expertise is being developed throughout the school system, and people within schools have begun to work with their colleagues and introduce them to the new instructional techniques. This has been the essence of the third area of emphasis in Halton's strategic plan:

- To attract, select, develop and retain the highest calibre staff.

A Partners in the Classroom programme for first year teachers partnered with mentor teachers has already proved successful. This has included sessions on instructional skills and strategies, classroom management and programme modification, attended by both partners, who work together between sessions. Programmes have also been introduced for administrators and for consultative staff, entitled Leadership Effectiveness Assisted by Peers (LEAP). These use a coaching model (Joyce and Showers, 1982) to increase transfer of information. Participants work with a peer coach during and between sessions. Evaluations have been particularly positive with regard to the benefits of working with a coaching partner. Participants have commented on the opportunity to clarify concepts, share experiences and solve problems together.

To help teachers and schools fulfill the strategic directions, additional consultative support is being offered to schools. The number of consultants has been increased for the 1990–91 school year, and these people, who provide instruction, curriculum and special education support, have been located in area offices rather than at a geographically remote central office. Furthermore, until September 1989, curriculum, special education and staff development operated as autonomous units. These three have now been integrated to form Instructional Services. Its mandate is to provide a coherent and cohesive service to the area teams and to the schools and to ensure that schools address government and Board expectations. It also provides leadership and inservice support to schools. In order to fulfil these responsibilities, this group of staff, which operates out of the central office, must re-orient its thinking from that of top-down programme development and delivery to that of service provision and response to school-identified needs.

Some reluctance to change has been encountered on the part of existing central office staff. The necessity for changes in location, role and, in some cases, style, have provoked anxiety. It is a continuing challenge to deal with concerns with regard to the increase and broadening of responsibilities, a decrease in leadership, and a perceived lack of communication. Many opportunities have been offered for concerns to be aired, and feedback has been used to make amendments to the original implementation plan. Team-building was a major focus in the 1989–90 school year, and staff development activities involved all consultative staff. An attempt was also made to involve the special services personnel to a greater extent, although this is an area that requires further attention.

Through an evaluation process we hope to discover that the increased support makes a real difference to the learning process, and to the school's capacity to implement its growth plans and solve its own problems as demonstrated elsewhere (Louis and Miles, 1990). Through this large-scale reorganisation of the school system, implementation of school effectiveness characteristics through a growth planning process, and an increase in consultative support and staff development activities, it is felt that the schooling process can be enhanced. But can this major change in Halton meet the needs of all children? Hopefully, the answer will be 'yes', because special educators have also provided significant input into this process.

Special educational services review

While the School Effectiveness Task Force was developing its plans, detailed reviews of curriculum, staff development and special education were being carried out. In 1986, the Special Educational Services Review Committee highlighted the importance of good instruction for all students. They argued that every student is unique and differs along a continuum of intellectual, physical and psychological characteristics. This should be recognised before educators are so quick to classify and label students. A need was perceived for collaboration between educators to focus on prevention of learning difficulties:

> Learning problems would be viewed as opportunities for further instruction within the wide breadth of the curriculum ... classroom teachers, special educators, and support staff would work in a partnership, sharing knowledge and skills to develop appropriate educational strategies for all pupils (p. 3).

In a follow-up report in 1987, they added:

> In all cases, the primary concern is that all students have an equal opportunity to learn (p. 7).

The committee had examined existing practice, findings of a case study of integration carried out in Halton (Stoll, 1987), and had received input from special educators and other Halton staff. After consideration, they believed that the merger of regular and special education should occur over a period of time. Furthermore, students with special needs should be integrated into mainstream classes. In this way, the needs of all students could be met appropriately through effective instruction and support within the classroom. This idea was captured in a statement of philosophy that read:

> Striving for the optimal growth of all students in the most enabling environment by recognizing individual strengths and needs.

> ● Every student is a special student
> ● Every teacher is a special teacher
> ● Every class is a special class
> ● Every program is a special program.

The successful integration or inclusion (Stainback and Stainback, 1988) of students with special needs into regular classes, however, depends upon effective instruction that is challenging and yet appropriate, adequate support, and the ability of all concerned to work together.

Effective instruction

Regular learning environments have been accused of failure to accommodate the educational needs of many students (Wang *et al.*, 1986). Students' withdrawal to special education classes, say Wang *et al.* (1986), is also based on a misperception that poor adjustment and performance can be attributed entirely to their background characteristics, rather than the quality of the educational environment. This was the argument outlined and refuted earlier: the schools and teachers can make little difference given a disadvantaged home background. Although differences in home circumstances can have a considerable impact upon pupils' educational outcomes, in an effective school with quality classroom instruction, all children, irrespective of social class differences, can make more progress than all children in an ineffective school with poor teaching methods (Mortimore *et al.*, 1988). What is required is a better understanding of the best practices highlighted by school and teacher effectiveness research (see, for example, Good, 1983; Mortimore *et al.*, 1988; Rutter *et al.*, 1979) and by other studies that have examined teaching strategies (for example, Johnson *et al.*, 1978; Slavin and Madden, 1989). If teachers, both those in special education and regular classrooms, could be encouraged and supported in the endeavour to become more reflective concerning their own practice (Fullan *et al.*, 1990; Sebba, 1990; Schon, 1983), and more knowledgeable with regard to successful teaching techniques and modification of programmes, the needs of many more students can be met within ordinary classrooms.

Student assessment is another area where changes need to be made. Profiles or records of achievement (see Hargreaves, 1989b) can provide a viable alternative to the standard reporting process. They also offer a greater opportunity for pupils to be involved in self-assessment. In Ontario, Ward and Cooper (1989) have used a similar framework to develop assessments for vocational students in secondary schools, many of whom have special needs. Rather than use traditional assessments that test what these students do not know, they have focused on students' work habits and interests, as well as their performance. Each student is assessed individually, and helps select and set targets for future meetings. In this way, students are more involved in the assessment process.

Adequate support

Workshops on teaching skills and strategies and classroom management described earlier, have been offered to special education teachers as well as other classroom teachers. Indeed, a special series was organised for the special education and special services personnel, who include psychologists, social workers, child and youth counsellors, and speech pathologists. Thus, all people in the system are learning the same language. It is hoped that this will enable special educators to provide better support to students with special needs, both within regular classrooms and when they are withdrawn for extra help, as will continue to be the case for the immediate future.

Paraprofessional support is also provided for students with severe disabilities when they are integrated into regular classrooms. It is important that this support be ongoing. At this time, few classroom teachers are trained to provide all the necessary classroom support for a severely handicapped child in addition to organising a challenging work programme that meets all the individual needs of 30 pupils.

All consultants who have been hired to the area support teams have additional qualifications in special education. Specialist consultants for pupils with severe learning difficulties, physical disabilities and gifted pupils will continue to work on the teams but will also have responsibilities for instructional support to all students in one or two schools. In essence, existing consultants, both subject specific and those who provide special education support, now have a much broader job description. New consultants also need to be able to provide a wide variety of instructional, subject, special education and staff development support to schools. This will be a challenge for them and, in some cases, has provoked anxiety that accompanies change. Ongoing assistance and inservice is also being provided for these people.

Collaboration

Collaboration underpins the strategic plan, the School Growth Plan, and integration of students with special needs. The development of closer partnerships between teachers within schools, support staff, and between teachers and support staff is essential to the success of this project. Collaborative work cultures within schools have been demonstrated to have a positive impact upon school improvement (Little, 1982; Nias *et al.*, 1989; Rosenholtz, 1989), even though it has also been stressed that teachers' individuality should not be suppressed (Hargreaves, 1990). Already, the role of Special Education Resource Teacher (SERT) within Halton schools is focused on collaboration as well as support. Each school has a SERT, whose responsibilities include:

- support in classrooms to instruct, aid, monitor or observe children
- assistance in the resource room through provision of withdrawal of individuals or groups
- assistance with adaptation and planning of programme to meet the needs of *all* pupils
- liaison with outside agencies and support staff.
- acting as curriculum leader and consultant within the school
- being a resource to staff, students and parents through provision of resource materials
- assistance in staff development
- being an active team member on the school team.

The School Resource Team is a problem-solving group that considers the strengths and needs of students and suggests programme modifications that will help students learn. It consists of the school's administrators, the SERT, special service personnel, for example the school's psychologist and child and youth counsellor, the pupil's classroom teacher, the school's consultant and, when appropriate, parents. The school team provides an opportunity for school and support staff to work and grow together through the sharing of knowledge skills, strategies and resources. Training workshops have been developed around the operation of the school team and support for students with special needs. All school teams have attended this in-service.

The Collaborative Planning Network has also fostered greater co-operation between classroom teachers and SERTs. It was developed in one area of Halton, and has now spread more widely as several schools have selected collaborative planning as a goal in their Growth Plan. Release time is provided for teachers and support staff to work together to plan units.

Conclusion

Although Task Force members considered themselves familiar with the research on change and how long it takes (Fullan, 1982), only now is its truth realised. In the four years since the inception of the School Effectiveness Project and the Special Educational Services Review in Halton, much has been achieved. A common language has been developed in Halton, and schools are now perceived by most as the basic unit of change. Support services have been reorganised to assist schools to meet their needs. At the same time, the importance of effective instruction and programme modification for all students has been recognised.

For every step forward, steps back have also been taken. Momentum is not easy to maintain, and coordination and communication within a relatively large school system needs to be ongoing. A detailed evaluation plan has been developed. It will take some time to see the precise impact of this reorganisation, although progress will be measured every year. There has, however, already been a major philosophical shift and a commitment to making Halton's schools more effective for all students through the application of the effective schools characteristics, integration of special needs students, quality instruction and school-based planning.

References

Bashi, J. and Sass, Z. (1989) 'Factors affecting stable continuum of outcomes of school improvement projects'. Paper presented at the Second International Congress for School Effectiveness, Rotterdam, The Netherlands.
Bennis, W. and Nanus, B. (1985) *Leaders*. New York: Harper and Row.

Bollen, R. and Robin, D. (1985) 'School improvement context', in Van Velzen, W. G. *et al.* (Eds) *Making School Improvement Work*. Leuven, Belgium: W.G. Academic Publishing Company.

Chrispeels, J. and Pollack, S. (1990) 'Factors that contribute to achieving and sustaining school effectiveness'. Paper presented at the Third International Congress for School Effectiveness and Improvement, Jerusalem, Israel.

Coleman, J. S., Campbell, E., Hobson, C., McPartland, J., Mood, A., Weinfeld, F. and York, R. (1966) *Equality of Educational Opportunity*. Washington: National Center for Educational Statistics.

Edmonds, R. (1979) 'Effective schools for the urban poor', *Educational Leadership*, 37,1:15–23.

Essen, J. and Wedge, P. (1982) *Continuities in Childhood Disadvantage*. London: Heinemann.

Fullan, M. (1982) *The Meaning of Educational Change*. Toronto: OISE Press.

Fullan, M., Bennett, B. and Rolheiser-Bennett, C. (1990) 'Linking classroom and school improvement', *Educational Leadership*, 47, 8:13–19.

Gardner, H. (1983) *Frames of Mind*. New York: Basic Books.

Good, T. L. (1983) 'Classroom research: A decade of progress', *Educational Psychologist*, 18:127–44.

Goodlad, J. (1984) *A Place Called School: Prospects for the Future*. New York: McGraw-Hill.

Hallinger, P. and Murphy, J. (1986) 'The social context of effective schools', *American Journal of Education*. 94,3:328–55.

Halton Board of Education (1986) 'Report of the Special Education/Services Review Committee'. Unpublished report.

Halton Board of Education (1987) 'Special Education Review Committee: follow-up report'. Unpublished report.

Halton Board of Education (1988) 'Building a school growth plan'. Unpublished report.

Hargreaves, A. (1989a) 'Cultures of teaching: A focus for change: Part 1 and Part 2', *OPSTF News*, February and April.

Hargreaves, A. (1989b) *Curriculum and Assessment Reform*. Toronto: OISE Press.

Hargreaves, A. (1990) 'Individualism and individuality: Reinterpreting the teacher culture'. Paper presented at the Annual Meeting of the American Educational Research Association, Boston.

ILEA (1986) *Primary School Development Plans: A Support Booklet*. London: Primary Management Studies, ILEA.

Jencks, C. S., Smith, M., Ackland, H., Bane, M. J., Cohen, D., Gintis, H., Heyns, B. and Micholson, S. (1972) *Inequality: A Reassessment of the Effect of Family and Schooling in America*. New York: Basic Books.

Johnson, L. C., Johnson, R. T. and Scott, L. (1978) 'The effects of cooperative and individualized instruction on student attitudes and achievement', *Journal of School Psychology*, 104:207–16.

Joyce, B., Hersh, R. and McKibbin, M. (1983) *The Structure of School Improvement*. New York: Longman.

Joyce, B. and Showers, B. (1982) 'The coaching of teaching', *Educational Leadership*, 40,2:4–10.

90

Lezotte, L. W. (1989a) 'Base school improvement on what we know about effective schools', *The American School Board Journal*, **176**,8:18–20.

Lezotte, L. W. (1989b) 'Introductory letter', *Effective Schools Research Abstracts 1988–89 Series*, **3**,1.

Lezotte, L. W. and Bancroft, B. A. (1985) 'Growing use of the effective schools model for school improvement', *Educational Leadership*, **42**,6:23–7.

Little, J. W. (1982) 'Norms of collegiality and experimentation: Workplace conditions and school success', *American Educational Research Journal*, **19**,3:325–40.

Loucks, S. F. and Hall, G. E. (1979) *Implementing Innovations in Schools: A Concerns-Based Approach*. Austin: Research and Development Center for Teacher Education, University of Texas.

Louis, K. S. and Miles, M. B. (1990) *Improving Urban High Schools: What Works and Why*. New York: Teachers College Press.

McMahon, A., Bolam, R., Abbot, R. and Holly, P. (1984) *GRIDS Handbooks*. York: Longman/Schools Council.

Mortimore, P., Sammons, P., Stoll, L., Lewis, D. and Ecob, R. (1988) *School Matters: The Junior Years*. Somerset: Open Books, and *School Matters*. Berkeley: University of California Press.

Nias, J., Southworth, G. and Yeomans, R. (1989) *Staff Relationships in the Primary School: A Study of Organizational Cultures*. London: Cassell.

Ontario Ministry of Education (1984) *Ontario Schools: Intermediate and Senior Divisions (OSIS)*. Ontario: Queen's Printer for Ontario.

Purkey, W. W. and Novak, J. (1984) *Inviting School Success: A Self-concept Approach to Teaching and Learning*, 2nd edn. Belmont, CA: Wadsworth.

Reynolds, D. (1982) 'The search for effective schools', *School Organization*. **2**,3:215–37.

Reynolds, D. (1985) (Ed.) *Studying School Effectiveness*. London: Falmer Press.

Reynolds, D. and Creemers, B. P. M. (1989) 'School effectiveness and school improvement: A mission statement', *School Effectiveness and School Improvement*, **1**,1:1–3.

Rosenholtz, S. J. (1989) *Teachers' Workplace: The Social Organization of Schools*. New York: Longman.

Rutter, M., Maugham, B., Mortimore, P. and Ouston, J. (1979) *Fifteen Thousand Hours*. London: Open Books.

Sackney, L. E. (1986) 'Practical strategies for improving school effectiveness', *The Canadian School Executive*, **6**,4:15–20.

Sammons, P., Kysel, F. and Mortimore, P. (1983) 'Educational priority indices: a new perspective', *British Educational Research Journal*, **9**,1:27–40.

Scheerens, J. (1987) *Enhancing Educational Opportunities for Disadvantaged Learners: A Review of Dutch Research on Compensatory Education and Educational Development Policy*: Amsterdam: North Holland Publishing Co.

Schon, D. (1983) *The Reflective Practitioner: How Professionals Think in Action*. New York: Basic Books.

Scriven, M. (1967) 'The methodology of evaluation', in Stake, R. E. *et al.*

(Eds) *Perspectives on Curriculum Evaluation, No 1*. Chicago: Rand McNally.

Sebba, J. (1990) 'Teacher Training for Effective Schooling for Pupils with Severe Learning Difficulties'. Paper presented at the Third International Congress for School Effectiveness and Improvement, Jerusalem, Israel.

Slavin, R. E. and Madden, N. A. (1989) 'What works for student at risk: A research synthesis', *Educational Leadership*, **46**,5:4–13.

Smith, W. F. and Andrews, R. L. (1989) *Instructional Leadership: How Principals Make a Difference*. Alexandria, V A: ASCD.

Stainback, S. and Stainback, W. (1988) 'Educating students with severe difficulties', *Teaching Exceptional Children*, **21**,1:16–19.

Stoll, L. (1987) 'The Effects of Integration on Student Self-Concept'. Halton Board of Education, unpublished report.

Stoll, L. and Fink, D. (1988) *An Effective Schools Project: The Halton Approach*, in Reynolds, D., Creemers, B. and Peters, T. (Eds) *School Effectiveness and Improvement*. University of Wales College of Cardiff and Rion Institute for Educational Research, The Netherlands.

Stoll, L. and Fink, D. (1989) 'Implementing an Effective Schools Project: The Halton Approach'. Paper presented at the Second International Congress for School Effectiveness, Rotterdam, The Netherlands.

Stoll, L. and Fink, D. (1990) 'Reorganization for Effectiveness: The Halton Approach'. Paper presented at the Third International Congress for School Effectiveness and School Improvement, Jerusalem, Israel.

Teddlie, C. and Stringfield, S. (1985) 'A differential analysis of effectiveness in middle and low socioeconomic status schools', *The Journal of Classroom Interaction*, **20**,2:38–42.

Wang, M. C., Reynolds, M. C. and Walberg, H. J. (1986) 'Rethinking special education', *Educational Leadership*, **44**,1:26–31.

Ward, F. and Cooper, D. (1989) *Basic English: Handbook. The Ontario Assessment Instrument Pool*. Toronto: Ontario Ministry of Education.

CHAPTER 5

Changing Ineffective Schools

David Reynolds

There is no doubt that special education has witnessed a revolution in its basic approaches towards the explanation of pupils' needs over the last decade or so. Explanations of pupils' problems in schools used to 'individualize' their causes by relating learning or behavioural problems to perceived deficiencies in pupils' home backgrounds, in patterns of community life and in the socialization processes that children experienced prior to their school life. Examples of the work that was carried out within this conventional, and now dated, 'paradigm' or way of thinking would be that conducted into truancy (reviewed in Reid, 1986), that conducted into behavioural problems (reviewed in Upton, 1982) and that conducted into learning difficulties and problems (Davie *et al.*, 1972; Douglas, 1968).

More recently, though, an analysis of the causation of pupils' educational needs has grown up which stands opposed to the basic tenets of the old paradigm. The new paradigm, first, sees the institution of the school, and often indeed the special and/or residential school, as one of the key defining mechanisms, which is regarded as actually *creating* pupils' problems and pupils' needs for help of various kinds, a view reflected in the works of numerous researchers and writers (Galloway, 1985; Reid *et al.*, 1986; Reynolds, 1985). Second, the new paradigm builds upon the integrational emphasis of the Warnock Report (Department of Education and Science, 1978) by proposals that children with special needs should not just have their education with others but that 'whole school approaches' should be followed which attempt to improve the quality of the school experience for all children in schools. Given Warnock's

92

massive redefinition of the prevalence of pupils with special educational needs (which expanded the size of the group tenfold from a 2 to a 20 per cent prevalence rate), an approach which saw institutional modification and improvement as a key policy for the amelioration of special educational needs is easy to understand (see Reynolds and the other contributors in Ramasut, 1989).

The increased links between the special education community and those researchers and practitioners involved in the field of school effectiveness have, of course, come some time after the growing enthusiasm for 'whole school' institutional change, which is of course to be regretted since school effectiveness researchers have had to struggle against the same intellectual hegemony of the individualized or 'pathology'-based explanations for pupils' problems as have special educational needs researchers and practitioners. For both communities, the dominance of psychologically-based 'defect' models also led to policy approaches which focused upon initiatives with 'abnormal' pupils and to an assumption that the institution of the school within which the so-called 'abnormal' children were located was itself essentially 'normal'. Policy measures therefore have in education generally, and in the special educational needs field particularly, included the development of special units for disruptive pupils, 'sin bins', alternative schools, schools within schools, separate residential provision and the targeting of educational psychologists at individual pupil cases. Policies that attempted remediation of the schools within which pupils were, or were not, socialized and developed of course only emerged from the early 1980s onwards.

The common intellectual history and common individualized policy approaches which each of the school effectiveness and special educational needs communities have had to struggle against are now increasingly widely recognized, as other contributors in this volume make clear. What is not acknowledged, and what is the subject of this chapter, is the difficulty for the special educational needs researchers and practitioners of successfully translating the findings of school effectiveness research into changed and improved practice within schools. Simply, we now know what makes a 'good' school but, unfortunately, we don't yet know how to make schools 'good'.

The context for school improvement

It is clear that the need for programmes of 'whole school' school improvement to deal with ineffective schools is likely to grow rapidly,

94

since a number of important factors will continue to increase the influence that schools have over the development of young people in the 1990s and beyond. First, the school populations of primary and, especially, secondary schools are now changing rapidly as children with special educational needs (physical, behavioural or learning problems) are re-integrated into schools with other children. The movement is common to all the major industrialized nations of the world (with the exception of some Scandinavian countries who were integrating already) and, whether the integration is total or partial, will put into schools groups of pupils highly sensitive to their school and classroom environment. Assuming all other factors remain unchanged and particularly that variation between schools continues to exist at least at its present levels, the result of this changing pupil population will be a substantial increase in the influence of the school.

Second, and again this is an international phenomenon, the increased policy concern to keep troublesome, delinquent or disturbed children within the normal school setting (rather than utilizing specialist, expensive and clearly highly ineffective special residential homes or units) will put into mainstream schools another group of pupils whom the evidence suggests also to be highly influenced by their schools (Graham, 1988). Indeed, there is a substantial volume of literature (for example, Gottfredson, 1987; Reynolds and Sullivan, 1981) which suggests that educational failure, and the effects of schools in the generation of this failure, may lie behind many of the antisocial demeanours that concern virtually all industrialized societies in the 1990s. Again, schools' influence on young people will increase because of the greater recruitment of young people highly sensitive to the quality of what they are being offered within their educational settings.

The school effectiveness knowledge base

The *need* for research and development in the general disciplinary area of school effectiveness is therefore, in my view, likely to be even greater in the 1990s than it has been in the 1980s and 1970s. The customary increased pressure for educational systems to attain results will be there, but the school systems themselves are likely to have become more heterogeneous in their quality and probably will be presented increasingly with 'at risk' young people who are likely to have very sensitive reactions to their schools, and over whom they probably are to have a substantial influence.

The development of the field of school effectiveness over time has been extensively described by myself and others elsewhere (Creemers and Scheerens, 1989; Creemers *et al.*, 1989; Reynolds *et al.*, 1989) so only an outline seems necessary here. In both the United States and in Britain, studies such as that by Coleman *et al.* (1966), the work of Jencks *et al.* (1971) and the British Plowden Report (Central Advisory Council for Education, 1967) all concluded that schools bring little independent influence to bear upon the development of their pupils. This period has been gradually followed in both societies by the emergence of a wide range of 'effective schools', 'school effectiveness' or 'school effects' studies which argue for the importance of school influence, beginning in the United States with various case studies and moving on to a wide range of quantitative studies, and beginning in Britain with work by Power *et al.* (1972), Gath (1977), (Reynolds, 1976; 1982; Reynolds *et al.*, 1987), Rutter *et al.* (1979), Galloway *et al.* (1985) and Gray *et al.* (1986). Subsequent studies have been by Mortimore and his colleagues (1988) in primary schools and the recent work of Smith and Tomlinson (1989) in multicultural secondary schools. Work in these two societies has been joined recently by that from the Netherlands, Australia, Canada, and by a resurgence of studies done in and about Third World societies.

From studies in this wide range of countries, it seems that a number of early simplistic assumptions that were frequently based upon school effectiveness research are now no longer tenable:

● On the size of school effects, it seems that early beliefs that school influence might be as large as family or community influences were misplaced, since a very large number of studies in the last five years show only 8–15 per cent of the variation in pupil outcomes as due to between-school differences (Bosker and Scheerens, 1989; Cuttance, 1991).

● On the causes of school effects, it seems that early beliefs that school influences were distinct from teacher or classroom influences were misplaced, since a large number of studies utilizing multi-level modelling show that the great majority of variation between schools is in fact due to classroom variation and that the unique variance due to the influence of the school, and not the classroom, shrinks to quite small levels (Scheerens *et al.*, 1989).

● On the consistency of school effects, it seems that early beliefs that 'effective' or 'ineffective' schools stayed so over quite considerable time periods of five to seven years were invalid, since it now appears that school performance can vary quite rapidly over two or three years (Nuttall *et al.*, 1989). (The proposed publication of the academic outcomes of schooling like the results of British national assessment procedures involves utilizing only one year's figures and is clearly a worrying policy if school performance is unstable).

- On the relative consistency of the performance of schools across a range of outcome measures, it used to be thought that the 'effective school' was so across a range of both academic and social outcomes, yet now we have much evidence that schools need not be effective or ineffective 'across the board'. The recent Junior School Project of Mortimore *et al.* (1988) showed, for example, a virtually complete independence of schools on different outcome measures, strongly suggesting that academic effectiveness is not necessarily associated with social or 'affective' effectiveness.

- On the question of effectiveness across different groups of pupils, the traditional belief that schools are effective or ineffective for all subgroups of pupils within them is no longer tenable, in view of the evidence that there can be different school effects for children of different ethnic groups, ability ranges and socio-economic status within the *same* school (Aitken and Longford, 1986; Nuttall *et al.*, 1989).

What processes make some schools effective?

Although the resolution of the above issues concerning the size of school effects, their consistency over time, their consistency for different types of children and their consistency on different outcomes measures may require much further research, it is clear that schools *do* have substantial effects upon pupils and that there are processes which 'work' across schools to maximise their outcomes. In the important secondary school study of Rutter *et al.* (1979), the factors that were linked with effectiveness could be grouped under the following broad headings:

- *the pupil control system*, with effective schools using rewards, praise, encouragement and appreciation more than punishments;
- *the school environment provided for pupils*, with effective schools providing good working conditions for pupils and for their teachers, being responsive to pupil needs and also providing buildings that were well cared for and well decorated;
- *the involvement of pupils*, with effective schools giving ample opportunities for pupils to take positions of responsibility and to participate in the running of the school and in the educational activities within the classrooms;
- *the academic development of pupils*, with effective schools making positive use of homework, setting clear and explicit academic goals, and with the teachers in these effective schools having high expectations of, and positive views of, the capabilities of their pupils;

- *the behaviour of teachers*, with effective schools providing good models of behaviour through teachers exhibiting good time-keeping and a clearly apparent willingness to deal with pupils' personal and social problems;
- *management in the classroom*, with effective schools possessing teachers who prepared lessons in advance, who kept the attention of the whole class, who managed to maintain discipline in an unobtrusive way, who focused upon the rewarding of good behaviour and who were able to take swift action to deal with any disruption by pupils;
- *the management structure*, with effective schools combining firm leadership by the headteacher with a decision making process in which all teachers felt that their views were represented.

Our own work in Wales (see references above) is parallel in many of its findings to those of the Rutter study, although our limited data on the intakes into our sample of schools made us less able than the Rutter team to prove conclusively that the large differences between our secondary schools were in fact due to the effects of what was going on within the schools themselves.

Our detailed observations on our schools over a decade showed a number of features that were associated with being an effective school. These were:

- *high levels of pupil involvement*, as shown by the co-option of a large proportion of pupils into a prefect system for example, and as shown by the use of pupil monitors in lesson time that helped with the distribution of books and equipment;
- *low levels of certain institutional controls*, as shown by a tolerant attitude towards the enforcement of certain key rules covering pupil dress and the like;
- *a low concentration upon punishment* (particularly physical punishment), and the use of more informal, verbal sanctions;
- *high expectations of what pupils could achieve*, both academically and in terms of their behaviour, linked to a positive view of the pupils' home backgrounds and communities.

Our observations over the years revealed important differences between the schools which we attempted to summarize under the headings of the schools' utilization, or not, of an 'incorporative approach' to the ways in which they attempted to generate order and pupil learning within school. The more effective schools that took part in the research appeared to be utilizing the incorporative strategy, of which the major components were twofold; the incorporation of pupils into the organization of the school and incorporation of their parents into support of the school. Pupils were incorporated within the classroom by encouraging them to take an active and participative role in lessons and by letting them, to an extent, intervene verbally without the teacher's explicit directions. Pupils in schools which utilized this strategy were also far more likely to be allowed and encouraged to work in groups than their counterparts in schools utilizing the coercive strategy.

Outside formal lesson time, attempts were made to incorporate pupils into the life of the school by utilizing other strategies. One of these was the use of numbers of pupil prefects and monitors, from all parts of the school ability range, whose role was largely one of supervision of other pupils in the absence of staff members. Such a practice appeared to have the effect of inhibiting the growth of anti-school pupil sub-cultures because of its effects in creating senior pupils who were generally supportive of the school. It also had the latent and symbolic function of providing pupils with a sense of having some control over their within-school lives; the removal of these symbols also gave the school a further sanction it could utilize against its deviants.

Attempts to incorporate pupils were paralleled by attempts to enlist the support of their parents by the establishment of close, informal or semi-formal relations between teachers and parents, the encouraging of informal visits by parents to the schools and the frequent and full provision of information to parents that concerned pupil progress and governor and staff decisions. Another means of incorporation into the values and norms of the school was the development of *inter*personal rather than *im*personal relationships between teachers and pupils. Basically, teachers in these incorporative schools attempted to 'tie' pupils into the value systems of the school and of the adult society by means of developing good personal relationships with them. In effect, the judgement was made in these schools that internalization of teacher values was more likely to occur if pupils saw teachers as 'significant others' deserving of respect. Good relationships were consequent upon minimal use of overt institutional control (so that pupil behaviour was relatively unconstrained), low rates of physical punishment, a tolerance of a limited amount of 'acting out' (such as by smoking or gum chewing for example), a pragmatic hesitancy to enforce rules which may have provoked rebellion and an attempt to reward good behaviour rather than punish bad behaviour. Within this school ethos, instances of pupil deviance evoked therapeutic rather than coercive responses from within the school.

Applying the school effectiveness knowledge base

In certain contexts like those identified by Louise Stoll in another chapter in this volume, it is clear that applying school effectiveness knowledge into school improvement programmes can be undertaken extremely effectively. In a British context, it is clear that although we have now made considerable progress in our understanding of what makes effective schools, it is perhaps in the *application* of school effectiveness knowledge that we have encountered most problems. There is no doubt that the character of the research described above has not helped its rapid translation into practice in schools. There are high levels of abstraction and use of jargon in some of the effective schools' process factors mentioned. The administrative implications of the research for teachers are often unclear, and the school effectiveness knowledge base is weak on the management and the 'technology' of schooling. The focal concerns of most practitioners – the curriculum and their instructional practices within classrooms – are not areas in which school effectiveness researchers have been much interested. Practitioners have every right to cry of the effectiveness research that, like Gertrude Stein's description of California, 'The trouble is that there is no there, there', since it is often not clear from the research what teachers should actually *do* in schools to make them effective.

It is understandable, then, that getting the effective schools knowledge base to 'take root' in schools has been a difficult process, judging by the experience of those researchers and practitioners in Britain who have tried it. Rutter and his colleagues (Maughan *et al.*, 1990; Ouston and Maughan, 1991) attempted major and lengthy intervention work with three of the schools that had formed the basis of their earlier school effectiveness research, using the findings of this earlier work in a direct attempt to improve school practice. Of the three schools involved, only two showed some improvements and even these were in what the researchers called 'restricted areas'. By comparison with some control schools which changed rapidly because of the appointment of a new headteacher, ' . . . change at these schools was less wide ranging, affecting either only one or other of our main outcome measures or being focused primarily on particular segments of the pupil intakes' (Maughan *et al.*, 1990, p. 207).

Other somewhat disappointing results have occurred when 'consultancy' methods have been used to bring the school effectiveness knowledge into ineffective schools, since the knowledge base is often threatening to established ways of thinking within schools. It is also likely that the school effectiveness knowledge may be *personally* threatening to staff groups in ineffective schools and that the arrival of new knowledge in these schools may create disturbance, both individually and collectively amongst the whole staff group.

The following example will, I hope, illustrate this point in more depth. More detailed accounts of this attempt to improve a school can be found elsewhere (Reynolds, 1987; Reynolds and Murgatroyd, 1984) and are forthcoming, but briefly, a team from University of Wales, College of Cardiff was invited by a local school that perceived itself as ineffective and underperforming to join with them as 'consultants' to resource the school's improvement efforts. Our consultancy role was to bring to the school the best available knowledge and evidence on school effectiveness, discuss with the school what aspects of the knowledge base were seen as appropriate to its local context and then evaluate the success or failure of the change attempt, to be followed by a process of feed back of the results to the school for further consideration.

As we began our work with the teachers in the school, many processes began about which the existing literature on school improvement had given us no warning. Taken in turn:

(1)   The staff of the school were unused to discussing educational matters, other than in the context of individual children who might have been 'problems' or who had perhaps distinguished themselves in conventional terms. Introducing into the school educational ideas, the language in which these ideas were couched and their related modes of conceptualization, caused immense problems, because staff inexperience resulted in their being unable to separate the personal from the political. They were unable to argue educational 'points of view' without getting personally involved in the process, due to a deficiency of interpersonal and communication skills. Increased interpersonal conflict, a breakdown of some pre-existing relationships and much interpersonal hostility in some cases were the results of our attempt to introduce outside ideas into a school.

(2)   We attempted to 'open up' the culture of the school by employing various devices. We tried to end the 'behind the closed door' mentality, whereby teachers had few contacts at a professional or intellectual level with other teachers, by the introduction of 'pupil pursuit'. This technique involved a member of the teaching staff shadowing an individual pupil through that pupil's entire morning or afternoon of schooling, in order to understand what the school experience and its shortcomings must have looked like for the 'consumer' of education. This tactic too generated a rapid further deterioration in interpersonal relations.

Many staff realized for the first time the incompetence of their colleagues, having experienced it at first hand rather than merely encountering it through rumour or innuendo.

There were other strategies which we utilized that eventually helped to solidify the staff group and make it re-form around the new body of knowledge that we had interpreted as 'good practice'. We opened up the school's management team through greater democracy, more openness, the keeping of minutes of meetings, etc., thereby encouraging the staff to 'take on' their management and thus solidify in terms of interpersonal relationships as they did so. We introduced some quasi-group work, small group sessions and experiential interventions to try to repair interpersonal damage. Eventually, although there were numerous individual casualties of the change process (including the headteacher who retired with an apparent breakdown), the school emerged a stronger and more effective institution and is now more able to handle the complex interpersonal difficulties that applying school effectiveness knowledge brings.

The world that we encountered at this school was very different to that which we had expected. We had anticipated, using the insights of the North American school improvement literature (for example, Fullan, 1991) to be able to adopt the 'rational/empirical model' in which teachers and their organization generate personal and institutional change because of the acknowledgement that the school effectiveness knowledge *is* in fact a better or more valid way of running their school. However, the staff culture and belief system of the school exhibited a marked 'non-rational' quality which made it possible for the staff to escape the adoption or implementation of the new organizational practices that were suggested to them by the school effectiveness knowledge base. The staff culture actually exhibited many of the characteristics of the inadequate, insecure or ineffective person, namely:

- projections of individual teachers' deficiencies onto the children or the surrounding community and its parents, as excuses for their ineffectiveness;
- 'clingons' of past practice (we've always done it this way!);
- defences, where teachers built walls to keep out threatening messages from outsiders;
- fear of attempting change because it might fail, associated with a reluctance to risk;
- the fantasy that change is someone else's job;

● the 'safety in numbers' ploy, whereby persons retreated into a ring-fenced mentality.

The school culture, then, was somewhat weary, fatalistic, used to failure and unused to the risks necessitated by potentially changing organizational practices. It was that defensive apparatus which is employed by the ineffective and the insecure to protect themselves from any outside influences which may expose them and their inadequacy.

Conclusions

The aim of this chapter has been to explore some of the potentialities and problems that exist in the increasingly close relationship between practitioners and researchers in the two areas of special needs education and school effectiveness. Both educational communities share a common history of the ideological hegemony of psycho-logically-based individualizing of pupil problems and the individually orientated and pathology-based policy models that sprang from it. Both educational communities now appreciate the need for 'whole school' improvement strategies that modify the institutional functioning of schools that actually *creates* special educational needs by being ineffective in their operation.

Major blocks exist, though, on the extent to which the school effectiveness knowledge base may be utilized within programmes of school improvement and development, since it assumes the applic-ability of 'rational-empirical' models of change and since schools may have numerous non-rational strategies for avoiding whatever empirical truths that they may be exposed to.

The challenge now for those involved in the school effectiveness and special needs fields is both to analyse in greater detail the further, unexplored characteristics of the 'ineffective' schools which may restrict their ability to act on the knowledge they are given, and to develop more successful ways of bringing the effectiveness knowledge to the schools. To take the first of these issues, it is important that our descriptions of ineffective schools move beyond the two-dimension-ality that has characterized them so far. Researchers in the British tradition have described the formal organizational processes of the school and the culture, values or 'ethos' of the institution that is related to the organizational level, but have not described that third dimension of schooling concerned with the 'emotional' or 'relational' areas of school life such as interpersonal relationships, self-perception and self/other perception. It is easy to understand why this dimension has not been a focus, since it is hard to collect data upon it and even harder to persuade teachers in schools that such aspects of school life should be disclosed or talked about. Furthermore, the effective schools movement has customarily operated with a research model which has started by looking at effective schools and subsequently moved on to see what factors in these schools were missing in the ineffective schools, rather than looking at what factors may exist in the ineffective schools that are not evident in the effective ones! The characteristics of ineffective schools that may *only* be in existence in the ineffective schools (inter-group conflict, negative self-perceptions, group and individual projections, and even group and individual self-delusion) would not be picked up by these existing research designs.

To look at the second of the issues – the difficulty of actually applying the knowledge in ineffective schools – it is clear that additional techniques may be necessary to ensure take-up. If schools have some of the characteristics noted above such as irrationality, defences, projections, anxieties and insecurities, then techniques derived from the psychological and psychiatric literature, together with insights from social work programmes and techniques, could be used to deal with the problems that the knowledge base may generate. Alternatively, it may be that bringing the knowledge base to schools through the 'Trojan Horse' of training school teachers as school change agents may be effective, since there is some evidence that teachers training other teachers in techniques of improving school effectiveness may lead to improved take-up in schools (Reynolds *et al.*, 1989). Whilst it is unclear which body of knowledge within the psychological/psychiatric field would be of greatest use (behavioural analysis or insights from Freudian psychoanalytic concepts for example), it is highly likely that the techniques for changing the non-rational and disturbed world of the ineffective school will come from the disciplines which have made great progress in understanding the non-rational and disturbed individual.

References

Aitken, M. and Longford, N. (1986) 'Statistical modelling issues in school effectiveness studies', *Journal of the Royal Statistical Society, Series A*, **149**, (1):1–43.
Bosker, R. J. and Scheerens, J. (1989) 'Issues in the interpretation of the results of school effectiveness research', *International Journal of Educational Research*, **13**, (7):741–51.

104

Central Advisory Council for Education (1967) *Children and their Primary Schools* (The Plowden Report). London: HMSO.

Coleman, J. *et al.* (1966) *Equality of Educational Opportunity*. Washington DC: US Government Printing Office.

Creemers, B. and Scheerens, J. (Eds) (1989) 'Developments in school effectiveness research', *International Journal of Educational Research*, special issue, **13**, (7):685–825.

Creemers, B., Peters, T. and Reynolds, D. (1989) *School Effectiveness and School Improvement: Proceedings of the Second International Congress, Rotterdam, 1989*. Lisse: Swets and Zeitlinger.

Cuttance, P. (1991) 'Assessing the effectiveness of schools', in Reynolds, D. and Cuttance, P. (Eds) *School Effectiveness*. London: Cassell.

Department of Education and Science (1978) *Special Educational Needs* (The Warnock Report). London: HMSO.

Davie, R. *et al.* (1972) *From Birth To Seven*. London: Longmans.

Douglas, J. W.B. (1968) *All Our Future*. London: Panther.

Fullan, M. (1991) *The New Meaning of Educational Change*. London: Cassell.

Galloway, D. (1985) *Schools and Persistent Absentees*. Oxford: Pergamon Press.

Galloway, D., Martin, R. and Wilcox, B. (1985) 'Persistent absence from school and exclusion from school: the predictive power of school and community variables', *British Educational Research Journal*, **11**:51–61.

Gath, D. (1977) *Child Guidance and Delinquency in a London Borough*. London: Oxford University Press.

Gottfredson, G. (1987) 'American education: American delinquency', *Today's Delinquent*, **6**:5–70.

Graham, J. (1988) *Schools, Disruptive Behaviour and Delinquency: A Review of Research*. London: HMSO.

Gray, J., Jesson, D. and Jones, B. (1986) 'The search for a fairer way of comparing schools' examination results', *Research Papers in Education*, **11**, (2):91–122.

Jencks, C. *et al.* (1971) *Inequality*. London: Allen Lane.

Maughan, B., Ouston, J., Pickles, A. and Rutter, M. (1990) 'Can schools change 1 – Outcomes at six London secondary schools', *School Effectiveness and Improvement*, **1**, (3):188–210.

Mortimore, P., Sammons, P., Ecob, R. and Stoll, L. (1988) *School Matters: The Junior Years*. Salisbury: Open Books.

Nuttall, D., Goldstein, H., Prosser, R. and Rasbash, J. (1989) 'Differential school effectiveness', *International Journal of Educational Research*, **13**, (7):769–76.

Ouston, J. and Maughan, B. (1991) 'Can schools change 2' *School Effectiveness and School Improvement*, **2**, (1) (in press).

Power, M. J., Benn, R. T. and Morris, J. N. (1972) 'Neighbourhood school and juveniles before the courts', *British Journal of Criminology*, **12**:111–32.

Ramasut, A. (1989) *Whole School Approaches to Special Needs*. London: Falmer Press.

Reid, K. (1986) *Disaffection from School*. London: Methuen.

Reid, K., Hopkins, D. and Holly, P. (1986) *Towards the Effective School*. Oxford: Blackwell.

Reynolds, D. (1976) 'The delinquent school', in Woods, P. (Ed.) *The Process of Schooling*. London: Routledge and Kegan Paul.

Reynolds, D. (1982) 'The search for effective schools', in *School Organisation*, **2**, (3):215–37.

Reynolds, D. (Ed.) (1985) *Studying School Effectiveness*. Lewes: Falmer Press.

Reynolds, D. (1987) 'The consultant sociologist: a method for linking sociology of education and teachers', in Woods, P. and Pollard, A. (Eds) *Sociology and Teaching*. London: Croom Helm.

Reynolds, D. and Murgatroyd, S. J. (1985) 'The creative consultant', in *School Organisation*, **4**, 3:321–335.

Reynolds, D. and Sullivan, M. (1981) 'The effects of school: a radical faith restated', in Gillham, B. (Ed.) *Problem Behaviour in the Secondary School*. London: Croom Helm.

Reynolds, D., Creemers, B. and Peters, T. (1989) *School Effectiveness and Improvement: Proceedings of the First International Congress, London, 1988*. Groningen: University of Groningen, RION.

Reynolds, D., Davie, R. and Phillips, D. (1989) 'The Cardiff programme – an effective school improvement programme based on school effectiveness research', in Creemers, B. P. M. and Scheerens, J. (Eds) *Developments In School Effectiveness Research*. (Special issue of the International Journal of Educational Research), **13**, 7:800–814.

Reynolds, D., Sullivan, M. and Murgatroyd, S. J. (1987) *The Comprehensive Experiment*. London: Falmer Press.

Rutter, M., Maughan, B., Mortimore, P. and Ouston, J. (1979) *Fifteen Thousand Hours: Secondary Schools and Their Effects on Children*. London: Open Books.

Scheerens, J., Vermeulen, C. J. and Pelgrum, W. J. (1989) 'Generalisability of instructional and school effectiveness indicators across nations', in *International Journal of Educational Research*, **13**, 7:789–799.

Smith, D. and Tomlinson, S. (1989) *The School Effect: A Study of Multi Racial Comprehension*. London: Policy Studies Institute.

Upton, G. (1982) *Educating Children With Behaviour Problems*. Cardiff: Faculty of Education, University College.

CHAPTER 6

Special Needs and School Improvement: The Role of the Local Education Authority

John Clarke

Introduction

It is now twelve years since the publication of the Warnock Report (DES, 1978) and nine years since the enactment of the 1981 Education Act. Since that time there has been a high level of interest in English and Welsh schools in the provision for children with special educational needs (SEN) in the mainstream context and a number of important changes in practices in secondary schools.

Typically, before 1981, pupils who were considered to be 'slow learners' or the 'less able' encountered, for some of the time, a separate provision within their secondary schools. Discrete 'remedial' groups were to be found following a curriculum which was substantially different from that followed by other children of the same age. This separate curriculum, generally, had at its focus more 'basic skills' work and in the 14–16 age range often was expressed in terms of a variety of courses which did not attempt to prepare pupils for academic CSE or GCE examinations but were concerned rather, with what was known as 'life skills'.

In those schools where children with learning difficulties were assimilated into other mainstream classes, they tended to be withdrawn from those classes by specialist SEN teachers who gave them further instruction in basic skills. Frequently they were withdrawn for this more individualised work from other areas of the curriculum, for example, foreign languages or some aspects of science. These strategies contributed to a lack of balance in the curricula of many children with special needs and this frequently produced limitations in continuity and progression.

There is much evidence that throughout the 1980s patterns of provision for children with SEN in mainstream schools changed, radically and quickly in some schools and more slowly in others. The trend has been toward in-class support and towards placing the responsibility for the education of all children in the class on the shoulders of the subject teacher. There has been a consequent change in the organisation of special needs departments. The special needs teacher has been seen in many schools as much more of a consultant on teaching and learning and in respect of particular difficulties which individual pupils may have. Advice has been provided to departments on teaching methodology, on resourcing and on assessment (c.f. Bines, 1986). Nevertheless, many schools continue to withdraw children from their mainstream classes for particular aspects of their work. A relatively small scale survey (DES, 1989a), found that while a growing practice in about a quarter of secondary schools was to provide support teaching for pupils with SEN within mainstream classes, three quarters of the schools visited extracted pupils with SEN from mainstream classes for varying periods of time each week to work in small special groups on 'an often limited range of language and computation skills' (p. 2). It may be, in fact, that there is a large discrepancy in secondary school provision for pupils with SEN between the rhetoric and the reality.

During the 1990s three important factors are likely to affect the provision in mainstream secondary schools for children with special educational needs. These are the introduction of a National Curriculum in England and Wales, the move towards school development planning and the growing body of research on effective schools. This chapter draws these strands together and describes the work of one Local Education Authority in England in assisting secondary schools with their development.

Special educational needs and the National Curriculum

In the first instance the 1988 Education Act has had, and will continue to have, great implications for all schools in England and Wales. The notion of a National Curriculum, prescribed very tightly in some subject areas, is a revolution in the education system of England and Wales. Moreover, the intention of the National Curriculum is that this is a curriculum for all. Although machinery exists for disapplication and modification of the curriculum for individual children according to need, the spirit of the legislation is that as many as possible should be entitled to receive the National Curriculum. As the National Curriculum Council's Guidance has indicated:

> All pupils share the right to a broad and balanced curriculum, including the National Curriculum. The right extends to every registered pupil of compulsory school age attending a maintained or grant maintained school, whether or not he or she has a statement of special educational needs. This right is implicit in the 1988 Education Act (NCC, 1989, p. 1).

Professionals in the field have taken this message to heart and there are, for example, important initiatives in accessing the National Curriculum to children with severe learning difficulties (Ashdown *et al.*, 1990 and Fagg *et al.*, 1991). It is unlikely, although still legally possible (DES, 1989b), that many Headteachers or Governing Bodies in mainstream schools will attempt to unpick the complicated regulations for disapplication or modification, and that therefore the vast majority of pupils will be following the National Curriculum.

This, in itself, has a number of important implications. All pupils will follow the three core subjects (English, mathematics and science) and seven other foundation subjects (technology, history, geography, a modern foreign language, art, music and physical education) plus religious education from the age of 5 to 16. The notion of creating non-examination groups in the 14–16 age range or designing particular courses in that age range which in the past have been intended to meet the needs of children for whom a range of academic subjects is deemed inappropriate, will cease. Moreover, the practice of withdrawing some pupils from lessons to work on basic skills in English or in maths will be not only inappropriate, but illegal if the lessons from which they are withdrawn are those following a National Curriculum subject.

Since most curricular time in secondary schools will be taken up by courses which follow the National Curriculum there is a clear implication for the operation of special needs departments. Special needs teachers have two choices. They could become increasingly expert in each of the National Curriculum subjects and withdraw pupils to work in smaller groups on the same courses as their peers in ordinary classes. Alternatively, they will have to develop methods to support classroom teachers in the delivery of the National Curriculum to a range of children with different previous attainments, in each subject. Moreover, these attainments will be recorded much more thoroughly than in the pre-National Curriculum era. Government regulations which come into force in 1991 are insisting that each school, in addition to reporting to parents annually as a baseline minimum on the performance of each pupil in the ten National Curriculum subjects are also insisting that schools must have information on the performance of each child in each attainment target within each subject of the National Curriculum which must be available for scrutiny by the pupil's parents (DES, 1990). For the first time the attainments of all pupils in England and Wales will be assessed and recorded in great detail. There are 36 attainment targets in the 'core' subjects alone, most expressed in terms of ten 'levels' and teachers will be continually assessing the progress of all pupils against the statements of attainment within these levels.

The impact of this legislation taken as whole is clear. The notion that there is a definable group of pupils who have special educational needs in the mainstream context is likely to be less than helpful. Schools will not be able to make separate provision in curricular terms for particular groups of pupils. They will not be able to emphasise one area of the curriculum at the expense of another because the concepts of breadth and balance are to be applied to all. The entitlement curriculum will become a reality and the job which teachers will face in classrooms is to make that curriculum accessible to all and to take pupils on from where they currently are to where they ought to be on their individual journey through the National Curriculum.

It has always been the job of teachers to move pupils on from where they currently are to where they might be next but the National Curriculum gives this process a much sharper focus. When 11-year-olds arrive in their secondary schools they will do so with a profile of attainments which will resemble an urban skyline – soaring skywards in some areas of attainments but not far off the ground in others. In addition, each individual's profile, which will be documented and available to parents, will be unique. The teacher's task will be to build on that profile and to offer a range of curricular experiences which is appropriate to that individual. The real issue, then, is concerned not with special educational needs but with individual educational needs. In this sense the notion that there is a continuum of need among pupils is emphasised by the National Curriculum. Pupils and parents will expect progress through the attainment targets irrespective of the baseline from which children start. Parents of a pupil who had attained at Level 3 in history by the age of 11 would have a reasonable expectation that he or she would be further on than Level 3 by the age of 14. If this progress has not been made parents and school would, justifiably, begin to talk in terms of the pupil having particular needs in history. The pupil fell within the 'normal' range for the age group which is defined in statute but had failed to make progress over a three-year period. Whether the need of the pupil is individual or special, in these circumstances, is irrelevant.

In the National Curriculum context the challenge for all schools and for all teachers is to develop further teaching strategies which recognise the different previous attainments of pupils who still, never-theless, will be taught in groups. All needs will have the same relevance and will be concerned with assisting children to move from one level to the next through a curriculum which has a built-in progression. This is not to imply that there will be no place for teachers who, in a previous culture, were specialists in special needs. Their role is likely to be enhanced in the search for the truly differentiated currciulum for all, rather than for a few. There is no less need for specialists but there is a need for them to be integrated into the planning and operation of the mainstream school (c.f. Wang *et al.*, 1986). They will, however, need to employ their expertise in advising on teaching and learning rather than on 'special' needs. They will need to advise on planning for differentiation, on resource production to ensure that there is material available in each class to support the learning of all pupils irrespective of their previous attainments. They will need to advise on classroom strategies in terms of the balance between individual and collaborative work and they will need to assist other colleagues with assessment and the process of accurately matching the curriculum offered to each pupil's previous attainment. These will be challenging tasks. The structure of the National Curriculum is unhelpful. There are major differences in the way each subject is currently described in the statutory orders and this is likely to mean that the ways in which differentiation is achieved within each subject will vary. In some subjects, for example, the design and technology component of technology, English and history, it will continue to be possible for whole classes of pupils to study the same thing at the same time. Differentiation will be achieved by the provision of resources to support learning at a variety of levels. In other subjects, science and geography for example, this is unlikely to be possible. There will be times when different small groups of pupils within the same class will be studying different content in order that all can achieve. This is a major challenge for the classroom teacher and undermines many of the traditional assumptions about how, particularly, secondary schools are organised. The specialist special needs teacher will need to advise on classroom management and organisation if he or she is to assist specialist subject colleagues in providing for differentiation.

In summary, what will be important for schools is not to ensure that their special needs policy or department is responding to the identified needs of one-fifth or one-sixth of the population but rather that the school as a whole is an effective institution for learning. The recent HMI report (DES, 1990) has demonstrated that special needs practice tends to be effective in effective schools and that where the general practice in the school is ineffective, so is the practice with pupils who have SEN. 'It was equally evident that the features of good practice applied to the teaching of all pupils and not just to those with Special Educational Needs' (p. 8). These features of good practice occurred in those schools where classroom or subject teachers, often supported by the special needs teachers, had begun to tackle the issue of differentiation in order to provide a curriculum which had meaning for all pupils in the group because all could make progress. In those schools where practice was less than good this issue had still to be addressed. In classes in these schools two large groups were being disadvantaged – those who were unable to cope with the tasks set by the teacher and those who could do the task before it was set. The fate of children with special needs in these classes was the same as that for many other children because the practice, taken as a whole, was ineffective. By definition an effective special needs policy cannot be operated within an ineffective school. The challenge for the future which is being highlighted by the introduction of the National Curriculum, although it has always been there, is to improve the effectiveness of schools for the benefit of all pupils. This chapter argues that in that process Local Education Authorities (LEAs) can have an important role and outlines what one LEA in England, Suffolk, has done.

Effective schools

Until fairly recently, attempts to improve the effectiveness of schools have been handicapped by the simple fact that not much has been known about the nature of effective schools. That situation has, to a degree, been remedied and we are now in a better position to advise schools much more on what school-based factors seem to have tendencies towards effectiveness.

In common with many LEAs in England and Wales, Suffolk established, some time ago, procedures for internal and external evaluations of its schools. These, dating from 1981, reflected the very tentative nature of much of this work. A scepticism that there were any 'right' answers to effectiveness in schools characterises much of this early work. The early documentation merely suggested the dimensions about which judgments could be made but established no criteria for effectiveness. For example, schools were invited to outline their practices but it was not easy to perceive entirely what the view of the LEA was in terms of effective practice:

'What is the school's assessment policy?'

- continuous assessment, formal examination
- objective testing
- impression assessment
- written work, practical work, skill development
- assessment methods reflecting curricular aims
- assessment results modifying teaching content and method
- review and revision of assessment procedures
  (Suffolk LEA, 1983, p. 8).

Not only was this true for the internal evaluations carried out by schools in their annual self-appraisals but also for the more formal reviews of practice in schools carried out by teams of the LEA's advisers. It was certainly not possible in advance of a formal review for teachers and schools to be sure to what criteria individual advisers were working. There was no guarantee, moreover, that schools or individual teachers within them would share with the advisers a common view of what constituted good practice. In addition, in the absence of briefing notes for advisers which were expressed in terms of criteria for successful practice, it was not possible to be sure that all advisers shared the same view.

By the end of the 1980s a number of important developments had taken place and there was an increasing expectation that local authority advisers should operate more in an inspectorial mode, and at the same time apply criteria to the practice they observed (Audit Commission, 1989). In Suffolk it became evident that the writing of criteria for school effectiveness was an important way forward.

In addressing this task the LEA was aided considerably by the volume of research findings on the nature of effectiveness. There are some dangers in this approach. Research on effectiveness is competent only to provide indications of what factors are likely to produce greater effectiveness. As Gray (1990) has pointed out, in about 30 per cent of cases 'schools seem to achieve "good" results without scoring particularly highly on all the "key" factors identified by researchers' blueprints' (p. 17). Nevertheless, the alternative is to consider not process factors but outcomes. Many schemes of evaluation rely solely on quantifiable data against 'performance indicators' which are concerned almost exclusively with outcomes. Any link between such schemes and school development and improvement is tenuous. The results of these evaluations may set the agenda for institutions in terms of suggesting which aspects need attention but cannot suggest to those institutions how such improvement can be secured. In their design therefore, despite the dangers, the writing group decided that, as a first principle, the Suffolk criteria should be concerned with process, with what schools and teachers actually do, and, in that context, emphasise the link between evaluation, effectiveness and development. Accordingly, they are based on the available research evidence on school effectiveness (notably, Brighouse, 1988; DES, 1977; HMI, 1979, 1985; Mortimore *et al.*, 1988; Clift *et al.*, 1987; Oakes, 1987; Reid *et al.*, 1987 and Rutter *et al.*, 1979).

Other important principles were followed. The criteria apply to all schools – primary, secondary and special. Schools are bound by common ethical, educational and organisational concerns. More importantly, perhaps, the National Curriculum has provided for all schools a common language in the way in which the greater part of the curriculum is described in terms of Attainment Targets and Programmes of Study and in terms of seeking to ensure effective continuity by seeing the educational process as a whole. By producing universal criteria for all schools it is possible to reinforce these notions of commonality and progression. Moreover the intention has been to demonstrate that special schools and by implication pupils with special educational needs in the mainstream school are no different from any other school or pupil. In this respect the LEA has received strong support from the Headteachers of special schools and from special needs coordinators in mainstream schools.

Thirdly, the criteria are not specific to particular subject areas. There is a possibility that producing separate criteria for separate subjects would have diluted the whole and been divisive within schools. It is for individual departments in secondary schools and individual subject specialist advisers to put their own complexion on the criteria by use of subject-specific examples which can be derived from the general criteria. The intention has been to stress that there are certain things about teaching and learning which are universal in terms of effective practice. If this is true of different subjects, it is also true of children of different previous attainments.

From the common features identified in the literature, five key areas emerge as a framework for the evaluation of effectiveness in schools. These are:

- aims
- ethos
- curricular organisation and assessment
- curricular implementation
- management and administration

To a degree the choice of these five areas is arbitrary and there are many overlaps. For example, assessment must be seen as an integral part of curricular implementation as well as sitting naturally within curriculum organisation; there are aspects of the school's ethos which are affected by the teaching and learning styles employed; aims, ethos, curriculum organisation and curriculum implementation are all affected by the quality of management. However, it was necessary to split the working of a school into broad headings for the purposes of producing a manageable document.

In the next stage the research evidence from a variety of studies was built into the criteria. The twelve key characteristics from the Inner London Education Authority Junior School Study (for example) were interwoven here along with other findings (e.g. Wang *et al.*, 1986). The outcome of this process was the production of key characteristics for each of the five areas listed above which relate to school effectiveness. For example, in terms of curricular implementation, key characteristics in effective schools tend to be:

- learning activities are purposeful
- learning activities are varied
- active learning is taking place
- pupils are encouraged to take responsibility for their own learning
- the learning environment is of a high standard
- practice seeks to ensure equal opportunities

The next task was to try to identify 'second order' statements which relate directly to each of these characteristics which, in themselves would stand as success criteria. For example, in terms of the key characteristic 'learning activities are purposeful' identified success criteria were:

- teachers have high expectations of their pupils
- learning is sequential and builds upon previous pupil achievement
- pupils are asked to perform productive tasks
- pupils are aware of the purpose of individual schemes or lessons and how each fits into the overall scheme
- progress is reinforced by regular feedback from teachers to pupils; praise is used to reward and motivate.

The final task was to identify examples of what might constitute evidence for each of these success criteria. For example, for the success criterion 'the pace and scope of work provides a real and continuous challenge for pupils' some evidence which might be adduced would be:

- that a sense of purpose and direction exists, work and progress are valued and pupils understand that time needs to be used wisely
- resources and tasks are differentiated to take account of pupils' abilities and needs
- that pupils are engaged on work which is demanding, stimulating and provides opportunities to succeed.

The way in which these last statements are phrased raises an important point. It is not possible in this model of evaluation to remove entirely a subjective view of what, for example, is meant by a 'sense of purpose and direction exists' or 'work is demanding and stimulating.' In this respect classroom observation, discussion with teachers and local knowledge of schools and their population remains important. The intention is that discussion between the evaluators, whether senior managers in schools or external evaluators will be more about the evidence on which judgements are made than the criteria themselves which underpin those judgements. Through this process of discussion about evidence, schools are presented with opportunities to become more reflective institutions and to engage in debate about quality. Both of these are likely to create the conditions in which schools can become more effective.

In terms of special needs, these criteria are for all schools and all pupils. There may be very minor modifications required. For example, it is not reasonable to assume that the total population of a school for children with severe learning difficulties should know the purpose of each activity and how it relates to what has gone before and what is to come. That aside, however, no modifications are required in terms of the application of these criteria. Throughout the entire document the term 'special needs' does not occur. In an important sense the Suffolk Criteria for School Evaluation are concerned with effective schooling

116

as a whole and with effective strategies in schools to ensure that each pupil receives his or her entitlement within the whole curriculum in general and the National Curriculum in particular. In that sense an assumption underpins the criteria. In an effective school the needs of all pupils are catered for and this includes those who, traditionally, have been described as having special needs.

School effectiveness, supported self-evaluation and school development planning

The last section of the chapter describes the use to which the criteria for school review have already been put. All schools within the LEA are required to produce school development plans annually. These incorporate school self-appraisal, the National Curriculum development plan, the Technical and Vocational Education Initiative (a nationally funded 14–19 curriculum project) plan in 11–16 or 11–18 schools and the budget plan concerned with the Local Financial Management of Schools. The processes which the schools go through in order to produce this plan are in line with those set out in the DES guidance (DES, 1989c). They undertake an audit of current practice, identify priorities, targets and tasks, set success criteria, implement and evaluate. The end-of-cycle review becomes part of the audit for the following year's plan.

A crucial first stage in the production of this plan is clearly the audit. This is intended to establish where the school is now. This is an important part of any planning but in school planning, there often have been difficulties. In the absence of criteria for effective practice individual schools have to rely on their own perceptions in order to determine what is currently going well and what is going badly. The Suffolk Criteria for School Evaluation fill that gap. Moreover, since they make no reference to special needs as such, the presumption is that, eventually, schools will cease to identify special needs as a priority in the school but instead will begin to identify differentiation or teaching and learning styles. In this, schools are aided by advice on the school development planning process. In an occasional paper for LEAs on the management of development planning (Hargreaves *et al.*, 1990) there is a very helpful metaphor which has particular merit when applied to special needs in schools. Hargreaves and his colleagues introduce the notion of root changes and branch changes which are discussed and brought about by the school development planning process. Root innovations are those which generate the base on which other, or branch, innovations can be sustained. In these terms changes related to the provision for children with special needs are frequently branch changes. If the root culture of a truly differentiated curriculum with the accompanying staff perception of the teaching methodologies likely to achieve it does not exist, the branch change concerned with special needs cannot be sustained. There is some evidence from the 1990 Action Plans that schools in Suffolk are already beginning to see that strategies for teaching and learning throughout are a school development priority rather than special needs. This is a major step forward, but only a step on a very long journey.

Moreover, the LEA's policy for monitoring and evaluation of school provision is intended to support schools in these developments. There is a regular cycle of whole-school reviews undertaken by members of the Advisory Service. These range from small-scale events, two advisers for two days in small primary schools to larger operations, six advisers for five days in large secondary schools. The purpose of each review is to assess the overall effectiveness of the school in meeting its own aims and objectives and to evaluate the quality and standard of provision for pupils. While there is a measure of accountability in the review, its primary purpose is to evaluate the school so that it can develop further. In essence it is an external audit and in the same way as in the process of internal school development planning it can set the agenda for future development. All judgements are made against the Suffolk Criteria for School Evaluation which schools already have and most of the review period is spent in classroom observation. Although the team leader of the review identifies particular aspects of the school on which the team will focus, equally, the Headteacher may, through discussion with the team leader, direct the attention of the team to particular issues on which the school itself feels it would like some data.

In addition to the report which is written for the school which, in essence, identifies what has been achieved and what further developments can now be planned, an annual report is produced which is a summary of the reports on all schools which have been reviewed in that year. This report is divided into the same sections as the Suffolk Criteria for School Evaluation and distributed to all Headteachers and Chairs of Governing Bodies. This is a summary of the collective judgements of the Advisory Service on the schools reviewed – about 20 per cent each year – and can therefore provide another stimulus to other schools in terms of self-evaluation. There is evidence

118

that schools, other than those reviewed, are using this document to set the agenda for their own evaluations.

It is a truism that schools improve themselves and are not improved by outsiders. However, the use of common criteria for evaluation, the external review process which supports self-evaluation, the advice to schools on development planning and the publication of summary reports are all important factors in establishing a culture within schools where the notion of special needs disappears and is replaced by the notion of individual need in the context of effective schools for all.

References

Ashdown, R., Boviar, K. and Carpenter, B. (1991) (Eds) *The Curriculum Challenge*. London: Falmer Press.
Audit Commission (1989) *Assuring Quality in Education: A Report on Local Education Authority Inspectors and Advisers*. London: HMSO.
Bines, H. (1986) *Redefining Remedial Education*, London: Croom Helm.
Brighouse, T. (1988) *The Effective School*. Oxford: Oxford LEA.
Clift, D. S., Nuttall, D. and McCormick, R. (1987) *Studies in School Self-Evaluation*. London: Falmer Press.
Department of Education and Science (1977) *Ten Good Schools*. London: HMSO.
Department of Education and Science (1978) *Special Educational Needs* (The Warnock Report). London: HMSO.
Department of Education and Science (1989a) *A Survey of Pupils with SEN in Ordinary Schools*. London: HMSO.
Department of Education and Science (1989b) *Education Reform Act 1988: Temporary Exceptions from the National Curriculum* Circular 15/89. London: HMSO.
Department of Education and Science (1989c) *Planning for School Development*. London: HMSO.
Department of Education and Science (1990) *Records of Achievement* Circular 8/90. London: HMSO.
Fagg, S., Aherne, P., Skelton, S. and Thornber, A. (1991) *A Broad, Balanced and Relevant Curriculum for Children and Young People with Severe and Complex Learning Difficulties in the 1990*. London: David Fulton Publishers.
Gray, J. (1990) Inaugural Lecture, University of Sheffield, March 7, 1990.
Hargreaves, D. H., Hopkins, D. and Leask, M. (1990) *The Management of Development Planning*. Cambridge: School Development Plans Project.
HMI (1979) *Aspects of Secondary Education*. London: HMSO.
HMI (1985) *Quality in Schools*. London: HMSO.
Mortimore, P., Sammons, P., Stoll, L., Lewis, D. and Ecob, R. (1988) *School Matters – The Junior Years*. Wells: Open Books.
National Curriculum Council (1989) *Curriculum Guidance Two: A Curriculum for All*. York: NCC.

Oakes, J. (1987) *Conceptual and Measurement Issues in the Construction of School Quality*. California: Centre for Policy Research in Education, The Rand Corporation.

Reid, K., Hopkins, D. and Holly, P. (1987) *Towards the Effective School*. Oxford: Basil Blackwell.

Reynolds, D. (1985) *Studying School Effectiveness*. London: Falmer Press.

Rutter, M., Maughan, B., Mortimore, P., Ouston, J. and Smith, A. (1979) *Fifteen Thousand Hours: Secondary Schools and their Effects on Children*. London: Open Books.

Suffolk Local Education Authority (1983) *Secondary Schools' Self Appraisal*. Suffolk: Suffolk LEA.

Wang, M. C., Reynolds, M. C. and Walberg, H. J. (1986) 'Rethinking special education', *Educational Leadership*, **44**:1, 26–31.

CHAPTER 7

The Quality of Classroom Learning Experiences for Children with Special Educational Needs

Neville Bennett

Theoretical background

The prime focus of our research on teaching-learning processes in classrooms over the last decade has been on the quality of children's learning experiences, and the classroom factors which aid, or hinder, these. For this focus we have adopted a constructivist approach to learning, deriving from insights provided by cognitive psychology. This perspective views learners as active and interpretive, and learning as a covert, intellectual process involving the development and restructuring of existing conceptual schemes. In this view, teaching affects learning through pupil thought processes, i.e. teaching influences pupil thinking, and pupil thinking mediates learning. Learning from teaching is not automatic (Wittrock, 1986).

The way in which teaching affects learning in classrooms is typically through the curriculum tasks that teachers present to children (or allow them to choose). As such, the activities of learners on tasks are critical to their cognitive development. To understand classroom learning thus requires an understanding of children's performances on their tasks, and the appropriateness of task demands for the individual learner.

Also, since learning takes place within complex social settings it is necessary to assess the impact of social processes on children's classroom experiences. The model of social processes that we have drawn on is that of Doyle (1979a; 1979b; 1983) which suggests that teachers and pupils are in a continuous process of adaptation to each other and the classroom environment, a process involving reciprocal accommodation. In Doyle's view the assessment system in operation in the classroom is at the heart of the process. Pupils must learn what the teacher will reward, and the teacher must learn what the pupils will deliver. Mutual accommodation leads to cooperation between teacher and taught, and cooperation, in Doyle's theory, is the keystone to a classroom life acceptable to the participants. His perspective emphasizes the complex social interactions involved in classroom life, assigns a crucial role to pupils in influencing the learning processes that teachers seek to manipulate, and emphasizes the role of assessment.

From these perspectives, studying classroom task processes and their appropriateness entails observing the tasks teachers assign, how and why they assign them, how and why pupils interpret and work on them, and how and why teachers respond to pupils' work. Our typical methodological approach is, therefore, after selecting appropriate samples of teachers and pupils, as follows:

(1) Interview the teacher(s) prior to classroom observations in order to ascertain what tasks have been planned and prepared, their rationale and intentions, and how they fit into the on-going curriculum.
(2) Observation and recording of teachers' assignment or presentation of tasks, and the classroom management structure operating.
(3) Observation and recording of pupil activities on the task(s) assigned.
(4) A post-task interview to ascertain pupils' understanding of completed task(s).
(5) Post-session interview with the teacher to ascertain, on the basis of the pupils' work, their judgements of the quality and appropriateness of the task(s) assigned, and future task intentions.

Since 1982 we have carried out five studies using this perspective, covering the age range 4–14 years, and the full ability range. Three of these five studies concentrated specifically on the lowest attaining children in the mainstreamed sector, and one followed children through the mainstreaming process, as they transferred from special schools to ordinary comprehensive schools (Bennett and Cass, 1988, 1989; Bennett and Kell, 1989; Bennett et al., 1984; Bennett et al., 1987).

Classroom task processes

The purpose of this chapter is to consider the findings of these diverse studies, with particular reference to the lowest attaining children in the classes, i.e. Warnock's 20 per cent, to ascertain common patterns

122

or issues. These findings are organised around the heuristic model of classroom task processes shown in Figure 7.1.

Figure 7.1 A model of classroom task processes

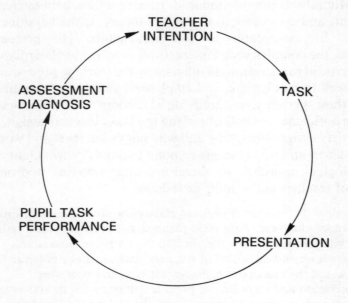

This is a summary model, derived from our several studies, and is cyclic. Briefly, teachers plan and perpare tasks for their pupils for particular purposes. These purposes, or intentions as they are labelled in the model, inform task selection. These tasks are presented to pupils in some way – a discussion, demonstration, experiment, TV programme, etc. in which is incorporated appropriate pupil activity – discussing, writing, making, etc. – here labelled 'pupil performance'. Pupils demonstrate their understanding (or misconceptions) of the task through their performances. Their completed work is assessed or diagnosed by teachers in order to judge children's developing competencies, and these assessments in turn should inform the next task planning cycle.

This brief description is deceptively simple, however. Teaching-learning processes in classrooms are extremely complex, and inconsistencies or inappropriatenesses can occur between every element of the model. Each element and its linkages are now considered with particular reference to low attaining children.

Teacher intentions

Two definitions of intention are necessary here. The first, broader, definition concerns what curriculum the pupil shall follow, i.e. what subjects, time allocations, and the subject balance achieved. The second definition is as described above – the purposes underlying the selection of specific tasks within a given curriculum area.

The broader definition was of particular importance in our study of mainstreaming. In this study we followed children formerly categorised ESN–M, through their transitions from special to ordinary schools. We observed them through the last term of their special school and the first year of secondary school. For some children the curriculum provided after transfer was very narrow. One child, a 14-year-old, spent nearly 60 per cent of his week on maths and English. The only other subjects available to him were of a practical kind – art, PE, woodwork, housecraft and care. Other children suffered a similar restricted curriculum, and in every single case, curriculum continuity between the two schools involved in the transfer was poor, either because the work in the ordinary school offered no extension to the work in the special school, or because there was marked discontinuity in demand, which left children floundering.

With regard to the narrower definition of intention two trends are apparent from our studies. First, and not infrequently, the tasks that children perform are not those which the teacher intended, and second, that when tasks are observed over a long period of time there is a clear difference in the actual curriculum received by low and high attainers.

That children end up working on tasks different from those intended is usually caused either by task design problems (i.e. the task chosen does not actually embody the teacher's intention), or by diagnostic errors, where an intention for enrichment, for example, actually turns out to be practice, because the child is already thoroughly familiar with the content and demand in the task. Generally high attainers suffered more than low attainers in this regard, although one finding of possible concern is that very similar opportunities for consolidation are accorded high and low attainers, possibly creating delays for the former and confusion or incompetence for the latter.

Task appropriateness

The task selected or designed by the teacher has to incorporate intellectual demands commensurate with the capabilities of the pupils. The mismatch between tasks and children is an aspect of classroom practice which has most concerned Her Majesty's Inspectorate. This mismatch is defined in the Plowden Report (1967) as teachers avoiding 'the twin pitfalls of demanding too much and expecting too little'. HMI have argued in all of their reports over the last decade or so that too often the level of demand and pace of work are directed towards children of average ability in the class. Lack of differentiation in demand has led to underestimation of high attainers and a corresponding overestimation of low attainers.

The data from our studies support this trend. In our first study of 600 maths and language tasks among 6–8-year-old children approximately 40 per cent of all tasks were matched, 28 per cent too difficult, and 26 per cent too easy. Children at different levels of attainment, however, had radically different experiences. High attainers were underestimated on 41 per cent of all tasks assigned to them. Low attainers were overestimated on 44 per cent of tasks assigned (Bennett *et al.*, 1984) (see Table 7.1).

Table 7.1 Matching by attainment level – maths

Attainment	Match	Too Easy	Too Hard
High	41	41	18
Average	43	26	26
Low	44	12	44
Total			212

If children at the extremes of attainment in each class are sampled, the effect of mismatching is even more noticeable. In a study of 8–11-year-old children, 500 tasks were observed in four curriculum areas, in which we targeted the three highest, and three lowest attaining children in each class. The extent of mismatch was greater, as can be seen in Table 7.2, and the pattern of over- and underestimations identical in each curriculum area (Bennett *et al.*, 1987).

Table 7.2 indicates that nearly two thirds of all tasks for lowest attainers were over-estimated. This is obviously a cause for concern,

Table 7.2 Matching for low and high attainers (per cent)

Attainers	Matched	Too Easy	Too Hard
Low	27	8	65
High	38	48	13

and in investigating this further it became clear that they found less difficulty with practical than with written tasks. In practical work the proportion of unsuitable tasks fell from two thirds to one half.

Pupil reactions to overestimation have been similar in our studies. In responding to written tasks the children typically had limited memory for the stimulus to writing. They were slow to get to the task, and the preliminaries of writing the date took up much of the time available. Performance on the task was slow: less than one word per minute of allocated time was produced. They made persistent demands on the teacher's time, notably with requests for spellings. Consequently, a large proportion of their time was spent waiting for help. Error rates were high, even when copying words from the blackboard or from their work books. Despite this, the children had every appearance of working hard.

On mismatched mathematics tasks work was completed very slowly. On average, the children took 3 minutes to complete each calculation. Most of the time was spent industriously on task, but much of the effort was concentrated on the production features of the task rather than on progress through the exercise; that is, a lot of time was spent copying out the calculation, going over figures, and rubbing out or boxing answers. Although most of the calculations were done correctly, post-task interviews revealed limited understanding of the processes used.

Pertinent examples of under- and overestimation, and their impact, came from both the pupils and their parents in our study of mainstreaming. For example, the mother of Timothy, a 14-year-old, felt that in general his experiences in the special school had not been beneficial to him, indeed she felt that standards had deteriorated in his final year. 'He might as well have not gone to school', she said. 'We might as well have kept him at home.... He was just sitting there playing games'. Timothy had complained of boredom and resented what he saw as simplistic work. His mother concluded 'He got more and more bored because, you know the ABC books?, he had them, which was making him the mind of a 4-year-old really.... He used to throw them down the side of the couch and say "I'm sick of them" '. Jonathan's mother similarly recorded his boredom and wanting to do more demanding work.

On transfer to the ordinary school the parents of Anna and Timothy present vivid examples of overestimation. Anna's parents cited examples of her difficulties in several areas of the curriculum including mathematics, religious studies and geography. Of one piece of geography homework her mother said, 'It was absolutely amazing. They had these sentences, and they had to fill in the missing word using geographical terms. . . . Some of them, unless you were doing sorts of O-level geography, you wouldn't really have been expected to know. She (the teacher) had just given out this sheet and she said to them, "If you don't bring this back I'll twist your heads around". Now you can imagine', continued the mother, 'how we felt sitting at home looking at this sheet and knowing that no normal 11-year-old should have been given it, never mind a remedial 11-year-old, and knowing what this woman had said. We daren't send it back and say "This is a load of rubbish", we felt we had to complete it'.

What these, and similar case studies show is the powerful supportive role that parents play, and what distressing effects the lack of adequate planning and differentiation by the teacher can have.

Presentation

A good intention transformed into an appropriate task can, however, fail due to poor presentation. What the teacher says in presenting the work clearly circumscribes what is required. And what is required is not always what the teacher says. In each of our studies we have been struck by the frequency with which children have been confused by poor specification of the task through inadequate teacher explanation or demonstration, or through lack of necessary curriculum materials. And poor presentation does of course differentially affect low attainers (Carroll, 1963).

One extreme, but true, example of this was observed with a class of very young children. The teacher had decided to do country dancing in the hall as a PE lesson. She used a tape which included the music as well as a voice-over calling out instructions for the children to follow. The tape was run through once and the children enjoyed the directed dancing. The teacher decided to repeat it. The observation log reads as follows:

> 10.25. Tape on again: at the beginning. But the dance they have to do is not the same as the instructions on the tape. Instead the teacher calls out different instructions. So when the tape says *dance on the spot*, the children have to swing their partners! When the tape says *dance around the room*, they clap on the spot.

Not surprisingly, some children find this extremely confusing (Bennett and Kell, 1989).

More mundane examples of poor presentation involve children not being able to read necessary instructions, or not being able to write quickly enough to copy procedures from the blackboard.

Implementation

The demands in the task carry demands for appropriate pupil activity, be it listening and responding in a discussion, or carrying out necessary procedures in an experiment. There also needs to be a classroom management system capable of sustaining high levels of pupil involvement, because without effective involvement there can be no effective learning.

The available evidence would indicate that in general low attainers have lower levels of on-task activity: and when grouped with other low attainers indulge in talk which is less task-enhancing, e.g. fewer explanations, knowledge sharing, etc. Their profile of involvement also differs from that of high attainers: involvement is sustained for much shorter periods of time, and they take longer to settle down after transitions (c.f. Bennett, Andreae, Hegarty and Wade, 1980).

Levels of involvement range widely from class to class, and from our study of mainstreaming it also varies either side of transfer. Our findings indicate an increase in on-task activity after transfer to ordinary schools, although there was a tendency for involvement to decrease through the first year. The reasons for this increase appear to be a combination of teaching approach, being much more directive in the ordinary schools, and the level of pupil interest in their work. The children and their parents all reported that the work in the special schools was both too easy and too boring.

Teacher behaviour also has a bearing on pupil involvement. There is observational evidence to show that pupil involvement is highest when an adult or teacher is in close proximity, and declines substantially when there is not. This argues for teacher mobility in supervision and monitoring rather than being stationary at the front of the class. Interestingly we have also found a slight tendency for improved matching when teachers were mobile.

In mainstreamed primary classes stationary teachers tend to be associated with increased queuing, an unfortunate management strategy which eats up both pupil and teacher time. We have, for example, timed pupils in queues for up to 20 minutes before they have received attention. In this situation children's time is wasted, the teacher has limited time to deal with any one child's problem, and is also unable properly to supervise the remainder of the class.

Assessment/diagnosis

'Assessment is at the heart of the process of promoting children's learning' (TGAT, 1988). Indeed David Ausubel (1968) once commented that if he had to reduce all of educational psychology to just one principle, he would say that the most important single factor influencing learning is what the learner already knows. Ascertain this and teach accordingly.

We have found it necessary in our observations in classrooms to differentiate between assessment and diagnosis. The former we define as verbal or written teacher comments concerning the quality of children's work. These tend to be limited to judgements of right and wrong, with associated ticks and crosses and minimal descriptive comment. Diagnosis, on the other hand, we have defined as teacher attempts to acquire a clear view of pupils' understandings or misconceptions through analysis of children's work and questioning. The common metaphor is to create a window into the child's mind.

Our consistent finding is that teachers are adept at assessment, which in our view is minimally useful for teacher and taught, but that they do not diagnose. There are probably good reasons for this in the mainstreamed sector. Teachers typically have no training in diagnosing children's understandings, and diagnosis undeniably requires more time, and a classroom organisation capable of sustaining uninterrupted lengthy interactions between the teacher and individual pupils. Nevertheless we did expect, naively in retrospect, that teachers in special schools or remedial/special needs departments in ordinary schools would demonstrate such skills. What we actually found were the worst assessment practices we have observed.

Few of the children we followed through the process of mainstreaming gained adequate assessment in the ordinary school. For example Timothy's spelling was very poor but no efforts appeared to have been made to improve it. His written stories were often no more than lists of points, and much of his project work was simply copied from newspaper reports or books. He had only rudimentary knowledge of grammar – capitals did not follow full stops and stories were a series of events of the 'and then' variety. Despite all this the teacher's comments on his work were of little or no value. A typical comment at the end of a story incorporating the above features would be a tick and 'you need to look at each sentence'.

Jonathan was similarly affected. His capital letters were randomly distributed, spelling errors were common, and basic words in letter writing were portrayed incorrectly. The teacher's consistent reaction to all these was to ignore them. Most were signified with a tick. None was graced with a single comment. Finally, the longest comment that Peter gained on his written work was 'a good try'.

It is not clear what conceptions of assessment these teachers had, if indeed they had any at all, but assessment is of no value unless it indicates to the learner how work could be improved, and indicates to the teacher what course of curriculum action ought to follow.

Lack of diagnosis is generally accompanied by a tendency among teachers in all sectors to limit the assessment to the product of the children's work. Rarely did they attempt to ascertain the processes or strategies deployed by children in coming to their finished product. This is also linked with a stress on procedural aspects of tasks, and mechanical progress through curriculum schemes, rather than on pupil understanding. Curriculum cover often seems more important than pupil learning.

The fact that many teachers limit their assessment to products, and allow queues to develop, leads to typical classroom scenes which were both amusing yet worrying. Many are the times I have observed low attaining children enter the queue with all the work wrong, but arrive at the teachers' desk with it all correct, through surreptitious checking and copying along the way. The teacher, unconscious of this process, marks the work as correct, often followed by lavish amounts of praise. In reality of course the child has no understanding of the work, but is often progressed on to the next exercise or workcard.

Diagnostic information is not only necessary for the purposes of effective feedback, but also for effective feedforward. Only by opening the window on to the child's mind can teachers gain sufficient information on which to plan the next optimal step. In this sense, then, poor assessment practices can lead to pedagogical planning blight.

The importance of the power of accurate diagnosis of children's understandings cannot be over-stressed. Nor can its links with other elements of the model. This can be seen most clearly in one of the conclusions of the Select Committee on Achievement in Primary Schools (House of Commons, 1986). It stated that 'The skills of diagnosing learning success and difficulty, and selecting and presenting new tasks, are the essence of the teacher's profession and vital to children's progress'.

Conclusion

The foregoing indicates that the quality of learning experiences for low attaining children is not the same as that for average or high attainers. They tend to receive too little consolidation, their tasks tend to over-estimate their capabilities, poor presentation of work by teachers affects them more acutely, their work rate is often poorer, and inadequate assessment and diagnosis can lead to superficial under-standing and less than optimal curriculum progression. It is of interest that those same features are apparent in mainstream schooling at every age range we have studied, from 4–14 years of age.

The critical question is of course 'How can improvements be sought for both teacher and taught?' First, of course, teacher educators have some explaining to do about the general absence of courses on the diagnosis of children's learning at either pre-service or inservice levels. Our response has been to argue that since inadequate diagnosis lies at the root of poor matching, and since inadequate classroom management lies at the root of poor diagnosis then matching, manage-ment and diagnosis should be tackled together. We have therefore developed inservice courses for teachers in which they consider the intellectual demands in tasks, and their design, together with strategies for pupil diagnosis in the classroom setting. These strategies involve focused task observations and clinical interviewing techniques. These have proved successful and have more recently been transformed into modules of a masters degree which can be studied in the university or in distance learning form.

Another recent initiative for improvement, influenced by our analyses of classroom organisation and the theoretical insights of Vygotsky and Bruner, comes from our work on cooperative learning. Vygotsky (1962) argued that a child's potential for learning is revealed and often realised in interactions with more knowledgeable others, and believed that cooperatively achieved success lies at the foundation of learning and development. Bruner has taken up some of these ideas, emphasising the role of dialogue in aiding intellectual growth. Bruner and Haste (1987) highlight this in contrasting the shift in conception of children from 'lone scientists' to 'social beings':

> It is not only that we have begun to think again of the child as a social being – one who plays and talks with others, learns through inter-actions with parents and teachers – but because we have come once more to appreciate that through such a social life, the child acquires a framework for interpreting experience, and learns how to negotiate

meaning in a manner congruent with the requirements of the culture. . . . 'Making sense' is a social process: it is an activity that is always situated within a cultural and historical context.

Before that, we had fallen into the habit of thinking of the child as an 'active scientist', constructing hypotheses about the world, reflecting upon experience, interacting with the physical environment and formulating increasingly complex structures of thought. But this active, constructing child has been conceived as a rather isolated being, working alone at her problem-solving. Increasingly we see now that, given an appropriate, shared social context, the child seems more competent as an intelligent social operator than she is as a 'lone scientist' coping with a world of unknowns.

The critical role of talk in learning has been stressed in many respects and by many authors (e.g., Newsom Report, 1963; Britton, 1972; Bullock Report, 1975; APU, 1986) but relatively few teachers have implemented classroom management systems designed to optimise dialogue.

Our work on cooperative grouping over the last eight years has moved through three stages – from description, to experimentation and now to implementation. This work with teachers has consistently demonstrated how powerful is the impact of social processes on pupil activity, the quality of group talk and of pupil understandings. We have shown in this work that implementing forms of cooperative grouping improves pupil involvement, pupil outcomes and, through appropriate classroom management strategies, creates the time necessary for effective pupil diagnosis.

The size of the effects is not small. Table 7.3 for example contrasts pupil involvement in primary classes where children sit in groups but do no cooperative work, with children working cooperatively.

The increases are substantial and significant and have a similar effect on the low and high attainers. However, a related finding of considerable

Table 7.3 Task related talk in individual and cooperative groupwork

	Individualised work in groups %	Cooperative group work %
Language	70	83
Maths	63	88
Technology	–	93
Computers	–	99
Total	66	88

132

importance for low attainers comes from our work on group composition. We have found that ability or homogeneous grouping, i.e. seating all low attainers together, has substantial negative effect on the quality of discourse. Low ability groups indulge in far less sharing of explanations or knowledge, both critical to effective group functioning, simply because they often do not have the knowledge or explanations to share. The poor quality of group interaction shows clearly in pupils' learning. Low attainers in heterogeneous or mixed ability groups on the other hand receive far more help from higher achieving colleagues, and benefit accordingly. There are clear implications here for classroom management.

A final thrust for improvement, as far as the British government is concerned at least, is the implementation of the National Curriculum. It is certainly our experience that children with special needs can experience a limited curriculum in the ordinary schools. Whether a wider curriculum will lead to 'considerable improvements in levering up standards in both the special and ordinary schools', as claimed by the government, is, of course an open question. My own view is that changing the curriculum alone will alter little. Teachers need the skills and knowledge to effectively implement that curriculum. And that is a job for the educational community, not for governmental dictat.

References

Assessment and Performance Unit (APU) (1986) *Speaking and Listening.* Windsor: NFER-Nelson.

Ausubel, D. P. (1968) *Educational Psychology: A Cognitive View.* New York: Holt Rinehart Winston.

Bennett, S. N. and Cass, A. (1988) 'The effects of group composition on group interactive processes and pupil understanding', *British Educational Research Journal,* 15:19–32.

Bennett, S. N. and Cass, A. (1989) *From Special to Ordinary Schools: Case Studies in Integration.* London: Cassell.

Bennett, S. N. and Kell, J. (1989) *A Good Start? Four Year Olds in Infant Schools.* Oxford: Blackwells.

Bennett, S. N., Roth, E. and Dunne, R. (1987) 'Task processes in mixed and single age classes', *Education 3–13,* 15:43–50.

Bennett, S. N., Andreae, J., Hegarty, P. and Wade, B. (1980) *Open Plan Schools.* Windsor: NFER.

Bennett, S. N., Desforges, C. W., Cockburn, A. and Wilkinson, B. (1984) *The Quality of Pupil Learning Experiences.* Hillsdale, NJ: Erlbaum.

Britton, J. (1972) *Language and Learning.* Harmondsworth: Penguin.

Bruner, J. and Haste, H. (1987) *Making Sense: The Child's Construction of the World.* London: Methuen.

Bullock Report (1975) *A Language for Life*. London: HMSO.

Carroll, J. B. (1963) 'A model of school learning', *Teacher's College Record*, **64**:723–33.

Doyle, W. (1979a) 'Classroom tasks and students' abilities', in Peterson, P. L. and Walberg, H. J. (Eds) *Research on Teaching*. Berkeley, CA: McCutchan.

Doyle, W. (1979b) 'Making managerial decisions in classrooms', in Duke, D. L. (Ed.) *Classroom Management*, pp. 42–74. Chicago: University of Chicago Press.

Doyle, W. (1983) 'Academic work'. *Review of Educational Research*, **53**:159–200.

House of Commons: Education, Science and Arts Committee (1986) *Achievement in Primary Schools*. London: HMSO.

Newsom Report (1963) *Half Our Future* (A report of the Central Advisory Council for Education). London: HMSO.

Plowden, B. (1967) *Children and their Primary Schools*. London: DES.

TGAT (1988) *Task Group on Assessment and Testing: A Report*. London: DES.

Vygotsky, L. S. (1962) *Thought and Language*. Cambridge: MIT Press.

Wittrock, M. C. (1986) 'Students' thought processes', in Wittrock, M. C. (Ed.) *Handbook of Research on Teaching*, pp. 297–314. New York: Macmillan.

CHAPTER 8

Adaptive Instruction: An Alternative Approach to Providing for Student Diversity

Margaret C. Wang

Schools today are facing the challenge of how to successfully teach the increasingly diverse student population in our educational system, using all forms of knowledge on how best to proceed with instruction. The purpose of this chapter is to synthesize this knowledge base and to discuss its implications for designing and implementing school programs that are effective in providing for student diversity in regular classroom settings. First, educational effectiveness is discussed in the context of the rights to schooling success for all students and current practices. The conceptual framework, the features, the implementation requirements, and the efficacy of the adaptive instruction approach are then discussed. The chapter concludes with a discussion of the implications of widespread school implementation of adaptive instruction for improving on the schools' capacity to effectively respond to student diversity.

Rights to schooling success

Equal access to public education has long been a goal of the civil rights movement worldwide. Indeed, providing public education for school-age children and youth has become the law of the land for all nations. However, progress falls far short of the goal of educational attainment for all of the diverse students schools today are challenged to serve. Providing opportunities to receive an education without being accountable for ensuring educational outcomes simply perpetuates inequity in a more subtle form. Fundamental to this conception is the principle that standards of educational outcomes must be upheld for every child.

Schools cannot simply provide educational opportunities for students and be satisfied with just creating special programs to address the equity issue. The fact is, an expanding number of students are not achieving well despite efforts to create 'increasing opportunities' to learn. Many students have serious learning problems and have difficulty in achieving learning success; they need better help than they are now receiving. There does not seem to be much argument about the provision of extraordinary resources and efforts to those requiring greater-than-usual educational and related service support. It is generally recognized that this is required to assure equity in schooling outcomes.

The many programs specially designed to provide these supports required by students with special needs, which have come to be viewed as a second system of education programs (Wang *et al.*, 1988), are examples of attempts to achieve equity of educational outcomes through extra resources and efforts. Special education and other types of remedial or 'compensatory' education programs, such as the Chapter 1 program in the USA, are widely implemented second-system programs.

Individual differences and learning

Students differ in interests, learning styles, and the amount of time needed for learning. These and other related learner differences require different approaches and amounts of instructional support. Some students require more direct instruction with the teacher, while others do better with very little intervention or direct teaching. Although these and related characteristics of learner differences have long been accepted as a given, advances in theories and research during the past two decades have provided substantial grounds for fundamental conceptual changes in the type of information about individual students and their learning that are examined and used for instructional planning. Among the significant developments is an increased recognition that differences in certain personal and learning characteristics are alterable (cf. Bloom, 1976). Some prime examples of variables no longer considered to be static are family characteristics, such as parental expectations and family involvement (cf. Walberg,

1984), cognition and processes of learning (cf. Chipman *et al.*, 1985; Snow and Farr, 1983) and student motivation and the roles students play in their own learning (cf. Stipek, 1988; Wang and Palincsar, 1989).

These advances have also resulted in a shift away from describing students based solely on grossly defined outcomes or measures of status. It is becoming more common to describe learner differences in the manner in which information is processed, mental mechanisms and rules that students bring to the learning situation, the motivation and affective response tendencies involved in the acquisition and retention of knowledge, and the knowledge competence of individual students (cf. Wang and Lindvall, 1984). The recognition of the alterability of these learner characteristics points to the wisdom of studying ways to modify the psychological processes and cognitive operations used by individual students (Bransford *et al.*, 1985; Feuerstein *et al.*, 1985; Palincsar and Brown, 1984), as well as of modifying learning environments and instructional strategies to accommodate learner differences (Glaser, 1977; Tobias, 1989; Wang and Walberg, 1985).

Student diversity and the role of the school

The growing research base and theoretical advances have led to an increasing recognition that it is the responsibility of the schools to structure educational programs in ways that are responsive to student diversity. The core of effective school programs is attention to alterable differences to ensure equity in educational outcomes. Schools are responsible for ensuring schooling success for every student, using the standard of mastering the 'common curriculum' of elementary and secondary education in the USA (Fenstermacher and Goodlad, 1983). If all students are to successfully complete a 'basic' education or common curriculum, today's schools must undergo major conceptual and restructural changes. We must abolish the current practice of 'compensating' for learner differences by lowering standards, or, to put it in other words, by making school success easier for selected students through establishing differential standards for schooling success.

Thus, effective schooling defined in the context of equity of outcomes requires a shift in our mind-set from a 'fixed' system for implementing the common curriculum to a flexible system that will allow all students to acquire the common curriculum. At the same time, we need to recognize that some students require more time and extraordinary instructional support to achieve mastery of the common curriculum and others require less time and little direct instruction; this latter group of students should have the flexibility to complete the common curriculum for basic education in less than twelve years.

Current practice: barriers and prospects for improvement

Schools' responses to learner differences

Despite the advances in theories and research on individual differences in learning and effective teaching during the past two decades, the knowledge base has had very little impact on how schools respond to individual differences in practice. There are serious problems in how individual differences are characterized and the way information is generated and used for instructional decision-making. In many cases, provisions designed to respond to student differences in learning have been counter-productive in promoting student learning (cf. Lipsky and Gartner, 1989).

Spurious classification. Students differ as individuals, not as groups. Very exceptionally talented students are about as heterogeneous across the range of learning characteristics as those having learning difficulties or considered to be low achieving or at risk of school failure. Programs designed to accommodate learner differences based on the assumption of group rather than individual differences tend to take different approaches and can result in very different outcomes. In current practice, learning differences among students are typically handled by classifying or labelling the perceived differences in terms of macro-level characteristics (i.e., children at risk, low-achieving children from poor families, children with learning disabilities, or socially/emotionally disturbed children). Then the 'identified' or 'certified' students are placed 'homogeneously' in narrowly framed categorical programs or 'special' educational arrangements.

Several recent research syntheses have revealed serious scientific and practical flaws in the current classification system for placing students in specially designed programs to receive their 'entitled' services. Most classification procedures are unreliable and irrelevant to instructional decision-making (Ysseldyke, 1987). Furthermore, there is also evidence that economics, program availability, race, and other factors having no valid implications for instruction have also entered into classification decisions. Children from cultural minority backgrounds

138

and from poor families are particularly vulnerable to being classified under the current system (Heller *et al.*, 1982; National Coalition of Advocates for Students, 1988). School districts arbitrarily change the classifications of children – for example, from 'mildly retarded' to 'learning disabled' – when one label becomes more stigmatic or less remunerative than another. Once students are placed in second-system programs such as special education, they are unlikely to return to regular classrooms. For example, in the United States, according to a recent report (Buttram *et al.*, 1986), 4.8 per cent of special education students enrolled in major urban schools in the USA were returned to general education placement during the 1984–85 academic year. The range was 0 per cent to 13.4 per cent. It is of interest to note these figures include all students enrolled in special education programs from preschool through age 21.

'Inequitable' outcomes of educational equity. The practice of grouping students with perceived similar instructional needs has been a commonly accepted programmatic (yet often instructionally meaningless) strategy for responding to student diversity. The strategy of placing students with similar classifications in specially designed programs is considered as an educational delivery strategy designed with the explicit objective to improve instructional effectiveness and efficiency, and thereby to ensure equity in student achievement and educational outcomes. However, these grouping practices have not worked very well for an increasingly large proportion of children and youth in our nation's schools. In fact, research suggests that these solutions have often limited, rather than enhanced the targeted students' opportunities for achieving educational equity, both in terms of access to knowledge and equity in educational outcomes.

There is substantial evidence to suggest that students may receive *less* instruction when schools provide them with specially designed programs to meet their special learning needs. For example, students provided with remedial reading programs often receive less actual reading instruction (Allington and Johnston, 1986; Allington and McGill-Franzer, 1989; Haynes and Jenkins, 1986). The classification and tracking practices schools now use to respond to differences in the learning characteristics and needs of students have not been shown to confer advantages. In fact, in many instances, they have led to further inequity in educational outcomes for students requiring greater-than-usual educational support (cf. Brandt, 1989; Heller *et al.*, 1982; Jenkins *et al.*, 1988; Williams *et al.*, 1986). In too many cases, the practice of grouping (or tracking) students for instruction based on certain perceived group differences involves the delivery of radically different and not always appropriate content to some students; there is a tendency to seriously neglect fundamental content (Oakes, 1985).

Schools themselves often contribute to children's learning problems. There is evidence of the so-called 'Matthew Effect' (Stanovich, 1984). Students who show limited progress in early phases of instruction in basic subjects, such as reading, tend to show progressive retardation over succeeding years. It has been estimated that in the middle elementary grades, the lowest achieving students may be reading only one-tenth as many words per day in school as students in a highly skilled reading group (cf. Reynolds, 1989).

Another version of the Matthew Effect occurs when teachers interact differently with students having special learning needs – for example, by giving less feedback on questions from them than from other students, calling on them less often, or waiting less time for them to answer (Cooper, 1983). Urban youth have been demonstrated to be less engaged in academic interaction with teachers than are students in suburban schools (Greenwood *et al.*, 1984). Similarly, less time is spent on regular reading instruction in schools with high rates of poverty than in other schools (National Assessment of Educational Progress, 1987). Such differences in school programs that work to the disadvantage of selected groups of students cannot be justified or permitted to continue if we aim to achieve educational equity for all of our students.

Research and practical bases for improvement

Clearly restructuring of the current two-systems approach to delivery of the greater-than-usual educational and related service supports within the schools is occurring. A major feature of the process has been described as progressive inclusion (Reynolds and Birch, 1988); that is, the gradual increase in the numbers and proportions of children with special needs who receive special education or other compensatory or remedial education services while enrolled in regular classes and schools. Although many policy-makers and educators believe that the field is ready to move and must move forward toward a restructured educational system that calls for an integrated approach to providing special education and other second-system programs (e.g., Gartner and Lipsky, 1987; Stainback *et al.*, 1989; Wang *et al.*, 1988), others see the current push for systematic integration of students with special needs and 'special' programs as based on arguable assumptions

Table 8.1 Variables important to learning: a consensus from the field

Variables	Number of variables in each variable category	Mean ratings* N = 1123	Percent of variables rated as important in each variable category
Category I: *State and District Variables*			
a. District Level Demographics and Marker Variables	(10)	2.08	0.30
b. State Level Policy Variables	(6)	2.06	0.50
Category II: *Out-of-School Contextual Variables*			
a. Community Variables	(3)	2.31	100
b. Peer Group Variables	(5)	2.44	100
c. Home Environment and Parental Support Variables	(9)	2.69	100
d. Student Use of Out-of-School Time Variables	(5)	2.19	0.60
Category III: *School Level Variables*			
a. Demographic Marker Variables	(8)	1.97	0.38
b. Teacher/Administrator Decision Making Variables	(6)	2.62	100
c. School Culture Variables (Ethos Conducive to Teaching and Learning)	(8)	2.55	100
d. School-Wide Policy and Organizational Variables	(13)	2.23	0.85
e. Accessibility Variables	(1)	2.28	100
f. Parental Involvement Policy Variables	(2)	2.26	100
Category IV: *Student Variables*			
a. Demographic and Marker Variables	(7)	1.97	0.57
b. History of Educational Placements	(3)	2.26	100
c. Social and Behavioral Variables	(5)	2.63	100
d. Motivational and Affective Variables	(9)	2.72	100
e. Cognitive Variables	(12)	2.48	100
f. Metacognitive Variables	(4)	2.66	100
g. Psychomotor Variables	(1)	2.18	100

Category		Mean	
Category V: *Program Design Variables*			
a. Demographic and Marker Variables	(4)	2.38	100
b. Curriculum and Instructional Variables	(15)	2.37	100
c. Curriculum Design Variables	(13)	2.45	100
Category VI: *Implementation, Classroom Instruction and Climate Variables*			
a. Classroom Implementation Support Variables	(6)	2.37	0.67
b. Classroom Instructional Variables	(26)	2.53	100
c. Quantity of Instruction Variables	(12)	2.36	0.92
d. Classroom Assessment Variables	(4)	2.31	100
e. Classroom Management Variables	(5)	2.67	100
f. Student and Teacher Interactions: Social Variables	(6)	2.59	100
g. Student and Teacher Interactions: Academic Variables	(5)	2.17	100
h. Classroom Climate Variables	(15)	2.52	100

*Respondents of the survey of variables important to learning were asked to rate the importance of the 228 variables on a scale from 1 (low) to 3 (high).

(e.g. Kaufman *et al.*, 1985; Vergason and Anderegg, 1989). Nevertheless, everyone appears to agree that if a high-quality integrated approach to delivery of 'special' programs is to be achieved, there must be strong teamwork by educators of all kinds based on a well-confirmed knowledge of best practices.

Findings from a recently completed 'meta-review' and research synthesis on the knowledge bases for regular and special education suggest a strong consensus on variables that are important to learning (Wang, Haertel and Walberg, 1990). The study examined the research literature in order to specify the well-confirmed knowledge about school learning and then asked various groups of educational professionals to make judgments about the importance of the identified variables or principles in their work. The object was to ascertain whether we have one or several distinct knowledge bases to be considered as progressive inclusion proceeds. Furthermore, it was reasoned that, to the extent that special and regular educators work from common bases of knowledge, there is added reason to press toward further collaboration, including teacher preparation, rather than for separation.

The questions addressed in the study were: What are the conditions that enhance the learning of children? To what extent are such conditions judged to be different by special education teachers, regular education teachers, and other education professionals? The review covered literature in both regular and special education, including, for example, the chapters in the review volume sponsored by the American Educational Research Association (AERA), *Handbook of Research on Training* (Wittrock, 1986); the three-volume *Handbook on Special Education: Research and Practice* (Wang *et al.*, 1987–89); *Designs for Compensatory Education* (Williams *et al.*, 1986); and the annual review series published in education, special education, psychology, and sociology. In total, 86 chapters from annual review series, 44 handbook chapters, 20 government and commissioned reports, 18 book chapters, and 11 review articles in journals were considered. Findings from this research synthesis formed the basis for a questionnaire surveying the opinions among education professionals on variables that are important to school learning. The survey was sent to six groups of professionals: educational researchers, policy makers, school psychologists, principals, regular education teachers, and special education teachers (Reynolds *et al.*, in press).

The approach to improvement of education drawn from the synthesis study calls attention mainly to alterable variables and to the practical realities of teaching, rather than to such practices as testing for IQs or hypothesizing about 'underlying deficits'. Findings from the study suggested remarkable agreement among regular and special education teachers, principals, school psychologists, and researchers on what variables or principles of instruction are important. Table 8.1 provides a summary of major findings from the survey. Briefly, of the six categories, the highest overall ratings were assigned to 'Program Design variables', followed by 'Implementation, Classroom Instruction, and Climate variables'. 'Out-of-School Contextual variables' ranked third in importance, closely followed by 'Student variables'. 'School Level variables', and 'State and District variables' received markedly lower ratings overall. Furthermore, there seems to be a consensus that, given the present state of knowledge about teaching and learning, instruction should be based on directly observable and manageable factors in the learning environment.

Adaptive instruction: an approach builds on diversity

The past two decades of research and innovative program development efforts suggest that it is possible to provide equal access to quality educational opportunities, that lead to equality in educational benefits for all students. Much can be gained by improving the current practice through rigorous efforts organized around principles identified as important to learning. The issue is not *what* to do, but the commitment to find ways to implement what we already know about making schools more productive for every child. Many of the current practices attempting to address the concern of student diversity would profit from rigorous efforts at improvement organized around principles identified as important to learning. Much of the work near term should involve increased collaboration among educational professionals in building a general education system inclusive of all the 'special' services, rather than building a disparate second-system of 'special' programs, disjointed and separated from the mainstream and from one another, that so characterize current practice. The adaptive instruction approach is one example among many of the widely used innovative approaches that systematically apply what is known from research about individual difference and effective conditions for learning to improve the schools' capacity to effectively respond to student diversity. The prospect for improving this capacity in ways that are effective and efficient in achieving equity in student outcomes through adaptive instruction is discussed next.

Programs using the adaptive instruction approach are designed with the basic premise that students learn in different ways and at different rates, and that effective instruction involves the recognition and accommodation of the unique learning needs of individual students, while enhancing each student's ability to achieve intended outcomes through building on the diversity of student characteristics and instructional approaches. Teachers who are effective in implementing the adaptive instruction approach use all forms of knowledge available on demonstrably effective classroom practices to accommodate their students' diverse learning needs. Although adaptive instruction calls for individualized planning, teachers not only work with students on a one-to-one basis but also incorporate small group instruction and other group tasks in the design of adaptive instruction programs when they are deemed particularly suited for achieving certain student outcomes (e.g., ability to engage in group discussion and collaborative learning tasks) and/or as ways to increase instructional efficiency (Glaser, 1976; Wang, 1980).

Successful implementations of the adaptive instruction approach as an alternative service delivery model for accommodating student diversity in regular classrooms have several salient characteristics. They are discussed in this section under four topical headings: educational philosophy, curriculum, instructional practice, and staffing patterns, professional roles and school-wide organizational and administrative supports.

Educational philosophy

Adaptive instruction as an alternative delivery system reflects a unique educational philosophy, which includes the following tenets:

- All children are 'special', and educators are responsible for getting to know the needs of each child and for providing school environments that promote meaningful and successful learning.
- Students classified in the various categories of mild or moderate handicaps, and those otherwise considered to be at risk of academic failure who require greater-than-usual instructional and related service support (e.g., students in such compensatory educational programs as Chapter 1, migrant education) can, and should, be successfully integrated in general education settings on a full-time basis with co-ordinated 'special' education and related service supports.
- General education teachers can develop the capabilities to take ultimate responsibility for the learning of all students, including students with

special needs, when the support of specialized professional staff and resources for providing special, remedial, or compensatory educational services are made available to them on an ongoing basis to meet the specific needs of the students requiring such services.

● There is a vast knowledge base on what makes teaching and learning more effective and efficient, as well as on research-based innovative instructional programs and classroom practices. When teachers are knowledgeable about how to incorporate these programs and/or practices to improve their instruction, they can serve all children better.

The curriculum

Under adaptive instruction programs, a variety of materials and learning activities are used to foster student motivation and enhance achievement. Curriculum materials are designed for both teacher-prescribed and student-initiated learning activities in the various subject-matter content areas. They also provide students with opportunities to develop social skills and ability to take on increasing self-responsibility for learning. Competencies to be learned are made explicit and the corresponding curriculum materials are organized in ways that allow each student to proceed with learning at his or her own pace.

Some curriculum refinement work is generally required for most schools when the adaptive instruction approach is first introduced. The amount of start-up effort needed to convert existing curriculum materials into suitable formats varies from school to school. For example, schools that rely exclusively on basal reading texts and workbooks may not have a great deal of flexibility. Thus, teachers interested in using the adaptive instruction approach will find it necessary to expand and refine their curricula to include some of the alternative strategies that are associated with the whole language approach to reading instruction in order to more effectively meet the diverse learning needs of their students.

Instructional practice

Effective instruction is a highly sophisticated process. It involves both subject-matter knowledge and pedagogical expertise. The design of demonstrably effective models of adaptive instruction emphasizes the development of teacher expertise in the following areas: ongoing formal and informal diagnosis and evaluation of student learning;

systematic monitoring of classroom processes; efficient management of classroom resources and time use; and prescription of appropriate learning activities based on the performance and needs of individual students in given curricular areas.

Teachers who are effective in implementing the adaptive instruction approach know the subject matter and their students. They know what individual students can do, their unique learning styles, and their characteristic behaviors in a variety of instructional-learning situations. They incorporate information about their students when adapting their instruction and prescribing learning activities that enhance students' ability to profit from instruction. In fact, effective teachers of adaptive instruction programs can be characterized as field-based researchers who are continually finding ways to improve their instructional effectiveness to enhance student learning. There is a strong link between diagnosis and instructional planning and intervention. Effective teachers practice interactive teaching processes, giving students timely feedback and reinforcement. Instructional prescriptions for individual students are modified as needed, based on frequent and systematic assessment and reassessment of their learning progress.

Staffing patterns, professional roles and organizational and administrative support

Current staffing patterns in many schools reflect disjointedness and inefficient use of professional expertise in the delivery of special services. For example, one corridor of a typical school building might contain a general education classroom, a full-time special education classroom, a resource room for part-time special education students, the school's Chapter 1 classroom, the room for the speech therapist, the migrant education program classroom, the gifted program classroom, the occupational therapist's room, the math lab, and the peer tutoring room.

Under programs using the adaptive instruction approach, functional and cooperative linkages are created between the regular education teacher and the various specialists, such as the special education staff. The roles of regular education teachers, special education teachers, principals, and other professional staff, such as school psychologists and social workers, are redefined to facilitate the coordinated delivery of services for all students in regular classroom settings. In addition, many adaptive instruction programs include an expanded role for students in the instructional process through co-operative learning and peer tutoring strategies.

Specifically, the role of the regular classroom teacher using the adaptive instruction approach is to serve all students with the co-ordinated support of all of the specialized professionals. Working together as a team, general and specialized professional staff represent a broad array of expertise and resources that can be utilized to meet the diverse needs of the students. One expected result of such collaboration would be a greatly reduced reliance on the 'pull-out' approach to special and related service delivery, which often tends to be carried out in a disjointed fashion.

Special educators and other specialized professionals functioning in this type of staffing pattern are able to spend concentrated time serving individual students who need the most intensive instruction, working either directly with the students or as consulting teachers. In addition to their instructional support role, they serve as an important link to relevant community resources. Their redefined role includes: developing functional assessments of the specific learning needs of individual students, working closely with teachers to develop and implement instructional strategies that improve students' motivation and learning of basic skills, and engaging in intensive interactions with individual students at the time when such support can be most beneficial to them.

Classrooms and schools with staffing patterns that build on the expertise and collaborative interactions among all of the professional staff in the school can be expected to generate creative ideas and new energy for solving instruction-related problems. Such innovative staffing patterns require ongoing systematic staff development, which is usually led by the principal, and is based on the training needs of individual teachers and other staff.

In addition to the change in staff roles from a self-contained mode to a collaborative mode, several organizational and administrative supports are important when using the adaptive instruction approach as an alternative delivery system for serving students with special needs in regular classrooms. These supports include flexible scheduling, alternative arrangement of space, and the instructional leadership of building principals.

School implementation of adaptive instruction: an illustration

One of the widely implemented adaptive instruction programs in schools is the Adaptive Learning Environments Model (ALEM). The design features of ALEM are briefly discussed in this section to provide an illustration of school implementation of adaptive instruction. The ALEM is a comprehensive educational model that aims to effectively respond to learner differences through the use of a variety of instructional methods and learning experiences that are adapted to the learning characteristics and needs of individual students. The ALEM was initially developed as an early learning program for pre-school and early elementary grades; it was field tested in a variety of schools in different geographic locations across the United States (Wang *et al.*, 1985).

Over the course of more than two decades, the ALEM has been extended to include elementary, middle, and high schools and has been widely implemented as a core general education program and/or as a mainstream program for special education students classified as learning disabled (LD), educably mentally retarded (EMR), and socially and emotionally disturbed (SED). The research base for the development and school-based implementation of the ALEM and its outcomes has been widely published (Manning and Quandt, 1990; Sobehart, 1990; Wang and Zollers, 1990). The ALEM, known as an adaptive education program that provides for student diversity in regular education settings, has been noted as a program uniquely suited for serving students with special needs in regular education settings (e.g., Brophy, 1986; Corno and Snow, 1986; Dawson, 1987; Epps and Tindal, 1987; Heller *et al.*, 1982; Lipsky and Gartner, 1989). Findings on the impact of ALEM on student outcomes have been quite consistent across a variety of school sites. In places where a high degree of implementation is observed, for example, students tend to show more significant academic gains and greater perception of self-competence than comparable groups not in the program (e.g., Manning and Quandt, 1990; Sobehart, 1990).

The ALEM has specific components or design features for providing adaptive instruction and supporting program implement-ation. Among the major features that facilitate the adaptation of instruction to student differences are: individualized progress plans; a diagnostic-prescriptive process for instructional planning and monitoring of student learning progress; and the classroom instructional-learning management system known as the Self-Schedule System. The features that provide district-, school- and classroom-level support for implementation of the ALEM are an adaptive program delivery system, the training sequence known as the Data-Based Staff Development Program, school and classroom organiz-ational supports, and a family involvement component.

Individualized progress plans

In ALEM classrooms, each student's educational experience is tailored to his or her particular learning characteristics and needs. Curriculum materials are modified when necessary for the development and implementation of individualized progress plans for each student. The plans are based on teacher observation and information from diagnostic tests and records of student progress rates. This information is used by teachers to prescribe appropriate amounts and types of tasks for each student and to support students' learning through individual and group instruction.

The learning tasks included in the individualized progress plans are generally organized around two complementary curriculum components. The first, the prescriptive learning component, consists of highly-structured tasks that foster basic skills mastery in academic subject areas (e.g. reading, mathematics, science, social studies, spelling). The basic skills curricula developed by individual schools or school districts, as well as commercially published materials (e.g., basal texts) currently used in classrooms, constitute the core of the prescriptive learning component. Examples of learning tasks in this component are: completing a written workbook assignment in a particular subject area, participating in a small-group teacher-guided science laboratory activity, and engaging in a one-to-one tutoring lesson with a teacher. The second curriculum component is the exploratory learning component. Tasks in this component are designed specifically to foster students' social and personal development, with a focus on enhancing their ability to plan and manage their own learning. These tasks also provide opportunities for basic skills enrichment. Examples of exploratory learning tasks are: writing a script for a class play, creating a poster, and playing a game of chess.

Diagnostic-prescriptive process

The adaptive instruction process under the ALEM begins with the diagnosis of each student's entering level of skills and knowledge in the basic subject matter areas. The program's diagnostic-prescriptive monitoring system uses criterion-referenced assessments (e.g., curriculum-based assessment procedures built into the various basic skills curricula) to ensure that appropriate educational tasks are individually assigned and lead to successful learning. This system calls for ongoing monitoring of each student's progress through recordkeeping procedures that incorporate paper-and-pencil or micro-computer formats to maintain up-to-date information.

Self-Schedule System

An instructional objective integral to the ALEM is developing each student's ability to play an active role in his or her education. The Self-Schedule System (Wang *et al.*, 1985) is designed to foster students' sense of responsibility and ability to become increasingly self-instructive in managing their own learning. Because the cognitive and social demands of assuming self-responsibility for school learning vary in complexity and requisite abilities, students are guided through a progression of relatively simple tasks to more complex ones. Through a series of hierarchically organized exercises, they learn to schedule prescribed and self-selected activities in order to complete their learning tasks within specified periods of time. For example, one of the first steps in the hierarchy might be to choose which of two teacher-prescribed activities in the same subject should be done first; a subsequent step might be to complete both activities within one hour; and finally, students might progress to selecting two out of five optional activities and deciding in what order to do the activities, along with all teacher-prescribed tasks, within a three-hour period. As with the development of any skill, not all students move through the hierarchy of the Self-Schedule System at the same rate. Therefore, instruction in self-management skills is adaptive to individual differences.

In addition to managing their learning activities, students learn to work within the constraints of the classroom by observing rules, following directions, managing materials, and requesting help from, and giving assistance to, teachers and peers. As students become increasingly proficient in managing and monitoring their own learning, teachers are freed from many routine management and instructional duties and are able to devote more time to instruction.

Adaptive program delivery system

The ALEM's approach to an effective program delivery system is to complement and supplement the existing characteristics of particular schools. School personnel are encouraged and assisted to adjust program implementation to their own improvement goals. The development of a school-specific program delivery system begins with a series of procedures to assess needs and plan implementation (Wang and Vaughan, 1987). Based on needs assessments of school features such as student population characteristics, staffing patterns, curricula, operating practices, record-keeping procedures, and physical resources, a site-specific implementation plan is developed. The plan, which includes an extensive awareness program for all relevant stakeholders (e.g., teachers, parents, school boards), eases the transition to the innovative educational approach and helps to ensure that the implementation of the ALEM meets schooling needs and goals.

Data-based Staff Development Program

Research and experience consistently suggest that staff development programs that include ongoing training support are features of effective school improvement in general and of effective mainstreaming in particular. Pre-implementation and ongoing support for the introduction and maintenance of the ALEM is provided through the Data-based Staff Development Program (Wang and Gennari, 1983). The training sequence for school personnel has three levels. The first, basic training, provides an overview of the ALEM and working knowledge of the program's implementation requirements. The second level, individualized training, is keyed to particular functions of each staff role. The third level, in-service training, consists of an interactive process of program assessment, feedback, planning, and staff development. The Data-based Staff Development Program is the core of the 'training-of-trainers' approach that is used to develop the competencies of local personnel for implementing the program in their own classrooms, schools, and districts. Local instructional leaders such as principals, building-level education specialists, and district-level staff development specialists receive systematic training in the functions of program development and implementation. The training prepares them for utilizing the structure of the Data-based Staff Development Program to provide ongoing, in-service training support for classroom teachers and other instructional staff.

The Implementation Assessment Battery for Adaptive Instruction (Wang et al., 1983) is one of the major tools available for monitoring the degree of implementation and identifying staff development needs. The Battery consists of a series of checklists, observation forms, and interview forms. It is routinely administered in ALEM classrooms to determine the presence or absence of critical program dimensions. There are twelve program dimensions: Arranging Space and Facilities,

Creating and Maintaining Instructional Materials, Establishing and Communicating Rules and Procedures, Managing Aides, Diagnostic Testing, Record Keeping, Monitoring and Diagnosing, Prescribing, Interactive Teaching, Instructing, Motivating, and Developing Student Self-Responsibility. The items in the Implementation Assessment Battery for Adaptive Instruction are based on 108 performance indicators of these critical dimensions. The reliability and validity of the Battery have been established for a wide variety of school settings and for the identification of both teacher-specific and school-specific staff development needs (Wang *et al.*, 1984).

School and classroom organizational supports

Adapting instruction to the needs of individual students requires flexibility in school and classroom organizational patterns. At the school level, the implementation of the ALEM supports staffing patterns that promote effective program implementation. In schools where the ALEM is used as a mainstreaming program, the roles of instructional personnel are redefined to achieve an interface between general and special education services. The role of special education teachers, for example, includes consultation with general education teachers as well as the provision of direct instructional services for students with special needs in regular classes. General education teachers function as the primary instructors for both the general education students and the students with special needs.

Principals play an integral role in creating a supportive organizational climate for implementation of the ALEM. Findings from recent research show that effective schools tend to have principals who function mainly as instructional, rather than administrative, leaders. As instructional leaders, principals work actively with teachers to influence instructional strategies. They involve themselves in identifying and solving classroom problems; they participate in in-service activities; they conduct both formal and informal staff development sessions; they observe classrooms and provide feedback to teachers; and they work closely with teachers to identify instructional goals and the means to achieve them. Because adaptive instruction programs require flexible scheduling, restructuring of relationships among teachers, and ongoing training support, all of these instructional leadership functions take on increased importance.

At the classroom level, the ALEM encourages the use of multi-age grouping and instructional teaming and organizational patterns that are often utilized to maximize the implementation of adaptive instruction. Multi-age grouping provides the necessary flexibility to accommodate the differences of individual students, particularly those who make unusually slow or fast progress, without the social consequences of repeating or skipping a grade. It also offers opportunities for spontaneous and planned peer modeling and tutoring, which enable teachers to spend more time with students who require greater amounts of teacher assistance. Instructional teaming allows increased use of various grouping methods and encourages teachers to apply their own interests and talents to the provision of alternative learning experiences.

Family involvement

Learning occurs at home as well as in school. Given the limited amount of time in the school day, even students in the most effectively implemented educational programs can benefit from instructional reinforcement at home. Thus, the ALEM encourages an active program of family involvement to increase the communication and cooperation between school and home. Activities are designed to induce family members to support their children's learning in concrete ways. Initial awareness sessions are conducted to inform parents of the design and goals of the program. As implementation of the program progresses, parents receive frequent formal and informal reports about their children's progress. Parents are encouraged to participate in designing and refining their children's educational plans and to provide home instruction in consultation with teachers. In addition, parents may work as classroom volunteers. Such activities ensure that families are knowledgeable about the school curriculum and about their children's learning plans and progress within the curriculum.

When all of the components of the program are well implemented, a unique classroom scenario is created. Students can be found working in virtually every area of the room at any given time, either in small groups or individually. Teachers circulate among the students providing instruction and evaluative feedback to individuals and small groups as needed. Academic skills are taught directly, based on diagnostic test results, and every student is expected to make steady progress through the curricula. Learning tasks are broken down into incremental steps, thereby providing frequent opportunities for evaluation. Each student's successes are recognized and acknowledged, momentary difficulties are pinpointed, and alternative instruction is provided before the difficulties become learning problems. Individual differences are viewed by teachers and students alike as the norm rather than the exception. Student responsibility is emphasized. Students are taught to plan and monitor their own learning. They are expected to take responsibility for planning, managing, and completing all their teacher-prescribed and self-selected learning tasks within the time limits agreed upon with the teacher.

Teachers spend more time on instruction than on managing students. Students tend to be highly task-oriented. Interactions among them, for the most part, are for sharing ideas and working together. The fluid and subdued, yet constant and steady, sound of productive interaction between teachers and students and among students replaces the passive learning mode typically found in conventional classrooms. Distracted behavior on the part of individual students is minimal and does not seem to interfere with the work of others.

Discussion

Several important strides have been made during the past two decades to ensure adequate and appropriate education for all students, including those with special needs and those otherwise considered to be at risk of school failure and dropping out of school unprepared for a productive life. One is the advances in research and innovative program development for increasing schools' capabilities to provide more effectively for student diversity. Another is a recognition that any reform aimed at improving the quality of education for all students cannot be fully realized without a broad restructuring of the current two-system approach to delivery of educational services. Demographic trends point to a clear and continuing increase in the number of the children who require 'special' education or other forms of greater-than-usual educational and related service supports – those with special education labels or with poor prognoses for academic achievement. The research base and practical experience of school personnel using the adaptive instruction approach have specific implications for the effective delivery of school programs that are responsive to student diversity. A high degree of implementation of adaptive instruction can lead to significant improvement of instruction and learning in school. The following brief vignettes of 'Scenarios for the Year 2000', quoted from Wang, Reynolds and Walberg (1990), provide illustrations of kinds of educational visions that can be achieved through applications of the research and practical bases addressed in this chapter:

> *Year 2000 Vignette – Teams of Educators.* Recent statistical reports show that more than 80% of special education teachers now work directly with teams of teachers in various kinds of 'regular' instructional environments. Many special educators have helped lead in the restructuring of schools and now serve in roles that are well-integrated into mainstream school operations. 'Mainstream' programs are now extremely diverse and different from the one teacher-one class operations of the past. In general, special education teachers provide high-density instruction to students showing the least progress, and they help to modify programs for those who learn most rapidly. They also tend to carry relatively heavy loads in pupil evaluation programs, reporting to and collaborating with parents and managing special studies of children who show special problems. Special education teachers work in full collaboration with other teachers in teams, at elementary, secondary, vocational-technical, and higher education levels (pp. 205–6).

> *Year 2000 Vignette – Child Study and Classification.* Studies of children with special needs now focus mainly on the necessary modification of instructional programs. Children are not labeled, except in terms of the kinds of instruction and services to be provided. It is common, for example, for selected primary-grade-level children to receive extended and intensive reading instruction. Others receive extended instruction in social and friendship skills. Children with poor vision are taught to read by braille methods. Classification is strictly in terms of the instructional level and methods needed; such classifications may 'hold' for only a brief time or throughout the schooling years, depending upon assessment of needs (p. 206).

> *Year 2000 Vignette – Monitoring Marginal Pupils.* Schools now regularly perform '20/20' analyses or use some comparable procedure to monitor progress of pupils showing most and least progress in school learning. The 20/20 plan involves a review of every student whose rate of progress toward important school learning goals is below the 20th percentile and above the 80th percentile. What are the characteristics of these students? What programs appear to serve them well, and what could be improved? Through such analyses, every child who shows learning problems is identified and studied. The procedure begins not by labeling or classifying the child in traditional special education style, but by identifying students in terms of variables reflecting progress toward important school goals and objectives.

> Procedures are similar for high-achieving students, on the assumption
> that they too need adapted school programs to permit them to proceed
> at high rates in school learning (p. 207).

As the authors of these vignettes noted, these scenarios from the Year
2000 'are not so much predictions as they are wishes for projects and
programs that might be helpful' (Wang, Reynolds and Walberg, 1990,
p. 205).

In conclusion, although we must be mindful that the vision of
educational equity for all students, as proposed in this chapter, is
complicated by many programmatic, administrative, and fiscal road-
blocks that may seem insurmountable, the past two decades of
experience in school-based implementation of innovative programs
such as the ALEM and others have shown that it is possible to
overcome many of the barriers. There is increasing evidence of a
movement toward a more coordinated and inclusive approach to
providing for the 'special' institutional and related service support
needs of many of the students who are currently served under the
second system programs. Imported steps toward such restructuring
include recommendations by various professional groups and top-
level government policy makers calling for educational reforms that
focus on better serving all children, especially those with special needs
and/or otherwise considered to be at risk of school failure or dropping
out of school unprepared (e.g., Council of Chief State School Officers,
1987; National Association of School Psychologists and the National
Coalition of Advocates for Students, 1986; Will, 1986; and discussion
at President Bush's Education Summit, held with the nation's
governors in September 1990).

The implications for improvement are clear. We know more than we
use. The challenge to educational researchers and practitioners in the
next decade is to develop practical ways to incorporate this research in
school-based implementations of improvement efforts that lead to
equity in educational outcomes for the increasingly diverse student
population schools are charged to serve today.

Note

The research herein was supported by the Temple University Center
for Research in Human Development and Education, which in part is
supported by the Office of Educational Research and Development of
the US Department of Education. The opinions expressed do not

necessarily reflect the position of the Center, and no official endorsement should be inferred.

References

Allington, R. L. and Johnston, P. (1986) 'The coordination among regular classroom reading programs and targeted support programs', in Williams, B. I., Richmond, P. A. and Mason, B. J. (Eds) *Designs for Compensatory Education: Conference Proceedings and Papers* (VI, pp. 3–40). Washington, DC: Research and Evaluation Associates, Inc.

Allington, R. L. and McGill-Franzer, A. (1989) 'School response to reading failure: Instruction for chapter one and special education students in grades two, four, and eight', *Elementary School Journal*, 89:529–42.

Bloom, B. S. (1976) *Human Characteristics and School Learning*. New York: McGraw-Hill.

Brandt, R. S. (1989) (Ed.) 'Dealing with diversity: Ability, gender, and style differences' (Special Issue), *Educational Leadership*, **46**,6.

Bransford, J. D., Vye, N. J., Delclos, V. R., Burns, M. S. and Hasselbring, T. S. (1985) *Improving the Quality of Assessment and Instruction: Roles for Dynamic Assessment* (Learning Technology Center Technical Report Series). Nashville, TN: George Peabody College of Vanderbilt University.

Brophy, J. B. (1986) 'Research linking teacher behavior to student achievement: Potential implications for instruction of Chapter 1 students', in Williams, B. I., Richmond, P. A. and Mason, B. J. (Eds) *Designs for Compensatory Education: Conference Proceedings and Papers* (IV, pp. 121–79). Washington, DC: Research and Evaluation Associates.

Buttram, J. L., Kershner, K. and Rioux, S. (1986) *A Study of Special Education: Views from America's Cities*. Philadelphia, PA: Research for Better Schools.

Chipman, S. G., Segal, J. W. and Glaser, R. (1985) (Eds) *Thinking and Learning Skills: Vol. 2. Research and Open Questions*. Hillsdale, NJ: Erlbaum.

Cooper, H. M. (1983) 'Communication of teacher expectations to students', in Levine, J. M. and Wang, M. C. (Eds) *Teacher and Student Perceptions: Implications for Learning* (pp. 193–211). Hillsdale, NJ: Erlbaum.

Corno, L. and Snow, R. E. (1986) 'Adapting teaching to individual differences among learners', in Wittrock, M. C. (Ed.) *Handbook of Research on Teaching*, 3rd edn., (pp. 605–29). New York: Macmillan.

Council of Chief State School Officer (1987) *Assuring School Success for Students at Risk*. November, Washington, DC: Author.

Dawson, P. (1987) 'Preface' in Canter, A., Dawson, P., Silverstein, J., Hale, L. and Zins, J. (Eds) *NASP Directory of Alternative Service Delivery Models*. Washington, DC: National Association of School Psychologists.

Epps, S. and Tindal, G. (1987) 'The effectiveness of differential programming in serving mildly handicapped students: Placement options and instructional programming', in Wang, M. C., Reynolds, M. C. and Walberg, H. J. (Eds) *Handbook of Special Education: Research and*

Practice: Vol. 1. Learner Characteristics and Adaptive Education (pp. 213–18). Oxford: Pergamon.

Fenstermacher, G. D. and Goodlad, J. I. (1983) (Eds) *Individual Differences and the Common Curriculum*. Chicago: University of Chicago Press.

Feuerstein, R., Jensen, M., Hoffman, M. B. and Rand, Y. (1985) 'Instrumental enrichment, an intervention program for instructional cognitive modifiability: Theory and practice', in Segal, J. J., Chipman, S. F. and Glaser, R. (Eds) *Thinking and Learning Skills: Vol. 1. Relating Instruction to Research* (pp. 43–82). Hillsdale, NJ: Erlbaum.

Gartner, A. and Lipsky, D. K. (1987) 'Beyond special education: Toward a quality system for all students', *Harvard Educational Review*, **57**,4:367–95.

Glaser, R. (1976) 'Components of a psychology of instruction: Toward a science of design', *Review of Educational Research*, **46**:1–24.

Glaser, R. (1977) *Adaptive Education: Individual Diversity and Learning*. New York: Holt, Rinehart and Winston.

Greenwood, C. R., Wharton, D. and Delquadri, J. C. (1984) 'Tutoring methods: Increasing opportunity to respond and achieve', *Association for Direct Instruction News*, **3**,3:4–7, 23.

Haynes, M. C. and Jenkins, J. R. (1986) 'Reading instruction in special education resource rooms', *American Educational Research Journal*, **23**,23:161–90.

Heller, K., Holtzman, W. and Messick, S. (1982) (Eds) *Placing Children in Special Education: A Strategy for Equity*. Washington, DC: National Academy of Sciences Press.

Jenkins, J. R., Pious, C. and Peterson, D. (1988) 'Exploring the validity of a unified learning program for remedial and handicapped students', *Exceptional Children*, **55**,2:147–58.

Kaufman, M., Agard, J. A. and Semmel, M. I. (1985) (Eds) *Mainstreaming: Learners and Their Environments*. Cambridge, MA: Brookline Books.

Lipsky, D. K. and Gartner, A. (1989) *Beyond Separate Education: Quality Education for All*. Baltimore, MD: Paul H. Brookes.

Manning, J. and Quandt, I. (1990) 'School-based innovation: Implementation issues and outcomes'. Paper presented at the meeting of the American Educational Research Association, April, Boston, MA.

National Assessment of Educational Progress (1987) *Learning by Doing: A Manual for Teaching and Assessing Higher-order Thinking Skills in Science and Mathematics* (Report no. 17-HO5-80). Princeton, NJ: Educational Testing Service.

National Association of School Psychologists and National Coalition of Advocates for Students (1986) *Position Statement: Advocacy for Appropriate Educational Services for all Children*. Boston, MA: Author.

National Coalition of Advocates for Students (1988) *100 Largest School Districts: A Special Analysis of 1986 Elementary and Secondary School Civil Rights Survey Data*. Boston, MA: Author.

Oakes, J. (1985) *Keeping Track: How Schools Structure Inequality*. New Haven, CT: Yale University Press.

Palincsar, A. S. and Brown, A. L. (1984) 'Reciprocal teaching of comprehension-fostering and comprehension-monitoring activities', *Cognition and Instruction*, **1**:117–25.

Reynolds, M. C. (1989) 'Children with special needs', in Reynolds, M. C. (Ed.) *The Knowledge Base for the Beginning Teacher* (pp. 129–42). Oxford: Pergamon.

Reynolds, M. C. and Birch, J. W. (1988) *Adaptive Mainstreaming: A Primer for Teachers and Principals*. New York: Longmans.

Reynolds, M. C., Wang, M. C. and Walberg, H. J. (in press) 'Changing the direction of research and practice in special education: A case of disjointedness'. *Exceptional Children*.

Snow, R. E. and Farr, M. J. (1983) (Eds) *Aptitude, Learning, and Instruction: Cognitive and Affective Process Analysis*. Stanford, CA: Office of Naval Research.

Sobehart, H. C. (1990) 'Implementing ALEM: An encouraging first year' (Special Issue), *PA Educational Leadership*.

Stainback, W., Stainback, S. and Forest, M. (1989) *Educating all Students in the Mainstream of Regular Education*. Baltimore, MD: Paul H. Brookes.

Stanovich, K. E. (1984) 'The interactive-compensatory model of reading: A confluence of developmental, experimental, and educational psychology', *Remedial and Special Education*, **5**,3:11–19.

Stipek, D. J. (1988) *Motivation to Learn: From Theory to Practice*. Englewood Cliffs, NJ: Prentice Hall.

Tobias, S. (1989) 'Another look at research on the adaptation of instruction to student characteristics', *Educational Psychologist*, **24**:213–29.

Vergason, G. A. and Anderegg, M. L. (1989) 'Save the baby! A response to "Integrating the children of the second system" ', *Phi Delta Kappan*, **71**,1:61–3.

Walberg, H. J. (1984) 'Families as partners in educational productivity', *Phi Delta Kappan*, **65**, 6:397–400.

Wang, M. C. (1980) 'Adaptive instruction: Building on diversity', *Theory into Practice*,**19**,2:122–7.

Wang, M. C. and Gennari, P. (1983) 'Analysis of the design, implementation, and effects of a data-based staff development program', *Teacher Education and Special Education*, **6**,4:211–26.

Wang, M. C. and Lindvall, C. M. (1984) 'Individual differences and school learning environments', in Gordon, E. W. (Ed.) *Review of Research in Education* (pp. 161–225). Washington, DC: American Educational Research Association.

Wang, M. C. and Palinscar, A. S. (1989) 'Teaching students to assume an active role in their learning', in Reynolds, M. C. (Ed.) *Knowledge Base for the Beginning Teacher* (pp. 71–84). Oxford: Pergamon Press.

Wang, M. C. and Vaughan, E. D. (1987) *Handbook for the Implementation of Adaptive Instruction Programs: Module 2. Needs Assessment and Implementation Planning*. Philadelphia, PA: Temple University Center for Research in Human Development and Education.

Wang, M. C. and Walberg, H. J. (1985) (Eds) *Adapting Instruction to Individual Differences*. Berkeley, CA: McCutchan.

Wang, M. C. and Zollers, J. Z. (1990) 'Adaptive Instruction: An alternative service delivery approach', *Remedial and Special Education*, **11**,1:7–21.

Wang, M. C., Catalano, R. and Gromoll, E. (1983) *Training Manual for the Implementation Assessment Battery for Adaptive Instruction*. Pittsburgh. PA: University of Pittsburgh, Learning Research and Development Center.

160

Wang, M. C., Gennari, P. and Waxman, H. C. (1985) 'The Adaptive Learning Environments Model: design, implementation, and effects', in Wang, M. C. and Walberg, H. J. (Eds) *Adapting Instruction to Individual Differences*. Berkeley, CA: McCutchan.

Wang, M. C., Haertel, G. D. and Walberg, H. J. (1990) 'What influences learning? A content analysis of review literature', *Journal of Educational Research*, **84**,1:30–43.

Wang, M. C., Reynolds, M. C. and Walberg, H. J. (1987–89) (Eds) *Handbook of Special Education: Research and Practice* (Vols. 1–3). Oxford: Pergamon.

Wang, M. C., Reynolds, M. C. and Walberg, H. J. (1988) 'Integrating the children of the second system', *Phi Delta Kappan*, **70**,3:248–51.

Wang, M. C., Reynolds, M. C. and Walberg, H. J. (1990) *Special Education Research and Practice: Synthesis of Findings*. Oxford: Pergamon.

Wang, M. C., Nojan, M., Strom, C. D. and Walberg, H. J. (1984) 'The utility of degree of implementation measures in program implementation and evaluation research', *Curriculum Inquiry*, **14**,3:249–86.

Will, M. C. (1986) 'Educating children with learning problems: A shared responsibility', *Exceptional Children*, **52**, 5:411–16.

Williams, B. I., Richmond, P. A. and Mason, B. J. (1986) *Designs for Compensatory Education: Conference Proceedings and Papers*. Washington, DC: Research and Evaluation Associates, Inc.

Wittrock, M. C. (1986) (Ed.) *Handbook of Research on Teaching* (3rd edn.). A project of the American Educational Research Association. New York: Macmillan.

Ysseldyke, J. E. (1987) 'Classification of handicapped students', in Wang, M. C., Reynolds, M. C. and Walberg, H. J. (Eds) *Handbook of Special Education: Research and Practice: Vol. 1. Learner Characteristics and Adaptive Education* (pp. 253–71). Oxford: Pergamon.

CHAPTER 9

Accommodating for Greater Student Variance

Jacqueline S. Thousand and Richard A. Villa

In this chapter, practices which appear to be associated with successful schooling of students in heterogeneous groupings are identified and described. Before discussing these practices, the authors believe it is important to clarify what, in their view, are some critical characteristics of successful heterogeneous public schools.

First, these schools are *comprehensive* in at least four ways. They are comprehensive in that they adopt a 'zero reject' principle (Lilly, 1971) by welcoming and educating *all* students of the community in local 'home' schools. Second, they accommodate the unique educational differences among students through fluid intructional options rather than the 'pigeonholing' of students into one of several standard programs or tracks of study (Skrtic, 1987). They also are comprehensive in that the body of decision-makers concerned with instructional, organizational, and individual student issues is expanded beyond the usual small, select group of administrators and teachers to include parents, students, teaching assistants, guidance and health personnel, human service agency personnel, community employers, and other interested community members. Finally, these schools are comprehensive in that academic achievement is considered only one of the purposes of schooling or criteria for student success. Social and life skills necessary for success in the vocational, domestic, and recreational domains of an increasingly international community (Benjamin, 1989; Wiggins, 1989) are appreciated and directly addressed as integral parts of the school curriculum.

The second characteristic of successful heterogeneous schools

161

concerns instructional effectiveness of the teaching staff. Great effort is put in to making available to all instructional and administrative staff timely and intensive training, coaching, and supervision in emerging 'exemplary educational practices'. The leadership of heterogeneous schools recognize the wisdom in attempting to not only implement but merge exemplary practices from both general and special education in order to take advantage of the knowledge base and demonstrated benefits of quality educational practices, regardless of their origins.

This chapter offers brief descriptions and specific examples of a few of the educational and organizational practices and beliefs which have been found to promote student success in heterogeneous schools (Thousand and Villa, 1989, in press b; Villa and Thousand, 1988, 1990). These examples are derived from the results of research and model demonstration efforts as well as the authors' own experiences in Vermont and other North American schools, where the commitment to educating *all* students in heterogeneous groups has been realized in practice.

Instructional practices

Recently there has been a proliferation of reviews regarding methods for 'individualizing' curriculum and providing 'individualized' instruction (e.g., Glatthorn, 1987; Nevin *et al.*, 1990; Slavin, 1987; Stainback and Stainback, in press; Stainback, Stainback and Forest, 1989; Villa and Thousand, 1988; Wang, 1989). Four sets of strategies considered appropriate and effective for responding to the individual needs of students in heterogeneous schools are discussed in this section. They are curriculum-based assessment models, outcomes-based instructional models, computer assisted instruction, and instructional practices utilizing peer power.

Curriculum-based assessment models

The term 'curriculum-based assessment' (CBA) represents a set of criterion-referenced assessment methods for identifying students' instructional needs by examining students' ongoing performance within the selected curricula used by the school. Unlike norm-referenced assessment, CBA is not concerned with comparing students with one another, but with examining each student's performance in comparison with a pre-set criterion or standard. CBA gives teachers information about what to teach, and in this way closely links assessment with instruction. To use CBA, school staff must create or identify and select curriculum sequences which are both appropriate and detailed enough to give teachers information for designing instructional programs. For in-depth descriptions of CBA methodologies, see Howell and Morehead (1987); Idol *et al.* (1986); and Shapiro (1987).

Outcomes-based instruction models

In Glatthorn's (1987) summary of research on methods for adapting curriculum and instruction to respond to individual student differences, three specific sets of approaches were offered as having very strong support of quality research. The first set of approaches identified were mastery learning models or outcomes-based instructional models (Block and Anderson, 1975; Brookover *et al.*, 1982; Guskey, 1985; Vicker, 1988). Common to all of these models are the following teacher behaviors: (a) frequent, brief diagnostic assessment of each student; (b) individualization of learning objectives with clear pre-set mastery criteria; (c) frequent specific feedback provided to students regarding their performance; and (d) supplementation or adjustment of teaching/learning method or practice time, for those students who do not yet meet their mastery criteria. An underlying assumption of outcomes-based instructional models is that all children can learn, given time and the appropriate resources. It is this assumption combined with the extensive effectiveness data that makes mastery learning models so compelling for use in classrooms which include students with diverse educational, psychological and emotional needs.

Computer assisted instruction

The second data-based approach identified by Glatthorn (1987) was computer assisted instruction (CAI). As Glatthorn noted, CAI is particularly useful in three areas of instruction: (a) tutorial, where new information is presented; (b) drill and practice, where old information is reviewed for the purpose of remediation or accelerating rate or level of mastery; and (c) simulations, where concept learning or more complex problem-solving is the focus. For students who are physically challenged, non-verbal, or verbally unintelligible to the general public, computers also may be used as an alternative or augmentative mode of communication as well as a learning tool.

164

Instructional practices utilizing peer power

Peer power may be defined as students supporting students in learning and socialization (Villa and Thousand, 1988). Peer power has proven to be one of the most valuable resources for facilitating the education of all learners within general education environments (Villa and Thousand, in press). Schools which effectively use peer resources do so in a variety of ways. Among the many strategies employed and described here are cooperative group learning models, partner learning or peer tutoring systems, peer buddies and peer support networks, and the inclusion of peers and members of planning teams for classmates with disabilities.

Cooperative group learning models. Cooperative group learning models (Johnson and Johnson, 1987a, 1987c; Slavin, 1983) were the third set of strongly researched adaptation approaches identified by Glatthorn (1987) in his review. As with effective collaborative teams, cooperative learning models share five common elements: (a) face-to-face interaction among the heterogeneous group of students, (b) positive interdependence (structured through common goals or products, joint rewards, division of labor and roles, division of materials or information); (c) teaching of small group interpersonal skills; (d) regular assessment and goal setting regarding the appropriate use of small group and interpersonal skills; and (e) individual accountability for achieving individualized academic and social objectives.

One question often asked by teachers new to cooperative learning is, 'How do I integrate a low achieving student or a student with disabilities into heterogeneous cooperative groups?' Johnson and Johnson (1987c) have described several proven strategies. One strategy involves assigning the challenged student a specific role which promotes participation and minimizes the student's anxiety about co-operating with more capable students. Examples of appropriate roles are checking that all members can explain the group's answer, summarizing the group's answers, and praising members for their contributions. A second strategy is to pre-train the target students in academic or collaborative skills so they have unique expertise to bring to the group. A third set of strategies involves adapting lesson require-ments for individual students. Different success criteria may be used for each group member; the amount of work expected of each member may be adjusted, or group members may study and coach one another on different words, problems, readings, and so forth. If the group is tested, the entire group may earn points based upon the degree to which each member exceeds *individual* success criteria.

A sample lesson designed by a Vermont teacher may best illustrate how adaptations may be made for students with intensive educational needs (Villa and Thousand, in press). John, an 8-year-old student with intensive needs who was a member of this teacher's combined first and second grade classroom, has spent his first years of schooling in a special class for students with multiple handicaps. He occasionally vocalized loudly, but did not yet use vocal behavior to communicate. One of John's educational goals was to develop his use of various electronic switching devices as a first step in developing his augmentative communication system. Other goals for John included remaining with a group throughout an activity, keeping his hands off others' materials, and refraining from making loud vocalizations during group times.

In this lesson students were assigned to groups of five students. All group members, John included, were expected to sit in a circle, stay with their group, and use an 'indoor' voice level. It should be noted that these social and behavioral expectations directly addressed two of John's educational goals. Groups first listened to a 'talking book' story tape and followed along with the illustrations from the story book. Each group had a copy of the story tape, a tape recorder, and the illustrated book. Each child in a group was assigned a specific job to perform during the lesson. One job was to turn the pages of the story book to correspond with the tape recording; another was to operate the tape recorder. John was assigned the role of tape recorder operator, and his tape recorder was adapted so that he could activate it by pushing on a panel switch attached to the recorder.

Being assigned the role of tape recorder operator gave John a valuable and needed role to his group. It also addressed two of his educational goals. First, it allowed for the assessment of a switch's potential for use in a meaningful real life situation. Secondly, it inhibited John's grabbing behavior, as one hand was busy, engaged in pushing the switch to turn on the tape recorder. A tape recorder also is a popular leisure time device among children and adults and appropriate for John to learn to use.

After listening to the story, groups generated and agreed upon answers to questions concerning the story. They then met as a large group and shared their responses. John's objectives for this part of the lesson continued to be behavioral in nature – to stay with the group and to refrain from making loud noises or grabbing other's materials.

Partner learning and peer tutoring systems. Same-age and cross-age partner learning or peer tutoring systems are two forms of peer power upon which heterogeneous schools are compelled to capitalize. As noted by Gartner and Lipsky (1990, p. 84) 'evidence of the instructional, social, and cost effectiveness of tutoring is mounting'. The many benefits for both the tutor and the tutee have been summarized in research reviews and a meta-analysis of research (Cohen *et al.*, 1982; Madden and Slavin, 1987; Pierce *et al.*, 1984). The documented benefits to both students giving and receiving instruction include learning gains, the development of positive social interaction skills with another student, and heightened self-esteem. Good and Brophy (1987) suggests that peers trained as tutors may, in some cases, be more effective than adults – they use more age-appropriate and meaningful vocabulary and examples; as recent learners of material being taught, they are familiar with the tutee's potential frustrations and problems; and they tend to be more directive than adults.

Same-age and cross-age partner learning systems may be established within a single classroom (Maheady *et al.*, 1988), across more than one classroom, or across an entire school. As with other instructional and peer support strategies which utilize peer power (Villa and Thousand, 1988) partner learning is a cost-effective way for teachers to increase the amount of individualized instructional attention available to their students (Armstrong *et al.*, 1979).

The following two examples from Villa and Thousand (in press) illustrate the power positive impact of partner learning on the social behavior of students identified as seriously emotionally disturbed (SED). Consider, the first student, Andrew. During his sixth grade year, Andrew was used as a cross-age tutor for the last 45 minutes of each school day in a second grade classroom. This privilege was dependent upon his making it through the day without outbursts, as defined in his behavioral contract. Although this young man often presented behavioral challenges to his own teachers and age mates, he was considered by the second grade teacher to be both a model of appropriate behavior and a valued instructional asset. His second grade tutoring time was one of two times during the day when an instructional assistant was *not* assigned to be available in case of disruptions. The importance to Andrew of the tutoring role was demonstrated the week before the Christmas holiday vacation, when he chose to give up his own class party in order to present individual gifts to the second grade teacher and each member of the second grade class.

For Rebecca, a fourth grader identified as SED, the tutoring role was intended to help her to identify and moderate her own anti-social behavior. Following each tutoring session with second grade students, she was asked to analyze her effectiveness in teaching and managing the students' behavior. Behaviors of her tutees which interfered with teaching and management were highlighted, and analogies were drawn to her own behaviors and their negative effects upon learning. Strategies then were discussed for effectively moderating her own social behaviors.

Peer support networks and peer buddies. Historically, some students – notably students with disabilities – have been excluded from certain aspects of school life (e.g., school clubs and other after-school activities, school dances, athletic events). Peer support networks or Circles of Friends (Forest and Lusthaus, 1989) have been established in many North American schools to enable peers with disabilities to more fully participate in school and after-school life. Peer support networks are different from peer tutor systems in that they are primarily non-academic in focus. In the words of a student organizer of a 'peer buddy' network:

> Peer support is a bunch of kids working together to break down the barriers that society has built into the public's idea of what the norm is. Teachers and peers need to . . . understand that the goal of peer support is not competitive academics. The goal is to belong, to meet new people, to learn to break down the barriers (Budelmann *et al.*, 1987).

The diversity of support which peer buddies can provide other students is limitless. A buddy might assist a peer with physical disabilities to get items from the hall locker or 'hang out' around the school halls before and after class. A buddy might accompany a peer to a school dance or athletic event or advocate for their interests by speaking to other students and adults about the unique learning, physical, or social challenges that their friend must face and overcome each day. Peer support networks have helped to make heterogeneous schools more caring places where learning outcomes have been expanded to include an understanding of one another's unique lives.

Students as members of the educational planning team for a peer. One of the challenges which teachers face in heterogeneous classrooms is determining meaningful curricular adaptations and instructional modifications to enable students with disabilities to simultaneously have their educational needs met and be active members of the daily classroom routine. Peers have proven to be invaluable members of the planning teams for classmates with handicaps, particularly because of their ability to identify appropriate social integration opportunities and goals for making their classmate with intensive educational challenges a genuine part of the school culture. The words of an administrator who now routinely includes peers in planning for the educational programs of students with intensive special educational needs emphasized this point:

> Although we have emphasized socialization and inclusion for years, it never really took off until we turned to the students and asked for their help. We previously were leaving out of the planning process the majority of the school's population (DiFerdinando, 1987).

In several Vermont schools, students as young as 6 years of age also have been trained in a creative problem-solving technique which they regularly employ to identify ways for meaningfully including a classmate with multiple handicaps or dual sensory impairments (i.e., deafness and blindness) in daily school routines and instructional activities (Giangreco and Cloninger, 1990). An elegantly simple variation of this technique involves the teacher introducing each upcoming lesson with a brief description of the objectives and activities involved in the lesson and asking, as a part of the routine introduction, 'How could we really make [student's name] a part of this lesson?'. Teachers who have used the creative brainstorming powers of children in this way report their students to be highly imaginative, effective, and efficient problem-solvers who generate a great many realistic and exciting modification strategies from which to choose.

Restructuring the school organization to create a climate of equity and equality

A number of characteristics of the organizational structure of traditional North American and European schools interfere with heterogeneous schooling. First, most schools continue to stratify students into low, medium, and high groups through heavy reliance upon 'tracking' systems and segregated or 'pull out' special education service delivery models. Secondly, many schools continue to take a 'lock step' curriculum approach, where students' objectives are not determined by their assessed individual needs, but the grade level to which they are assigned. Students are placed in a grade according to their age and expected to master a predetermined curriculum sequence by the end of the school year. Students whose needs do not match this curriculum are retained or referred for special services and pulled out of the general education program for part or all of their day (Thousand, 1990). Finally, teachers, regardless of their general or special education label, are expected to work alone. Few schools expect or structure opportunities for personnel to collaboratively plan and jointly deliver instruction in team teaching arrangements.

Schools committed to educating their students in heterogeneous learning arrangements have attempted to eliminate these and other organizational barriers. Specifically, they have redefined professional roles, created opportunities for collaborative teaming, and created a common conceptual framework and language through the structuring of continuing education opportunities for all school staff.

Dropping professional labels and redefining professional roles

'I used to think of myself as a speech and language pathologist; but now I think of myself as a *teacher* who happens to have training and expertise in the area of communication' (Harris, 1987). Redefining professional roles is viewed as a necessary step to shift from categorical educational services (e.g. general education, vocational education, special education classes and pull-out services) to a unified educational system in which support would be available to any student or teacher as needed.

Job titles and the formal or informal role definitions that accompany them influence the way in which people behave within schools (Brookover *et al.*, 1982). Take, for example, the American special education instructional title of 'resource room teacher'. This title carries with it a picture of a teacher working in a separate room only with those students eligible for extra support. This person, however, likely has extensive training and expertise in such areas as student assessment, task and concept analysis, behavior management, and instructional design – areas which, if shared with classroom teachers, would expand the range of teaching responses for maximizing learning of a heterogeneous student body.

Now suppose that the resource room teacher label were dropped and the role redefined as a provider of technical assistance to any number of educators through team teaching, consultation, and inservice training arrangements. Some schools have taken such a step in order to merge the instructional resources of general and special education. Among the schools in North America that have dropped professional labels and distributed job functions across a number of school personnel is the Winooski (Vermont) School District (Villa and Thousand, 1988). In Winooski, a single job description, labelled 'teacher', has been adopted for all professional educators. The new job description emphasizes collaborative planning and shared responsibility for the education of all of the community's children. The Winooski schools, along with other school districts, also have opened the teacher role to the entire adult and student community through the formation of *teaching teams* – 'organizational and instructional arrangement[s] of two or more members of the school and greater community who distribute among themselves planning, instructional, and evaluation responsibilities for the same students on a regular basis for an extended period of time' (Thousand and Villa, 1990, p. 152). Not only does the teaching team notion redefine the traditional view of who can be in the teaching role, but it increases the possibilities for individualizing instruction through enhanced teacher/student ratios and the ongoing exchange of knowledge and skill among team members.

Expecting and creating opportunities for collaboration

All schools have within them a natural yet frequently untapped reserve of expertise; each educator has unique skills and interests which may be brought to bear upon the challenges faced by another teacher. Having processes and opportunities for collaborating and sharing skills have been identified as a key to successfully meeting the needs of all students and teachers (Johnson and Johnson, 1987; Thousand *et al.*, 1986). 'The integration of professionals within a school system is a prerequisite to the successful integration of students. We cannot ask students to do those things which we as professionals are unwilling to do' (Harris, 1987).

Establishing a collaborative teaming process. Personnel of our most successful heterogeneous schools have consistently identified as the keystone to their success strong collaborative teams which utilize formal *collaborative teaming processes* (Thousand *et al.*, 1986). Teams which use these processes have found that formal professional roles and dividing lines dissolve as team members coordinate their work to achieve common, publicly agreed goals. The collaborative processes to which these teams prescribe are based upon the already articulated principles of cooperative group learning (Johnson and Johnson, 1987b, 1987c) – (a) frequent face-to-face interaction, (b) an 'all for one, one for all' feeling of positive interdependence, (c) a focus on the development of small-group interpersonal skills, (d) regular assessment of team functioning, and (e) methods for holding one another accountable for agreed commitments (Thousand and Villa, 1990).

The power of teams which employ collaborative teaming processes lies in their capacity to merge the unique skills of talented adults and students, enfranchise team members through the participatory decision-making process, and distribute leadership authority beyond the administration to the broader school community (Thousand and Villa, 1990). Effective collaborative teaming also promotes a climate of equality and equity in a number of ways. There is no one leader of the group; instead, leadership roles are distributed and rotated among all members. Everyone alternately plays the consultant/expert and the consultee/recipient roles, so that specialists have no extra authority. They are 'just another member' of the team (Thousand *et al.*, in press).

Creating opportunities for teams to meet. One big issue facing all schools interested in implementing collaborative teaming processes is how the school's organizational structure may be modified to allow staff the time it needs to meet in teams. In Vermont, some school districts have dealt with this issue by contracting a permanent substitute who rotates among schools to relieve general education teachers so they may attend meetings concerning students in their classrooms. Other schools have instituted a practice of reserving time blocks (e.g., one half-day per week, three 1-hour blocks per week) each week for team meetings. All support personnel (e.g., teachers with specialized expertise, nurses, counselors, teaching assistants) are expected to hold this time open until they are notified of scheduled meeting times for students with whom they are involved. During the times when they are not scheduled for meetings, they relieve general education teachers so they may attend meetings for students in their classrooms.

It is important for administrators to demonstrate appreciation for this type of collaborative time by setting an expectation that teachers will collaborate, coordinating the school's schedule so events are scheduled other than during teaming times, and arranging incentives and rewards for collaboration (Villa and Thousand, 1990).

Creating common conceptual frameworks, knowledge, and language through continuing education opportunities

Staff of schools committed to educating all of their students in the mainstream of regular education need to acquire a common conceptual

> framework, language, and set of technical skills in order to communicate about and implement practices which research and theory suggest will enable them to better respond to a diverse student body. If personnel employed within the school have not received this training through their teacher preparation program, it becomes the job of those responsible for planning inservice for the local education agency to facilitate the formulation and ratification of a comprehensive inservice training agenda. This agenda may need to extend across several years to ensure that instructional personnel have the opportunity to progress from acquisition to mastery (Villa, 1989, p. 173).

This statement acknowledges what many teachers have reported (Lyon *et al.*, 1988), that neither their professional preparation nor their relatively isolated teaching experiences have adequately prepared them to meet the needs of a heterogeneous student population. Fortunately, schools do not have to wait for higher education to respond; they can structure their own continuing education opportunities for empowering staff to collaborate in the education of all children.

The authors' personal experiences and reading of the literature have led them to identify at least four areas in which staff interested in heterogeneous schooling need instruction and practice (Villa, 1989). The first content area involves collaborative teaming processes (Johnson and Johnson, 1987b; Nevin *et al.*, 1990, Thousand *et al.*, 1986). As already emphasized, if school personnel are to effectively merge their talents through collaboration, they need to become skillful in implementing a collaborative teaming model and using interpersonal and small group skills.

The second area of training would introduce the school and greater community to the research and underlying values concerning emerging 'best educational practices' that promote heterogeneous schooling. This training would examine the characteristics of schools which general education researchers have found to be more effective than others in enhancing student learning (Brookover *et al.*, 1982) as well as that which special education researchers promote as best educational practice (Thousand and Villa, in press b). Armed with this information, school personnel and community members would be equipped to articulate the demonstrated benefits of these practices and argue for the establishment and merger of exemplary practices within their schools.

A third content area would include a variety of instructional and student management practices for accommodating diverse student needs, specifically: (a) curriculum-based assessment models (e.g., Idol *et al.*, 1986); (b) outcomes-based instructional models (e.g., Block and Anderson, 1975; Hunter, 1982); (c) computer assisted instruction (e.g., Heerman, 1988); (d) cooperative group learning models (e.g., Johnson *et al.*, 1984; Slavin, 1983); (e) partner learning or peer tutoring models (e.g., Pierce *et al.*, 1984); (f) classroom management strategies (e.g., Becker, 1986) and class-wide and school-wide discipline systems (e.g., Curwin and Mendler, 1988; Glasser, 1986); (g) methods for teaching and reinforcing students' use of positive social skills (e.g., Hazel *et al.*, 1981; Jackson *et al.*, 1983); and (h) the use of peers as buddies and members of education planning teams (Thousand and Villa, 1988).

Finally, school supervisory personnel may need training and practice in the use of a clinical supervision model (e.g., Cummings, 1985). If supervisors are effectively to provide teachers with the feedback and coaching they will need to become skilled in the use of the instructional strategies listed above, they must become skillful in observing, analyzing, and conducting conferences regarding teachers' instructional performance.

As Villa (1989) has pointed out, whatever the training content a school staff elects to study, the principles of effective teaching should be followed in the delivery of the content. Specifically, trainers must model multiple examples of the desired knowledge or skill, create guided practice opportunities for applying the knowledge or skill, require the application of the knowledge or skill in real instructional (or collaborative teaming) situations, and provide regular feedback regarding the application of the knowledge or skill (Joyce and Showers, 1980, 1988).

Beliefs

Although the instructional and organizational practices discussed thus far have been found to promote heterogeneous schooling, it is the *beliefs* held by parents and the school community which ultimately determine whether or not *all* of the community's children will be welcomed and successfully educated within general education environments. We make this statement, because of an emerging body of research (Fortini, 1987; Miller and Gibbs, 1984; Thousand and Burchard, 1990) supporting a *theory of reasoned action* which associates the voluntary behavior of people with their beliefs (Azjen and Fishbein, 1980). What follows are three frequently stated beliefs which, in the authors' view, influences a community's willingness in and success at creating heterogeneous schools (Thousand and Villa, 1989).

Heterogeneity is possible

For a school community to enthusiastically open its doors to a more diverse group of students and promote these students' learning in general education environments, it is important for them to believe or, at least temporarily, suspend disbelief that heterogeneous age-appropriate school experiences *can* meet the unique needs of each student (Nevin and Thousand, 1986; Thousand and Burchard, 1990). In other words, they must trust that they will be made capable of doing a quality job – that they will receive the technical assistance and training and the human and material resources they will need to do the job effectively.

Often, school and community members faced with the challenge of restructuring schools to accommodate a more diverse student population take a 'show me' posture of 'seeing is believing'. They are willing to entertain the possibility of heterogeneous schooling only *after* others have had successful experiences. They wait to hear whether support was provided when it was needed. Others embrace a belief in the possibilities of heterogeneous schooling only after they, themselves, have had positive first-hand experiences educating a diverse group of students. In either case, it is important to have some successes, to create successful demonstrations of hetereogeneous schooling. Fortunately, today many such demonstrations do exist in communities across North America (Nevin *et al.*, 1990; Thousand and Villa, in press b).

Heterogeneity is beneficial to all

Another belief supporters of heterogeneous schooling hold is that heterogeneous educational learning opportunities are beneficial to all students and school personnel. A kindergarten teacher who had integrated a student with moderate handicaps full-time into her classroom clearly articulated this belief. When asked why she chose to have this child in her classroom, she replied:

> I, as a teacher, have no right to limit the possible potential of this child. No one knows his limits. I like to think of [this child] as having no limits. Anything is possible for him. I feel fortunate to have had the opportunity to grow in a new direction by having [this child] in my classroom. I am learning and adapting along with the other students, accepting and believing that everyone is special (Donahue, 1988).

This response reflects both this teacher's appreciation of the student's human and educational rights and her belief that the student's presence in the classroom was beneficial – a catalyst for new learning both for herself and all of her students.

Another set of beliefs regarding the benefits of heterogeneous schooling concerns students with disabilities, who, in the past, would have been excluded from general education environments. These students have spoken out as to the positive effects of heterogeneous schooling on their own emotional well-being and sense of belonging. One high school student commented, 'I was in a special class. I've been in regular classes for five years. I'm more a part of the school now' (Budelmann *et al.*, 1987). Another young woman with disabilities who had always been educated with her peers stated: 'I feel like I am a part of the school. I am aware of the things that are going on. I've gone to the school car wash and homecoming. I have friends in and out of school, and this helps me feel better about myself' (Budelmann *et al.*, 1987).

Clearly, both students recognized their heterogeneous schooling experiences as a primary source of their feelings of inclusion.

Parents as equal partners

In successful heterogeneous schools, parents are considered valid and valued members of the collaborative teams supporting their children's education. To view parents otherwise limits the school's access to the resources parents offer in identifying their children's strengths and needs, designing realistic educational interventions, and evaluating the outcomes of their children's schooling. A mother's address to university professors and public school professional educators best conveyed this appreciation for parents' unique expertise: 'Parents should be thought of as scholars of experience. We are in it for the distance We see and feel the continuum. We have our doctorate in perseverance. We and the system must be in concert or the vision shrinks' (Sylvester, 1987).

Summary

'Student diversity is only a problem because of the kind of school organization we have' (The Holmes Group, 1990). As an illustration of this point, we offer Skrtic's (1987, 1988) description of the 20th century school as a professional bureaucracy which diminishes rather than enhances teachers' ability to individualize for a great many students.

The biggest problem is that schools are organized as professional bureaucracies . . . a contradiction in terms: professionalization is intended to permit personalization; bureaucratization is intended to assure standardization. To blame the inability to individualize instruction totally on the capacity or will of professionals is misguided in that it blames the teacher for the inadequacies and contradictions of the organizational structure. This is the same kind of distortion of reality we make when we blame particular students for not learning from the existing standardized programs of the school organization. These students are the ones we call 'handicapped', which is what I mean when I say that school organizations create 'handicapped students'. In both cases our tendency is to blame the victims – teachers who fail to individualize and students who fail to learn – for the inadequacies of the system (Thousand, 1990, p. 31).

The organizational, instructional, and attitudinal variables presented in this chapter have been offered as tools for enhancing the capacity of schools to individualize for students, to become less of a professional bureaucracy. We encourage all who are interested in or charged with the responsibility of school improvement to carefully examine the organizational structures, educational practices, and beliefs operating within their schools and assess whether they promote or impede continued progress toward meeting the diverse needs of all students.

We further propose that educators consider organizing into ad hoc collaborative teams (Patterson *et al.*, 1986) or *adhocracies* (Skrtic, 1987) so that they may 'mutually adjust their collective skills and knowledge to invent unique, personalized programs for each student' (Thousand, 1990, p. 32). In such collaborative teaming arrangements, teachers become inventors who have an implicit understanding that educational programs will have to be

. . . continuously invented and reinvented by teachers in actual practice with students who have unique and changing needs. The value of the adhocracy is that it is configured for diversity whereas the professional bureaucracy is configured for homogeneity, and so must remove diversity from the system through means like special education and other pull-out programs (Thousand, 1990, p. 32).

As a final recommendation, we encourage school communities to be optimistic, to embrace the belief that there are actions which each individual can take to create change and that it is the collective actions of individuals that result in change. It is the actions of ad hoc collaborative problem-solving and teaching teams in schools across North America that have resulted in the many heterogeneous-oriented schools which now exist, and just one decade ago would have been considered beyond reach (see Nevin *et al.*, 1990; Thousand and Villa, 1989, 1990; Villa and Thousand, in press).

References

Armstrong, S. B. Stahlbrand, K., Conlon, M. F. and Pierson, P. M. (1979) 'The cost effectiveness of peer and cross-age tutoring'. Paper presented at the international convention of the Council for Exceptional Children, April (ERIC Document Reproduction Service No. ED 171 058).

Azjen, I. and Fishbein, M. (1980) *Understanding Attitudes and Predicting Social Behavior*. Englewood Cliffs, NJ: Prentice-Hall.

Becker, W. (1986) *Applied Psychology for Teachers: A Behavioral Cognitive Approach*. Chicago, IL: Science Research Associates.

Benjamin, S. (1989) 'An ideascape for education: What futurists recommend', *Educational Leadership*, **47**,1:8–14.

Block, J. and Anderson, L. (1975) *Mastery Learning in Classroom Instruction*. New York: Macmillan.

Brookover, W., Beamer, L., Efthim, H., Hathaway, D., Lezzotte, L., Miller, S., Passalacqua, J. and Tornatzky, L. (1982) *Creating Effective Schools: An Inservice Program for Enhancing School Learning Climate and Achievement*. Holmes Beach, FL: Learning Publications.

Budelmann, L., Farrel, S., Kovach, C. and Paige, K. (1987) 'Student perspective: Planning and achieving social integration'. Paper presented at Vermont's Least Restrictive Environment Conference, April, Burlington, VT.

Cohen, P. A., Kulik, J. A. and Kulik, C. C. (1982) 'Educational outcomes of tutoring', *American Education Journal*, **19**:237–48.

Cummings, C. (1985) *Peering in on Peers*. Edmonds, WA: Snohomish Publishing Company.

Curwin, R. and Mendler, A. (1988) *Discipline with Dignity*. Alexandria, VA: Association for Supervision and Curriculum Development.

DiFerdinando, R. (1987) 'An administrator's perspective on the value of peer support networks'. Paper presented at Vermont's Least Restrictive Environment Conference, October, Burlington, VT.

Donahue, S. (1988) Examples of integration in Addison Northeast Supervisory Union. Paper presented at the Teaming for Creative Mainstreaming Conference, March, Ludlow, VT.

Forest, M. and Lusthaus, E. (1989) 'Promoting educational equality for all students: Circles and maps', in Stainback, S., Stainback, W. and Forest, M. (Eds) *Educating All Students in the Mainstream of Regular Education* (pp. 43–57). Baltimore, MD: Paul H. Brookes Publishing.

Fortini, M. (1987) 'Attitudes and behavior towards students with handicaps by their nonhandicapped peers', *American Journal of Deficiency*, **92**:78–84.

Gartner, A. and Lipsky, D. (1990) 'Students as instructional agents', in Stainback, W. and Stainback S. (Eds) *Support Networks for Inclusive Schooling: Interdependent Integrated Education*. (pp. 81–93). Baltimore: MD: Paul H. Brookes Publishing.

Giangreco, M. F. and Cloninger, C. J. (1990) 'Facilitating inclusion through problem-solving methods', *TASH Newletter*, **16**, 5:10.

Glasser, W. (1986) *Control Theory in the Classroom*. New York: Harper and Row.

Glatthorn, A. (1987) 'How do you adapt the curriculum to respond to individual differences?', in Glatthorn, A. (Ed.) *Curriculum Renewal* (pp. 99–109). Alexandria, VA: Association for Supervision and Curriculum Development.

Good, T. L. and Brophy, J. E. (1987) *Looking into Classrooms* (4th edn.). New York: Harper and Row.

Guskey, T. (1985) *Implementing Mastery Learning*. Belmont, CA: Wadsworth Publishing.

Harris, T., (1987) 'A speech and language pathologist's perspective on teaming to accomplish cooperation between and among regular and special educators for the provision of services in the least restrictive environment'. Paper presented at Vermont's Least Restrictive Environment Conference, October, Burlington, VT.

Hazel, J., Schumaker, J., Sherman, J. and Sheldon-Wildgen, J. (1981) *Asset: A Social Skills Program for Adolescents*. Champaign, IL: Research Press.

Heerman, B. (1988) *Teaching and Learning with Computers*. San Francisco, CA: Jossey-Bass Publishers.

Holmes Group The , (1990) *Tomorrow's Schools: Principles for the Design of Professional Development Schools*. East Lansing, MI: The Holmes Group.

Howell, K. W. and Morehead, M. K. (1987) *Curriculum-based Evaluation for Special and Remedial Education*. Columbus, OH: Charles E. Merrill.

Hunter, M. (1982) *Mastery Teaching*. El Segunda, CA: TIP Publications.

Idol, L., Nevin, A. and Paolucci-Whitcomb, P. (1986) *Models of Curriculum-based Assessment*. Rockville, MD: Aspen Publishers.

Jackson, N. F., Jackson, D. A. and Monroe, C. (1983) *Behavioral Social Skill Training Materials – Getting along with others: Teaching Social Effectiveness to Children*. Champaign, IL: Research Press.

Johnson, D. W. and Johnson, R. T. (1987a) *A Meta-analysis of Cooperative, Competitive and Individualistic Goal Structures*. Hillsdale, NJ: Lawrence Erlbaum.

Johnson, D. W. and Johnson, R. T. (1987b) *Joining Together: Group Theory and Group Skills* (3rd edn.). Englewood Cliffs, NJ: Prentice-Hall.

Johnson, D. W. and Johnson, R. T. (1987c) *Learning Together and Alone: Co-operation, Competition, and Individualization* (2nd edn.). Englewood Cliffs, NJ: Prentice-Hall.

Johnson, D. W. and Johnson, R. T. (1987d) 'Research shows the benefit of adult cooperation,' *Education Leadership*, **43**, 3:27–30.

Johnson, D. W., Johnson, R. T., Holubec, E. and Roy, P. (1984) *Circles of Learning*. Arlington, VA: Association for Supervision and Curriculum Development.

Joyce, B. and Showers, B. (1980) 'Improving inservice training: The messages of research', *Educational Leadership*, **37**:379–85.

Joyce, B. and Showers, B. (1988) *Student Achievement through Staff Development*. New York: Longman.

Lilly, M. S. (1971) 'A training based model for special education', *Exceptional Children*, **37**, 745–9.

Lyon, G. R., Vaassen, M. and Toomey, F. (1989) 'Teachers' perceptions of their undergraduate and graduate preparation', *Teacher Education and Special Education*, **12**:164–9.

Madden, M. A. and Slavin, R. E. (1987) *Effective Pull-out Programs for Students at Risk*. Baltimore, MD: John Hopkins University, Center for Research on Elementary and Middle Schools.

Maheady, L., Sacca, M. K. and Harper, G. F. (1988) 'Classwide peer tutoring with mildly handicapped high school students', *Exceptional Children*, **55**:52–9.

Miller, C. and Gibbs, E. D. (1984) 'High school students' attitudes and actions toward "slow learners"', *American Journal of Mental Deficiency*, **89**:156–66.

Nevin, A. and Thousand, J. (1986) 'Limiting or avoiding referrals to special education,' *Teacher Education and Special Education*, **9**:149–61.

Nevin, A., Thousand, J., Paolucci-Whitcomb, P. and Villa, R. (1990) 'Collaborative consultation: Empowering public school personnel to provide heterogeneous schooling for all', *Journal of Educational and Psychological Consultation*, **1**, 1:41–67.

Patterson, J., Purkey, S. and Parker, J. (1986) *Productive School Systems for a Nonrational World*. Alexandria, VA: Association for Supervision and Curriculum Development.

Pierce, M. M., Stahlbrand, K. and Armstrong, S. B. (1984) *Increasing Student Productivity through Peer Tutoring Programs*. Austin, TX: Pro-Ed.

Shapiro, E. S. (1987) *Behavioral Assessment in School Psychology*. Hillsdale, NJ: Lawrence Erlbaum Associates.

Skrtic, T. (1987) 'The national inquiry into the future of education for students with special needs', *Counterpoint*, **4**,7:6.

Skrtic, T. (1988) 'The crisis in special education knowledge', in Meyen, E. and Skrtic, T. (Eds) *Exceptional Children and Youth: An Introduction* (3rd Edn.) (pp. 415–48). Denver: Love Publishing Co.

Slavin, R. E. (1983) *Cooperative Learning*. New York: Longman.

Slavin, R. E. (1984) 'Review of cooperative learning research', *Review of Educational Research*, **50**:315–42.

Slavin, R. E. (1987) 'Ability grouping and student achievement in elementary school: A best-evidence synthesis', *Review of Educational Research*, **57**:293–336.

Stainback, S. and Stainback, W. (in press) *Teaching in the Inclusive Classroom: Curriculum Design, Adaptation, and Delivery*. Baltimore, MD: Paul H. Brookes Publishing.

Stainback, S., Stainback, W. and Forest, M. (1989) *Educating all Students in the Mainstream of Regular Education*. Baltimore, MD: Paul H. Brookes Publishing.

Sylvester, D. (1987) 'A parent's perspective on transition: From high school to what?' Paper presented at Vermont's Least Restrictive Environment Conference, October, Burlington, VT.

Thousand, J. (1990) 'Organizational perspectives on teacher education and renewal: A conversation with Tom Skrtic', *Teacher Education and Special Education*, **13**:30–35.

Thousand, J. and Burchard, S. (1990) 'Social integration: Special education teacher attitudes and behaviors', *American Journal in Mental Retardation*, **94**:407–19.

Thousand, J. and Villa, R. (1989) 'Enhancing success in heterogeneous schools', in Stainback, S., Stainback, W. and Forest, M. (Eds) *Educating All Students in the Mainstream* (pp. 89–103). Baltimore, MD: Paul H. Brookes Publishing.

Thousand, J. and Villa, R. (1990) 'Sharing expertise and responsibilities through teaching teams', in Stainback, W. and Stainback, S. (Eds) *Support Networks for Inclusive Schooling: Interdependent Integrated Education* (pp. 151–66). Baltimore: Paul H. Brookes Publishing.

Thousand, J. and Villa, R. (in press a) 'A futuristic view of the REI: A response to Jenkins, Pious, and Jewell', *Exceptional Children*.

Thousand, J. and Villa, R. (in press b) 'Strategies for educating learners with severe disabilities within their local home schools and communities', *Focus on Exceptional Children*.

Thousand, J., Villa, R., Paolucci-Whitcomb, P. and Nevin, A. (in press) 'A rationale for collaborative consultation', in Stainback, S. and Stainback, W. (Eds) *Divergent Perspectives in Special Education*. Boston, MA: Allyn and Bacon.

Thousand, J., Fox, T., Reid, R., Godek, J., Williams, W. and Fox, W. (1986) *The Homecoming Model: Educating Students who Present Intensive Educational Challenges within Regular Educational Environments* (Monograph No. 7-1). Burlington, VT: University of Vermont, Center for Developmental Disabilities. (ERIC Document Reproduction Service No. ED 284 406).

Vicker, T. R. (1988) 'Learning from an outcomes-driven school district', *Educational Leadership*, **45**,5:52–5.

Villa, R. (1989) 'Model public school inservice programs: Do they exist?', *Teacher Education and Special Education*, **12**:173–6.

Villa, R. and Thousand, J. (1988) 'Enhancing success in heterogeneous classrooms and schools: The powers of partnership', *Teacher Education and Special Education*, **11**:144–54.

Villa, R. and Thousand, J. (1990) 'Administrative supports to promote inclusive schooling,' in Stainback, W. and Stainback, S. (Eds) *Support Networks for Inclusive Schooling: Integrated Interdependent Education* (pp. 201–18). Baltimore, MD: Paul H. Brookes Publishing.

Villa, R. and Thousand, J. (in press) 'Student collaboration: The essential curriculum for the 21st century', in Stainback, S. and Stainback, W. (Eds) *Adapting the Regular Class Curriculum: Enhancing Student Success in Inclusive Classrooms*. Boston, MA: Allyn and Bacon.

Wang, M. (1989) 'Accommodating student diversity through adaptive instruction', in Stainback, S. and Stainback, W. and Forest, M. (Eds) *Educating All Students in the Mainstream of Regular Education* (pp. 183–97). Baltimore, MD: Paul H. Brookes Publishing.

Wiggins, G. (1989) 'The futility of trying to teach everything of importance', *Educational Leadership*, **47**,3:44–59.

CHAPTER 10

School Renewal as Cultural Change

Bruce Joyce, Carlene Murphy, Beverly Showers and Joseph Murphy

During the past two years we and our colleagues have developed a
school improvement programme based on principles derived from
research on:

- the culture of the school and the process of innovation
- the ways teachers learn new teaching strategies
- the ways teachers transfer new skills into the classroom, and
- models of teaching and teaching skills.

Our design restructured the workplace – organising teachers into
collegial study groups, providing regular training on teaching, and
inducing faculties to set goals for school improvement and strive to
achieve them.

We can now begin to report the degree of change that occurred and
the lessons we learned in the process. Some of the effects have been
dramatic. For example, in one middle school only 30 per cent of the
students reached promotion standards the year before the programme
began. That number rose to 72 per cent during the first year of the
programme and 94 per cent during the second year. However, because
the effects have not been uniform, we have begun to learn what factors
explain the varying degrees of success. For example, achievement rose
more rapidly in social studies and science than in the language arts.
This finding prompted us to inquire into the reasons and to try to
reorient future work for more rapid across-the-board results.

This chapter appeared originally in *Educational Leadership*, 47, 3. It is reprinted with
permission of the Association for Supervision and Curriculum Development.
Copyright © 1989 by ASCD. All rights reserved.

In addition, while virtually all the teachers learned to use the teaching strategies to a mechanical level of competence, some reached much higher levels of skill, and these differences were reflected in the achievement of their students. On portions of the Iowa Tests of Basic Skills, the median students of teachers who reached the higher levels of skill fell between the 85th and 90th percentiles of the students whose teachers reached only mechanical levels of use. This finding led us to search for ways to improve training to ensure that *all* teachers reach the level of skill that will provide their students with expert instruction.

In this report of our work, we describe the shape of the project, its results in the three schools involved from the beginning, and the first steps in our search to refine and improve our procedures.

An organic approach

We adopted an organic approach to school renewal, restructuring the workplace and introducing training to bring the study of research-based teaching strategies into the regular workday of teachers.

We subscribe to Fullan's (1982) thesis that it is the bond of shared understandings and common language that sustains innovations and reduces the stress of change. Also, we designed our training around the theory–demonstration–practice–coaching paradigm that has been found to bring about high levels of skill and implementation (Joyce and Showers, 1987). We used a 'peer-coaching' process: the teachers were organised into study groups and the faculties into problem-solving groups. The content of our training has focused on teaching strategies that increase students' learning by effecting their aptitude to learn (Joyce and Weil, 1986).

We intended that the development of shared understandings would develop vertical and horizontal social cohesiveness, thereby reducing administrator–teacher division while increasing cooperation between classrooms and teams of teachers. Our training paradigm was intended (a) to enable teachers to develop high levels of skill in the content of the programme, and (b) to bring teachers and administrators together in study groups committed to implementing instructional changes and achieving goals for school improvement. Another effect of the study groups was to contribute to faculty cohesiveness and, thus, to reduce isolation.

The models of teaching we selected had a research history indicating that they could bring about fairly rapid improvement in student learning. The initial models included cooperative learning, mnemonics, concept attainment, inductive reasoning, and synectics. The teachers studied how to organise classrooms into study teams, how to use link words to assist memorisation, how to classify information into categories, learn concepts, build and test hypotheses, and use analogies to reconceptualise problems and generate solutions to them. All of these models addressed student learning problems characteristic of the schools involved in the initial phases of the project.

These planned changes in the workplace are easy to describe and, on the surface, easy to implement. Organising staff into study groups, providing regular training in models of teaching, and making concerted efforts to achieve specific goals are changes that hardly call for radical rhetoric. For many of the teachers and administrators, however, these changes required difficult adaptations in patterns of behaviour and ways of thinking. In negotiating these changes, we have learned much about problems that must be solved during the period of change.

Context and planning

We implemented our programme in Richmond County, Georgia, USA where 50 schools and 1,800 teachers serve 33,000 students. The school district serves the city of Augusta and the surrounding county, with a combined population of about 200,000 people. The principal industries of the region are chemical processing, pulp processing, textile manufacturing, metal-working, brick and clay manufacturing, and food processing. The major employers are Fort Gordon, the Medical College of Georgia, and the Savannah River Plant located in neighbouring South Carolina. Many of the students in districts are economically disadvantaged. In the three participating schools, over two-thirds of the students received subsidised meals.

Low student achievement had long frustrated many of the schools in the district. Despite Chapter 1 and special education programmes, a variety of programmes for at-risk students, regular revision and up-grading of curriculum and instructional materials, and 14 years of staff development, many students remained in academic difficulty. In the middle school mentioned above, half of the students were receiving attention from special programmes, yet 70 per cent of the student body was achieving below the levels set by the state and district for promotion on merit.

We began our planning in January 1987 with intensive seminars for cabinet level staff. By March, district administrators had decided on the general dimensions of the project. During the first two years, the consultants (Joyce and Showers) would provide most of the training, but a cadre of teachers and administrators would be trained to offer service to other teachers and administrators – to bring other schools into the project on a regular basis in the future.

The development of the district cadre was critical to the project and to the relationship between the district and the consultants; it symbolised the intent to make permanent changes in the workplace. It made concrete the need for district personnel to possess the expertise of the consultants and to take over the functions of the consultants.

Our efforts during the first year (phase one) concentrated on three schools and the initial preparation of the cadre. During the second year (phase two), we added four more schools and prepared the cadre to add other schools during the following year. During the third year, two more entire faculties will be added; and teams from ten other schools will begin training to become leaders of the process in their schools. The cadre provides follow-up training throughout the school year, for study teams cannot be left to maintain themselves. Regular training will become embedded in the workplace.

Schools competed to participate in the first three phases. We asked principals to pool their staffs to determine interest in summer training and a closely monitored implementation effort throughout the academic year. We asked principals to submit letters of application if faculty interest was high. The first year, 12 of the 13 schools invited to participate submitted applications. The superintendent's cabinet and the department directors selected one middle school and two elementary schools for phase one and one high school and three middle schools for phase two. Each faculty member in these schools had made a written commitment to:

- attend summer training
- practice the new teaching strategies with peers regularly throughout the summer and share plans for implementation during the fall
- employ the new strategies regularly throughout the 1987–88 academic year
- work with peer study groups during the academic year in planning lessons and visiting one another in classrooms
- participate in regular training activities during the school year
- make videotapes of their teaching on a regular basis
- participate in a similar programme in the summer of 1988 and during the 1988–89 school year.

The summer programme included two weeks of intensive training, followed by six weeks of practice and design of lessons for the fall, and the organisation of study groups. We asked all participants to practice the teaching strategies no less than 30 times apiece during September and October and to strive to incorporate them into their active repertoires by the end of October. The study groups were to meet weekly; between meetings, members were to visit one another in their classrooms to study the children's responses to the teaching strategies and plan to teach the students to respond more powerfully. Our intent was to involve the faculties immediately in collective action that would have rapid effects on student learning.

Initiation and initial response

The training, practice, organisation of study groups, development of short-run school goals, and initial classroom use of the teaching strategies occurred more or less as planned.

(i) Learning to work together

Participants planned lessons they would teach, then shared their plans – and their scepticism about whether the plans were practical. The models of teaching were new to almost all the teachers and their students; they required substantial amounts of new learning. Administrators scheduled time for study groups to meet; they also practiced the strategies in classrooms as did counsellors and supervisors. Some study groups were comfortable planning and sharing, while others were anxious. New teachers hired at the last minute had to be integrated into the process.

The success of the study groups depended on the leadership of teachers. Because leadership was uneven – some groups had several energetic leaders while others had none – we reorganised the groups several times to distribute initiative throughout the schools. At the end of the second year, the study groups still depended on the leadership of a relatively small number of teachers and the stimulation of the cadre to help them learn new teaching techniques.

We asked the study groups to concentrate on teaching their students how to respond to the models of teaching they were learning. They had been told that, although the students might respond immediately to the new cognitive and social tasks presented by those models, it would take about 20 practices before students would become really proficient. The initial goal for student skill would be attained when a trainer could enter the classroom, announce the model to be used in a lesson, and students could respond efficiently and comfortably. The goal for teachers was to bring students to that level of proficiency as rapidly as possible. The study groups gradually learned to track student progress and design ways of accelerating learning.

As we had hoped, there were immediate and positive effects on students. Especially visible was the reduction in disciplinary referrals. Many teachers reported that their students liked the new teaching strategies and that classroom management was easier. Some of the teachers became very excited about the increase in cooperative activity and the positive responses of their students. Some were anxious as they altered their familiar classroom routines; they worried because they could not predict how their students would respond until both they and their students had experience with the new procedures.

(ii) Academic year training

At six-week intervals during the first and second years we provided regular assistance to the faculties, derived from our observations of the staff. Through direct observation and the examination of video-tapes, we gathered information about implementation and devised demonstrations and practicums to address the needs we saw. With the supportive relationship among the staff development director, consultants, and the principals of the schools, problems could be identified and approached.

(iii) Progress

By stages, the new teaching strategies became familiar and the study groups learned to function together. By the beginning of the second year, the operation in the phase one schools was relatively smooth. Each faculty has a few members who still hoped the project would go away, but teacher leadership within the faculties was dominant in maintaining and extending the study groups and practice.

(iv) The cadre

During the winter and spring of 1988, we selected candidates for the cadre. The candidates, who were teachers and administrators from throughout the district, submitted applications and videotapes of classroom teaching to demonstrate their competence with the models of teaching they had practiced.

Cadre training included assisting with the introductory workshops for the phase two schools. By the end of July, they had designed courses and workshops to be offered at the district level during the 1988–89 school year. They also provided assistance to phase one and two study teams, prepared training materials, developed video-taped demonstrations of teaching, and studied research on training and teaching.

Schoolwide objectives for improving the social climate of the schools were established only with difficulty, although two schools have made great progress. In both cases the schools had relied heavily on quasi-legal methods of control, chiefly suspensions. In one elementary school, there were nearly 200 incidents of suspension per year (in a student population of about 550). When disciplinary referrals began to drop, apparently as a result of students' increased involvement in learning, the building administrators seized the opportunity to induce the staff to reflect on the dynamics of management and the relationship between instruction and classroom control. Consequently, the staff worked hard to use instruction as the major mechanism of control and, during the second year of the project, only six students were suspended. The school had moved from massive reliance on suspension to minimal use, in extreme cases only. Nearly 1,000 days of lost instructional time were thus recovered, and management became a much less obtrusive feature of the school. The middle school had a similar problem and, although it still uses an in-house suspension programme, out-of-school suspensions have dropped from about 150 per semester (again in a population of about 550 students) to about 35.

The faculties are still individualistic in many ways but show their increasing willingness to attack common problems. The services of process-oriented consultants would perhaps be timely, to enable the faculties to capitalise more fully on the collegial settings.

The extent of change in the workplace has affected the degree of implementation by individuals. The concerted implementations that occurred when building administrators generated 'whole-school' goals became enthusiastic collaborations as faculties generated mnemonics to be employed throughout the school, or gave concentrated energy to 'metrics', or otherwise worked together. Concerted efforts helped teachers learn that they can be effective as a faculty. However, unified efforts continue to be a function of the active leadership of the building administrators and lead teachers. Only by being *very* active can they maintain collective activity.

Implementation of the teaching models

The administrators observed their teachers on a regular basis and collected records of their use of the teaching strategies. Predictably, use of the models of teaching varied widely, from tentative and minimal use to regular and appropriate use. Administrators reported extensive use by about three-fourths of the faculty members, with moderate use by most of the others. From each school six teachers were selected randomly and observed and interviewed regularly throughout the year to determine quality of use (see Showers, 1989). The 18 teachers were also videotaped near the end of the school year, and we analysed those tapes to determine the level of skill they had achieved.

The training and use of the study group format were designed to ensure that 75–90 per cent of the teachers would reach a mechanical level of use of at least two of the teaching strategies by the end of the first year. This goal was achieved during the first year. About one-third of the teachers developed a high level of skill in using three or four models of teaching. Another third learned to use at least two of them with a satisfactory level of competence. About half of the remainder were able to use one or more of them to a mechanical but not fluid level.

During the second year, the phase one teachers have continued to develop and consolidate skills. They are much more comfortable with the addition of new models but continue to struggle with new skills until they have practiced them about 20 times. The study groups and the use of peer coaching continue to be important as new models are introduced. More than 50 videotapes have been made to demonstrate aspects of the teaching strategies where the teachers have had difficulty. These, together with dozens of 'live' demonstrations, have helped greatly, but the road to executive control is a rocky one for many of the teachers. Because the reading and language curriculums of the district are tightly prescribed, most 'legitimate' use of the models of teaching has been in the social studies, mathematics, and, in the middle school, the sciences. In these curriculum areas the opportunity for use has been greatest; therefore, we understand the impact on student achievement that we have found there.

Student learning

Our study of student learning has had two objectives:

(1) to learn whether differences in teacher skill in using the new strategies is associated with student learning; and
(2) to learn whether our effort narrowed the gap between students from poor families and their wealthier counterparts.

The clearest test of the first question was in the elementary schools where, in self-contained classrooms, individual teachers have instructional responsibility for curriculum areas other than reading. To determine whether any differences in achievement were a function of developed ability to learn, we used reading level as an indicator of general competence. We compared the classes of the teachers who had reached executive control with those of the teachers who performed at the mechanical level, with respect to reading level. We found them to be about equal in both mean and range.

The social studies tests from the Iowa Tests of Basic Skills battery were administered to the 5th grade students at the end of the second year. The achievement of the classes whose teachers had reached executive control was compared with the classes whose teachers used them mechanically (and, thus, generally less than they could be used appropriately).

When the two distributions are compared, the median student in the 'executive control' classes is between the 85th and 90th percentiles of the 'mechanical use' classes. Compared to national norms, the median student of the 'executive control' classes was at the 76th percentile, compared to the 44th percentile for the 'mechanical use' classes. At the time the tests were given, the median grade-equivalent score for the national sample was 5.8. The median grade-equivalent scores for the 'executive control' classes range from 6.5 to 7.9, or from 0.7 to 2.1 above the national median. For the 'mechanical use' classes, the range was from 5.0 to 6.1. The distributions of the extreme classes barely overlap. Figure 10.1 depicts the comparison between the 'executive control' and 'mechanical use' classes in grade-equivalent terms.

The message is clear. Skillful implementation of these research-based teaching strategies can have a substantial impact on student achievement. However, to reach their full potential, these models must be used with considerable skill and frequency. The 'mechanical use' classes are not achieving badly in normative terms – in fact they are above average for schools equivalent in socioeconomic status – but

190

Figure 10.1 Comparison of 'executive control' and 'mechanical use'; 5th grade classes in the social studies

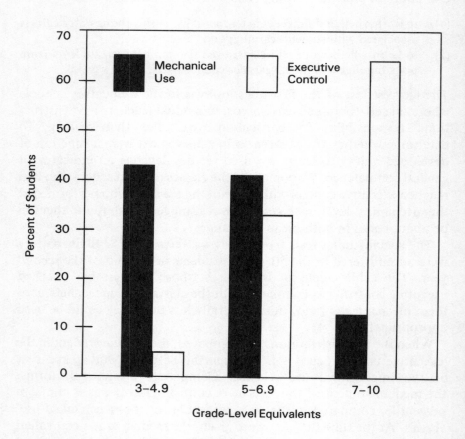

their students could have learned much more. Thus, we need to find ways of increasing the impact of training. We have many clues about how to achieve this, particularly for providing more explicit training for those teachers who require it; some of our previous research on the relationship between conceptual level of teachers and need for structure in training will be useful here (Joyce *et al.*, 1981).

The best answer to our second question – whether we narrowed the achievement gap between the children of the poor and their economically advantaged counterparts – lay in the study of the middle school. The promotion rate for the school rose from 30 per cent before the project began to 70 per cent at the end of the first year and 94 per cent at the end of the second year, using the same standards for promotion. The magnitude of the increase certainly indicates that student learning is on the rise.

Because the school district administrative staff and, reportedly, members of the board of education place more credence in 'standard tests' than on local tests and teacher judgement of achievement, the district's staff development unit administered the ITBS battery in science, social studies, mathematics, and one language test at the end of the second year to attempt to confirm the standards used for promotion in normative terms. This testing also provided us with the opportunity to explore whether the 8th grade students, who had been exposed to the programme for two years, had gained on their wealthier counterparts.

The analysis, which compared 6th and 8th grade students, dealt with our question about whether the students had nonetheless continued to fall behind 'middle class' students. It confirms our impression that the majority of the students are now making 'normal' progress.

The social studies scores of the 6th grade students indicate that, through the first six years of their schooling, the average student had been achieving the equivalent of about seven months of growth for each year in school (10 months of growth being, by definition, the average for the national sample). The mean score on the social studies test for the 6th grade was 1.5 grade equivalents below the national mean (5.3 compared with 6.8 for the national sample). If the students continued at that rate of growth, we would expect that in the 8th grade the mean would be 6.7. However, the 8th grade mean was 7.3 for social studies, still below the national average but six months higher than their past rate of growth had been (see Figure 10.2).

Their probable rate of growth was about average for the national sample. The mean grade equivalent was 7.5 for science and 7.7 for mathematics. In the 6th grade, only five 6th grade students scored as high as 7.0. By contrast, 13 8th grade students scored 10.0 or higher, indicating that the school had become an environment that would support above-average achievement.

Given the educational history of the school, it is quite an accomplishment for it to become a place where average achievement is now normal. Much remains to be done, of course, especially to increase the executive level use of the teaching models and to drive toward equality in overall achievement. However, if the current levels of achievement can be sustained, most of the these students will not be wiped out in the economic marketplace, as appeared to be their destiny before the programme was initiated. Moreover, if the students can

Figure 10.2 Predicted and actual achievement in middle school social studies

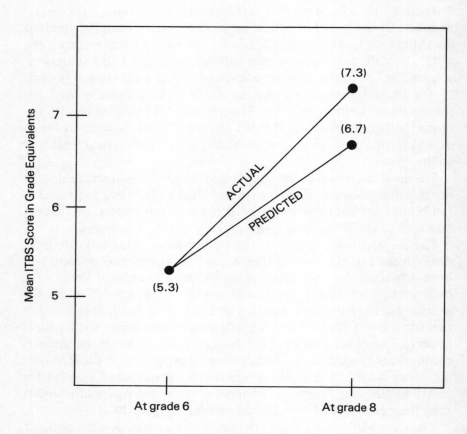

increase their learning rates as much as they appear to have done, there is no good reason why they cannot be helped to increase them still further.

From anxiety to pleasure

This project relies on staff development to reorganise the workplace and help teachers learn teaching strategies. Hence, it is different from a curriculum or technological innovation where a new programme of study or learning device is 'put into place' and its effects are studied. In our project, as appropriate implementation is achieved, effects are expected to be gradual but eventually large. The district has been able to bring about large changes in the workplace, and the cadre development has been splendid. The phase one teachers have practiced unfamiliar strategies until many of the teachers have reached a good level of skill with them. The study groups are functioning, and the school faculties as a whole are making concerted efforts to advance student achievement in specific areas. The students are learning more, and social control is more a function of instruction than of coercion.

The phase two schools are in about the same developmental stage as were the phase one schools a year ago, with uneven implementation and a great deal of scepticism on the part of many teachers. The pessimistic attitudes of many teachers about the possibility of improving student learning are not intractable, but success by peers has little apparent effect on it. The practice of collective action does have effect, albeit gradual, provided the workplace is changed to make cooperative behaviour the norm.

We do not believe that success in improving student learning will sustain the collaborative activity. Success makes it easier to reiterate the purpose for changing the workplace, but the schools will surely return to their previous states fairly rapidly unless they are well tended. Also, success in some schools does not inspire most teachers in other schools. The most active resistors fight the cadre as actively as they fight consultants from outside the district – and the cadre have less experience in dealing with resistance.

However, the changed organism offers many satisfactions – and the concerted schoolwide efforts are rewarding to those teachers who experience the power of working together and the real and immediate effects on the students. Better-planned lessons are more satisfying to teach, and borrowing the ideas and materials of others becomes a pleasurable source of success.

The collegial setting is least satisfying to the least-prepared teachers, whose shaky hold on subject matter and uninspired teaching are unmasked in the collegial environment. This is necessary but sad; and it takes a long time to remedy, for the least competent teachers learn both subject matter and teaching practices more slowly than do the others. It is natural that they would want to hide in their classrooms. Nevertheless, the charisma of the most inspired teachers should dominate the environment. Where it does, the learning climate can change quite rapidly – far more so than conventional wisdom would predict.

In the few schools we have been discussing, hundreds of students are daily experiencing success and can expect promotion rather than failure and, just as important, know they have earned that promotion.

194

Social control is becoming an effect of instruction rather than 'management'. Teachers are learning from one another and are welcoming the fruits of research into their repertoires. It is a pleasure to watch their transition from anxiety to pleasure in the company of their colleagues.

References

Black, J. (1989) 'Building the school as a center of inquiry: A whole-school approach built around models of teaching'. Doctoral project, Nova University, Fort Lauderdale, Florida.

Fullan, M. (1982) *The Meaning of Educational Change*. New York: Teachers College Press.

Joyce, B. and Showers, B. (1987) *Student Achievement Through Staff Development*. White Plains, NY: Longman.

Joyce, B., Peck, L. and Brown, C. (1981) (Eds) *Flexibility in Teaching*. White Plains, NY: Longman.

Joyce, B. and Weil, M. (1986) *Models of Teaching*. Englewood Cliffs, NJ: Prentice-Hall.

Lortie, D. (1975) *Schoolteacher*. Chicago: University of Chicago Press.

Showers, B. (1989) 'Research-based training and teaching strategies and their effects on the workplace and instruction'. Paper delivered at the annual meeting of the American Educational Research Association, San Francisco.

Sudderth, C. (1989) 'The social battleground of school improvement'. Paper delivered at the annual meeting of the American Educational Research Association, San Francisco.

CHAPTER 11

Reducing the Marginalisation of Pupils with Severe Learning Difficulties through Curricular Initiatives

Judy Sebba and Ann Fergusson

Introduction

This chapter briefly considers the traditional instructional model for working with pupils with severe learning difficulties and some of the more recent challenges to this in the light of research on effective schools. The applicability of the literature on effective staff development is then examined and parallels drawn between 'pupil as learner' and 'teacher as learner'. Current initiatives involved in the introduction of a National Curriculum in England, Wales and Northern Ireland provide a context in which to develop effective teaching and staff development in order to provide genuine entitlement to the curriculum for every pupil. Relevant aspects of effective teaching and staff development are identified and illustrated through the work of the National Curriculum Development Team (Severe Learning Difficulties) in schools in England. This chapter draws on work by other authors in this volume, in particular, that of Bennett (Chapter 7) and Joyce *et al.* (Chapter 10).

Three major premises underline the work described. First, that as Stainback and Stainback (1984) have suggested, effective instructional methods, or what might be termed the principles of effective practices, will benefit all pupils, including and especially those with special educational needs. Second, that the quality of the learning environment is, as Wang *et al.* (1986) suggest, a more appropriate focus for our energies than attributing failure to the characteristics of pupils. Hence, effective practices and effective schools will by definition *reduce* the impact of learning difficulties, even severe learning difficulties, and enable these pupils to be reconceptualised as having individual needs, as do each of their classmates.

Third, that staff development needs to link demonstration, practice and feedback in order to be effective, as suggested by Joyce *et al*. in Chapter 10, this volume. Hence, staff development should be school-focused with built in opportunities for practice and feedback, to be effective in terms of leading to change. Providing staff development in the school may be considered most likely to lead to transfer of skills since learning is taking place in context.

The National Curriculum Development Team (Severe Learning Difficulties)

The examples will be drawn from the work of the National Curriculum Development Team (Severe Learning Difficulties) based at the Cambridge Institute of Education, England, which is aimed at reducing the special needs of pupils by promoting effective practices through the framework of the National Curriculum. The main aim of the team's work is to provide access for pupils with severe learning difficulties to the curriculum to which all pupils are entitled, the National Curriculum. This might enable the special educational needs of these pupils to be seen as individual needs within a National Curriculum.

The model of staff development adopted by this team mirrors that described by Joyce *et al*. in Chapter 10, this volume, as likely to be most effective, involving school staff in a coaching process with team members. From the team of ten teachers, three or four meet with the staff of a school that has requested the team's involvement. Discussion between team and staff leads to identification of one or two issues from the action plan of the school's development plan for the forthcoming year. This sub-team then spends one day observing in the school prior to a two week 'block' period during which they work alongside staff planning sessions together, considering ways of broadening curriculum coverage within current activities, varying teaching strategies to increase access to the curriculum for all pupils, etc. In addition, spontaneous discussions can arise with some or all the staff which are pursued with the team during staff meeting times.

Following the block, the team meet with staff to invite some initial reactions to their involvement in the school. A draft report of the block is then prepared by the team and discussed with staff until agreement on the content is reached. The final report is produced for the school to use as a working document and might include, for example, copies of activity plans written by the teacher and the team member collaboratively during the block. On the school's request, a copy is sent to the special needs advisor for the local authority. The school may then circulate additional copies to anyone they wish, for example, a subject specialist advisor, in order to encouarge mobilisation of resources, identification of future staff development needs or other progress.

An attempt is made by the team to collect information which might provide evidence of longer-term effectiveness in terms of any changes begun or extended in the school during the block. This is done by evaluation sheets completed by staff, discussion with staff and collection of 'artefacts' indicating work carried out after the block. From one school, for example, we have collected a wide range of completed self-recording sheets indicating that our limited explorations with staff during the block have led to much more extensive and wider use of this method. One local authority (equivalent of school districts) is collecting its own evaluative material on the work done by the team.

Traditional instructional models of working with pupils with learning difficulties

Teaching strategies

Traditionally, behavioural approaches to teaching have been used much more widely with pupils in special schools than more open-ended 'topic' type approaches commonly used with many pupils in mainstream primary or elementary schools. This reflects the assumption that for topic approaches to be successful, pupils will need to initiate enquiry, exploration and first-hand experience. These are the identified elements of 'discovery learning' methods, but are rarely the skills attributed to pupils in special schools, particularly those with severe learning difficulties. Hence, behavioural methods were found to offer effective teaching strategies for pupils who, left to discover, appeared to discover nothing.

Structured behavioural approaches demanded criterion-referenced assessments since traditional psychometric tests had been largely discredited, particularly in their use with pupils with special educational needs. Furthermore, precise and detailed assessment enabled progress to be monitored even when this progress was slow. Relatively small class sizes and better staffing levels were introduced in special schools in recognition of the need for greater emphasis on individual work. The growth in objectives-based curricula was accompanied by the appearance of detailed, lengthy criterion-referenced checklists.

Breadth and balance in the curriculum

The curriculum in some special schools has tended to become narrower, focusing more on the priorities of self-help, communication and physical skills. This limited breadth has been highlighted in recent surveys by Her Majesty's Inspectorate in England and Wales (DES, 1989a, 1989b, 1990a). Lack of coverage in science and technology in particular was noted. The National Curriculum Team (Severe Learning Difficulties) has noted lack of attention to geography, history and technology, all foundation subjects of the National Curriculum in England and Wales and therefore an entitlement for every pupil.

In addition, this team has noted that within some subject areas the curriculum has narrowed in many special schools. For example, science work has focused on multi-sensory activities, technology on work with microcomputers and maths mainly on number work. In addition, pupils spend considerably more time listening to the teacher than communicating themselves, creating imbalance within the English curriculum.

The assumption cannot be made that a broader curriculum would necessarily be offered to these pupils were they to be mainstreamed into ordinary schools. Bennett notes (in Chapter 7, this volume) that for some children who transferred from special schools to ordinary ones, the curriculum provided after transfer was very narrow, being dominated by maths, English and practical activities (e.g., art, PE, etc.). Problems were also noted due to lack of curriculum continuity between the schools involved in the transfer.

School effectiveness and the challenge to traditional instructional models

Special education has been undergoing a considerable period of change during the 1980s. Behavioural approaches have been challenged and criticised (see for example, Bray *et al.*, 1988; Wood and Shears, 1986) with certain features of these approaches being particularly questioned. Pupils were taught out of context – for example, having their art session interrupted by the teacher demanding that they remove their shoes, in order to comply with the perceived priorities of a current educational programme in the self-help area of the curriculum. Teaching became too rigid, spontaneous initiations by the pupil being rejected in favour of completing the planned sessions. Too much emphasis was placed on one-to-one sessions with group work and collaborative learning opportunities undervalued or not acknowledged.

Pupils became dependent on the teacher, the structure, predict-ability of the routine and unable to voice an opinion or take a decision. They were ill-prepared for any further education opportunities that might be offered when they left school, within which the advocacy movement had led to greater negotiation of learning objectives, participation in recording their own achievements and student committees. Research on school effectiveness (e.g. Mortimore *et al.*, 1988) indicated that approaches which maximise communication between teacher and pupil rather than those which are heavily teacher-directed are associated with effective schools.

Moreover, Mortimore *et al.* had noted intellectually challenging teaching to be a factor in schools considered to be effective. Bennett (Chapter 7, this volume) has highlighted the evidence suggesting that tasks are frequently mismatched to the pupil and that the task performed is often not that which the teacher intended. Bennett's work has been predominantly carried out in primary/elementary schools although more recent studies included special schools. This led to the comment that the work in these schools was thought by children and parents to be too easy and boring.

The growth of alternative approaches

In this climate, it is not surprising that behavioural approaches to assessment and teaching have been rejected by some staff in special schools and, to some extent, by teachers with designated responsibility for special educational needs in ordinary schools. In addition, staff in special schools are having to adjust to increasing proportions of pupils with more severe and multiple difficulties (DES, 1990a). Approaches seen as offering an alternative instructional model to the behavioural ones, in particular the multi-sensory approach described by Longhorn (1988) and the 'interactive' approaches typified through the work of Nind and Hewett (Nind and Hewett, 1988; Smith, 1987) have gained popularity. These approaches re-emphasise the need to follow the pupil's lead and take every opportunity to develop skills without imposing set routines. To some extent they draw on features of good practice from traditional primary work, emphasising interactive learning, creativity and a more opportunistic approach to learning (in the sense that spontaneous, unplanned events can be pursued).

Research on the effectiveness of staff development

There is a widely held assumption that staff development will improve practice. However, it is evident from the extensive reviews of staff training (e.g. Fullan, 1982; Hopkins, 1989; Joyce *et al.*, Chapter 10, this volume; Showers *et al.*, 1987) that the relationship between training and institutional change is complex and the evidence suggests most training is of limited long-term effect. A variety of factors influence this relationship including characteristics of the individuals who participate in training, characteristics of the institutions in which they work and, perhaps most importantly, models of training offered. In addition, since most staff training and development is not evaluated, the information on its effects is limited.

Models of training

An important parallel can be drawn here between 'teacher as learner' and 'pupil as learner'. For many years the emphasis in explanations of why people with learning difficulties sometimes failed to learn was on the perceived characteristics of the individual, often using the label of a syndrome. More recently, explanations have focused to a greater extent, although importantly not exclusively, on the possible inappropriateness of the teaching approach. Staff development has been through a similar process. Initially, the explanation given for why staff failed to change was because they lacked motivation, did not understand the techniques, were too rigid, etc. Currently, staff trainers are much more critical of the approach to training that is adopted.

The gap between research and practice is as wide in this field as anywhere. The research evidence has been accumulating for years about the need to enter staff development with negotiated objectives between trainer and participants (e.g. Sebba and Robson, 1987). As Fullan (1982) reminded us, sustained change in curriculum and instruction depends heavily on a shared understanding about the nature of the innovation and what it can accomplish. Hence, staff training and development must seek to establish shared objectives from the outset and yet most initiatives which take place fail to address this fundamental issue.

From the 200 studies which Showers *et al.* (1987) analysed, it appeared that where or when training takes place or who the trainer is, are much less important than the training design. Many researchers and staff developers have been suggesting for years that staff development activities must be as close to the 'real life' work situations as possible. Showers *et al.* make it clear that the theory-demonstration-practice-feedback combination is vital to ensuring transfer of skills into the work situation. Joyce and Showers (1988) report that the magnitude of the effect is considerably enhanced when training involves two people observing one another's practice of the skills. Whether the trainer does the 'coaching' or it is done by a peer, it leads to the same level of effectiveness. More surprisingly, it has been found that peer coaching involving observation only, without any opportunity for discussion, is just as effective.

Staff development involving peer or trainer coaching is seen as creating the conditions under which sufficient levels of knowledge and skill are developed to sustain and support practice until transfer of skills has taken place. At this point it is assumed that the staff have cognitively assimilated the practice sufficiently for it to be re-selected and used at any time, approximately and integratively. However, surveys of staff development practice reported by Showers *et al.* (1987) suggest that only a small proportion of programmes offered combine the necessary components to sustain practice to the point of transfer.

The parallels with pupils' learning are clear. The pupil is noted by Bennett, Chapter 10, this volume, to learn most effectively when in heterogeneous groups of pupils on tasks set up to involve collaborative learning. Thus, opportunities for peer coaching are created which are more likely to result in learning. It appears that the strategies selected by teachers or trainers need to focus on how peer coaching can be facilitated. Examples of this process are described below.

Curricular initiatives associated with effective teaching and staff development that can be developed to reduce marginalisation of some pupils

There are many initiatives associated with effective teaching and staff development that could contribute to the process of reducing marginalisation of pupils with severe learning difficulties. Eight areas in which curriculum development work can contribute to this process have been selected here: entitlement, curricular audit, breadth and balance, integrated schemes of work, cooperative group work, planning and record-keeping, differentiation, and models of staff development. Each of these is now briefly considered.

Entitlement

The notion of a national curriculum which is for all pupils theoretically reduces the marginalisation of pupils with special educational needs. Teachers are required to identify exactly where every individual pupil is, in every subject area. In this sense, it could assist in the process of redefining special educational needs as individual needs. Furthermore, it potentially broadens the curriculum basis for pupils in schools where the curriculum has narrowed. Teachers have a common language and continuity should be easier. The problems identified by Bennett in relation to school transfer are likely to be reduced.

The subject specialisms needed by teachers in special schools and the skills in systematic, rigorous assessment and recording needed by those in mainstream schools may provide the basis for more collaboration and cooperation between teachers across what were traditionally separate areas of education. The scope for teachers coaching teachers is apparent. Hence, increasing similarities may develop in both curricular content and possibly instructional approaches across mainstream and special schools as a result of the national changes. Consistency among teachers within a school was noted by Mortimore *et al*. (1988) to be associated with school effectiveness but previously has not always been in evidence within special schools.

An assumption in this positive standpoint is that the content of a national curriculum is appropriate or sufficiently flexible to meet the needs of the pupils, even if they have profound and multiple learning difficulties. On the basis of the current documentation on the National Curriculum in England and Wales this is questionable, but progress implies extending the curriculum to meet the needs of all pupils not excluding them from it. It is only through this process that their marginalisation can be reduced.

Curricular audit

As noted above, Bennett in Chapter 7, this volume, draws the distinction between the tasks that the teacher intended and those that the children perform. Hence, the *perceived* curriculum can be contrasted with the *received* curriculum. The development team has been particularly interested in exploring ways of honestly evaluating what a sample of children are actually receiving, as opposed to what appears on the timetable or in the teaching plan.

This has been done by selecting a small number of pupils or one activity involving a small group and carrying out a detailed observation of the activity, noting down exactly what happened, what the teacher did and any responses by the pupil. The activities observed are then referenced to the programmes of study legally specified in the National Curriculum. We called this process 'shadowing' and it is similar to that referred to as 'pupil pursuit'. This type of information can be used by the class teacher to identify gaps or imbalances in curriculum coverage and match or mismatch between the intention and the practice. In addition, shadowing could provide a basis for two teachers working together to observe one another and discuss their work, a process similar to that described by Showers (1985) as peer coaching.

Another method of auditing we have initiated in some schools at their request is to provide record sheets for a child over a week for the teacher to complete. These record broadly which subject areas that child has covered in the perceptions of that teacher. It is important to note that no attempt has been made by the team to indicate which activities should be attributed to which subject areas. This approach cannot and should not be used as an external monitoring device, but to provide the basis for staff to self-review and discuss their shared definitions of subject labels as well as possible gaps or imbalances of coverage. It is, however, interesting to note that even these data collected on one child by the teacher, often reflect the same imbalances as identified in the national surveys by Her Majesty's Inspectorate, i.e., lack of science, technology, history and geography, etc.

The guidelines sent to every school in England and Wales for the school development planning process (DES, 1989c) specifies that an annual audit of the curriculum be undertaken. The need to collect information through shadowing or more global recording for classroom based planning, links to the overall needs of the school in the review and development process. Furthermore, the statutory requirement to be able to report, at the request of parents, specific levels of attainment in any National Curriculum subject implies the need for this type of detailed record.

Broadening and balancing the curriculum

The process of auditing described above has been undertaken in many schools in England and Wales recently and those with which the team have been working have requested assistance with specific subject areas as a direct result of these audits. The team has been working on a broadening of mathematical skills, activities designed to promote technology and introduce geographical or historical skills. In addition, many cross-curricular activities have been extended to give more scope and allow for greater differentiation in order to provide access for more pupils. Excellent examples of maths, science and English work have been published by the team based in Manchester, England (Aherne *et al.*, 1990a and b; Fagg *et al.*, 1990a and b) and further work is described by them and others in Ashdown, Bovair and Carpenter (1991).

Three major points emerge from this work. First, most teachers working with pupils with severe learning difficulties do not have a subject specialism in one of the National Curriculum areas. Hence, they may be undertaking activities that do in fact cover specific subject areas but their awareness of this is limited. If they can increase their awareness through work with the team, consideration of material from other sources, seeking support from their local advisory staff and working collaboratively with colleagues in mainstream schools, a broadening of coverage is likely to take place. This will reduce the difference between the curriculum received by pupils in special schools and those in mainstream, leading us nearer the notion of individual rather than special needs.

Second, subject areas traditionally regarded as irrelevant to the needs of pupils with severe learning difficulties are being recognised to have some value. For example, history, for which no final statutory orders yet exist but for which the Minister has just produced his final report for consultation (DES, 1990b), is often regarded as having nothing to offer pupils with severe learning difficulties. This may partly reflect our image, based on our own experiences, of the subject as being limited to the chronological dates of the accession of kings and queens.

A central historical skill that the authors certainly do not recall from their own schooling, is that of using evidence. In one class in which the team was recently working, the teacher produced a bag which she claimed to have found in the corridor. The pupils had to take items out of the bag and deduce from this evidence whose it was. The group considered whether it belonged to a man or woman, attempted to recognise and label a calculator and all showed great interest in pulling things out of the bag. Finally, one pupil identified a school dinner sheet which indicated it belonged to 'Sarah', the school secretary. They took the bag to her to verify that was indeed hers. A follow up activity the next day involved selecting an everyday item from a large collection on the table and deciding who uses it in their work in the school. Photographs of the school cook, secretary and caretaker were each pinned to large sheets of paper and the pupil indicated to which of the three people each item belonged. This activity was noted to be easier for the group than the previous one, perhaps because the handbag had acted to remove the link one step further between object and item.

Third, the coverage of subject areas within cross-curricular work is not always easily identifiable. In order to be more explicit about the areas of the curriculum covered, the team introduced, or further developed in some schools, planning sheets for each activity. The role of these in the overall process is described below.

Developing 'Integrated Schemes of Work

The dilemma facing the special needs community about how to deal with the scepticism in relation to behavioural approaches, yet maintain some form of curricular structure, led the team, and our colleague Richard Byers (1990) in particular, to develop the approach we have termed 'Integrated Schemes of Work'. What appeared to be required was an attempt to retrieve the most appropriate elements of behavioural approaches and synthesise these with the best aspects of traditional primary school 'topic' work. This may provide a more helpful and positive way to meet the needs of the National Curriculum while meeting the needs of every individual pupil.

Integrated schemes of work start, like so many planned topics, with a topic web in which an area is identified e.g. 'Colour'. Staff brainstorm every activity they can think of that might fit into this theme. In a traditional primary or elementary school context the ideas may come mainly from the pupils. In a school for pupils with severe learning difficulties they are more likely to be teacher-generated. Traditionally, teaching has then gone ahead based on the activities identified and any straying from the initial plan is often regarded as spontaneous and useful. This raises difficulties in relation to manageable record-keeping.

The team's approach has been to suggest that themes are selected which are specific enough to cover in a defined period of time, e.g. two

Figure 11.1 An example of a planning and recording sheet based on an activity from Howe, L. (1990)

ACTIVITY REFERENCE: Science (from Howe Primary Pack)	CLASS: 4M	GROUP: Paul, Steven, Rebecca, Michelle	TERM & YEAR: Autumn 1990

ACTIVITY PLAN: Investigation of what material lets water through. Design, make and evaluate something to drink out of

TEACHING STRATEGIES	CURRICULUM REFERENCES	MORE IDEAS
Part 1 1. Discussion of what happens when it rains What do we wear? How do we keep dry? 2. Purpose of activity explained. Children worked in pairs. For each item, each pupil was asked to 'predict' whether they thought it would let water through. 3. One pupil puts a piece of material on the large sheet of paper and spoons a few drops of coloured water on to it. After a minute, pupil lifts material. Both pupils to observe and comment as to whether the water went through and 'coloured' the paper. Tested plastic, tissue, foil, cord, paper, J-cloth, scourer and PVC. 4. When pair have decided whether the item let the water through, they stick the item in the appropriate column (let it through/does not let it through) on chart. *Part 2* 5. 'Here's the jug of squash but the cups have all gone missing. Can you make something to drink out of?' Jigsawed material: Steven-junk; Paul-scissors; Michelle-sellotape; Rebecca-glue. 6. When child has made something, get them to test whether it will hold the squash and whether they can drink from it. 7. When pupil satisfied with results, sticks container on chart.	*Science* – promote ideas and seek solutions – promote at first hand the exploration of objects and events – sorting, grouping and describing of objects and events – development of simple measuring (how much water?) – develop understanding of purposes of recording results – encourage interpretation of results – develop reporting skills. *Technology* – explore and use a variety of materials to design and make things – recognise that materials are processed in order to change or control their properties – recognise that many materials are available and have different characteristics which make them appropriate for different tasks – join materials and components in simple ways – use imagination and their own experiences to generate and explore ideas – evaluate their finished work against the original intention – make simple objects for a purpose. *Maths* – making predictions based on experience – comparing and ordering objects without measuring – using common words to describe a position – recording with objects – selecting criteria for sorting a set of objects and applying them consistently – sorting and classifying 2-D and 3-D shapes *English* – development of powers of concentration, grasp of turn-taking – discussion of their work with other pupils and the teacher – collaborative planning of activities in a way which requires pupils to speak and listen – giving and receiving simple explanations, information and instructions; asking and answering questions – appreciate that pictures and other visual media can convey meaning. *Geography* – investigate the effects which weather has on them.	Record pupil's predictions of which items will let the water through and compare with results. Test out a range of 'containers', eg, plastic bag, paper bag, egg cup, balloon, etc. to see if they hold water. Encourage pupils to suggest other items that could be tested. Record on chart. Present spilled water on table/floor as a problem. Get pupils to test what material will mop up most water. Ensure same amount spilled each time. Test blotting paper, duster, sponge, etc. Make 'waterproof' pictures on paper plates to hange from ceiling (candles or wax crayons with watery paint). When it rains, try coats of different materials to see which will keep you dry.

weeks, half a term, etc. The brainstorming is done with a planning sheet for each subject area in front of them, on which the activities can be noted against the legally specified programmes of study. Hence, at the planning stage, there is a real attempt to identify which areas of each subject and other important skills are likely to get coverage. A record sheet for planning and recording group work and individual activities related to the theme can then be used for each session. Objectives for individual pupils within group work can thereby be planned, woven into the group activity and recorded. An example of one planning and recording sheet currently used by the team is given in Figure 11.1.

We have noted that this approach can assist teachers to plan and record both individual objectives and National Curriculum programmes of study for one activity for a group of six to eight children (typical group size for a school for severe learning difficulties). Information would need to be transferred to additional sheets for recording of the specific attainments. This seems to meet some of the criticisms of traditional 'topic' work by being more rigorous, systematic and recording essential information. However, we have also used this framework to encourage teachers, who previously have based their work mainly on behavioural, individualised sessions, to explore teaching a more coherent overall programme within which activities are related. This is seen as preferable to teaching a series of individualised, unrelated objectives. In addition, the need to teach relevant skills in context is emphasised.

Cooperative group work

This approach is being used to promote more group activities without losing rigour, to establish a better balance between group and individual sessions and to encourage more collaboration and co-operation between pupils however limited their skills may be to do this. The principles of 'Jigsawing' described by Johnson and Johnson (1986) in which tasks are set up to structure positive interdependence among group members, are being explored with groups of pupils in which all or some are seen as having severe learning difficulties. In the activity described in Figure 11.1, each pupil was given different material (e.g. sellotape, scissors, etc.) all of which were likely to be needed to complete the task. Hence, positive interdependence was being fostered.

Bennett (Chapter 7, this volume) concludes that their studies consistently demonstrate the value of cooperative grouping of pupils in terms of improving pupil involvement and pupil outcomes. However, homogeneous groupings are found to have negative effects. The quality of group interaction is much improved in heterogeneous groupings in which cooperation is enhanced. Facilitating cooperative learning in heterogeneous groups is therefore likely to lead to a reduction in marginalisation for pupils with learning difficulties. However, there is clearly a need for some pupils in special schools to be taught the basic skills required to function in a group in order that they can benefit from these strategies.

Planning and record-keeping

In describing the Integrated Schemes of Work some examples of planning and recording have been given. This is the area in which the team's help is most frequently requested. The National Curriculum is seen by most schools as making excessive demands on record-keeping. In special schools in which the emphasis is on recording individual programmes, annual review reports to parents and subsequent revision to children's statements of special educational needs (legally required if there are any resource implications) extensive record-keeping systems are relatively well established. This bodes well in terms of the finding from the Mortimore *et al.* study (1988) that written records of pupils' progress was associated with effectiveness. In many cases, the schools are looking for ways of streamlining their record-keeping without losing valuable information.

The team has tried the strategies described above for recording group sessions. Greater use of pupil self-assessment and recording has also been introduced in the schools in which we have worked so far. Many National Curriculum documents encourage and indeed specify through the programmes of study that pupils should be encouraged to describe and record their own work. Clearly, for pupils with limited communication skills, special schools will need imaginative ways of tackling this. The teacher can add his or her comments below. An example is included here in Figure 11.2. This is a dual recording sheet inviting pupils to mark the activities completed which are represented by Makaton-like symbols. In addition, a few examples of software which enables teacher recording and in some instances self-recording of the National Curriculum Attainment Targets are being developed and trialled.

Figure 11.2 An example of a self-recording sheet

Name: _____ **Class:** _____

I can help to make flapjack

210

Differentiation

The National Curriculum Council for England and Wales defines differentiation in the curriculum as allowing for differences in the abilities, aptitudes and needs of children, even of the same age (NCC, 1990). This is a central concept in the successful implementation of any national curriculum and in the process of accessing the curriculum to all pupils. It is the aspect of teaching which appears least well practised from our own evidence.

When observed in schools, differentiation tends to be solely on the basis of outcome and rarely on the basis of task, presentation, organisation, physical environment or resources. Some exemplary work has been observed in a document on science for special schools produced by Humberside Local Education Authority (1990) in England, in which true differentiation by task within a range of activities in the science National Curriculum is illustrated. In the example of 'jigsawing' given above, differentiation was provided by giving each pupil different materials. In other examples we have observed, pupils have self-differentiated tasks, pupils allocating themselves or each other different roles within the task.

A key factor associated with effectiveness in the Mortimore *et al.* (1988) study was intellectually challenging teaching. Bennett, in Chapter 7, this volume, has exposed the dangers of presenting tasks for the mythically average child. Careful planning is a skill well established in many special schools but mainly in relation to individuals. Hence, arguably, differentiation should be regarded as no problem in these schools. The basis for differentiation must after all be the accurate assessment of each child's current skills, difficulties and preferred learning styles. However, Bennett found that in both special schools and designated special needs departments in ordinary schools, the assessment practices were the worst of those observed. If these pupils are not to be marginalised, the increasing emphasis in many schools on group work to be balanced with individual work, implies greater attention to differentiation.

Staff development

The brief consideration given above to work on models of staff development suggests the effectiveness of working alongside teachers in schools. Inevitably, this is not a cheap model but the feedback the team have received to date and evidence of changes being implemented in schools following blocks suggests that two weeks in a school may be worth far more than ten days lecturing. While this has been known for some years, the predominant method of staff development remains 'course'-based rather than work-based.

Constraints to reducing marginalisation through curricular initiatives

The major problem currently facing teachers in England and Wales is the sheer volume of change in which they are being expected to participate. Fullan *et al.* (1990) have noted that it is not always resistance to the innovation itself, but the lack of coordination between too many different innovations that results in incoherence, fragmentation and overload. Furthermore, it is clear that current practice prior to recent changes did not reflect what is known to be effective. For example, research on the effectiveness of cooperative group work has been available for a number of years and yet is relatively rarely apparent in teaching strategies adopted in special schools. This may be explained by the predominant attitude still prevailing that these children are different, and effective teaching strategies will not be enough to provide them with the skills they require. Hence, changes in attitude and the establishment of basic instructional skills may need developing in some schools before taking on new demands.

The adequacy of communication between staff in schools has been identified as a key factor in school effectiveness studies (see for example, Evans and Hopkins, 1988; Mortimore *et al.*, 1988). This is a major issue within the schools in which the team has worked. Good communication is hard to establish even with a relatively small staff group but without it innovation is severely hampered.

The problems are exacerbated by a particular feature of special schools: the large number of classroom assistants (not teachers). In schools where assistants outnumber teachers but the national system for provision of inservice training – the Local Education Authority Training Grants Scheme (LEATGS) – has been restricted to teachers, innovation is further limited. How can teachers introduce changes which more than half the staff have not had the opportunity to discuss, understand or contribute to the identification of implementation strategies? If pupils in these schools are not to be marginalised, a system for including assistants in school self-review, development planning and staff development will be needed. A more recent government circular has taken this problem into account (DES 1990a).

Conclusion

The curricular initiatives associated with the introduction of the National Curriculum in England and Wales have provided a context within which the marginalisation of pupils with severe learning difficulties can be challenged. This has been illustrated through examples from the work of the National Curriculum Development Team (Severe Learning Difficulties) which include assisting in the process of broadening the curriculum in special schools, increasing group work through cross curricular activities, exploring collaborative learning and self-recording, encouraging a more flexible approach to differentiation and establishing better use of mainstream resources. In addition, the involvement of special schools in the same processes of self-review and school development planning as all other schools further enhances the sense in which provision for pupils with special educational needs is merely an extension of a continuum of educational opportunities designed to meet the individual needs of every pupil. The factors relating to how effectively any schools can do this remain the focus of much current debate.

More than any other factor, it is the perceived gap between the needs of these pupils and those in mainstream primary or elementary schools that perhaps contributes to the perpetuation of notions of special needs. Yet many people claiming to work specifically with this population considered it in the interests of these children to be dis-applied from the National Curriculum as it was being introduced in England and Wales. It can be argued that since children with severe learning difficulties have only been included in the education system in England and Wales since 1970, it might be somewhat regressive to exclude them at this stage. If the National Curriculum is not appro-priate for these pupils as it stands, then it may be necessary to suggest ways in which it could be revised to meet the needs of all pupils rather than taking pupils out of the system. This is surely implied by an entitlement curriculum and will be a necessary step in ensuring marginalisation is reduced.

Finally, there needs to be a greater commitment to closing the gap between what are known to be effective models of staff development and what is delivered. Several countries are devolving more control of staff development resources directly to schools. This is likely to result in an increase of in-house staff development and training 'on-the-job', which is welcomed. However, special schools are usually relatively small and may need to avoid becoming further marginalised by this process. The trend towards several schools collaborating over development activities appears very positive in this respect. This will need to be accompanied by some method of involving assistants in this process.

References

Aherne, P., Thornber, A., Fagg, S. and Skelton, S. (1990a) *Mathematics for All: An Interactive Approach Within Level 1*. London: David Fulton Publishers.

Aherne, P., Thornber, A., Fagg, S. and Skelton, S. (1990b) *Communication for All: A Cross-curricular Skill Involving Interaction between Speaker and Listener*. London: David Fulton Publishers.

Ashdown, R., Bovair, K. and Carpenter, B. (1990) (Eds) *The Curriculum Challenge: Pupils with Severe Learning Difficulties and the National Curriculum*. London: Falmer Press.

Bray, A., Macarthur, J. and Ballard, K. D. (1988) 'Education for pupils with profound disabilities: issues of policy, curriculum, teaching methods and evaluation', *European Journal of Special Needs Education*, 3:207–24.

Byers, R. (1990) 'Topics: from myths to objectives', *British Journal of Special Education*, 17:109–12.

DES (1989a) *A Survey of Provisions for Pupils with Emotional/Behavioural Difficulties in Maintained Special Schools and Units*, Report by HM Inspectors, London: DES.

DES (1989b) *Educating Physically Disabled Pupils*, Report by HM Inspectors. London: DES.

DES (1989c) *Planning for School Development*. London: HMSO.

DES (1990a) *Special Needs Issues: A Survey by HMI*, Education Observed series. London: HMSO.

DES (1990b) *The Final Report of the History Working Group and its Annexe*. London: HMSO.

Evans, M. and Hopkins, D. (1988) 'School climate and the psychological state of the individual teacher as factors affecting the utilisation of educational ideas following an in-service course', *British Educational Research Journal*, 14:211–30.

Fagg, S., Aherne, P., Skelton, S. and Thornber, A. (1990a) *Entitlement for All in Practice: A Broad, Balanced and Relevant Curriculum for Pupils with Severe and Complex Learning Difficulties in the 1990s*. London: David Fulton Publishers.

Fagg, S., Skelton, S., Aherne, P. and Thornber, A. (1990b) *Science for All: Access to the National Curriculum for Children with Special Needs*. London: David Fulton Publishers.

Fullan, M. (1982) *The Meaning of Educational Change*. New York: Teacher's College Press.

Fullan, M., Bennett, B. and Rolheiser-Bennett, C. (1990) 'Linking classroom and school improvement', *Educational Leadership*, 47:13–19.

214

Hopkins, D. (1989) *Evaluation for School Development*. Milton Keynes: Open University Press.

Howe, L. (1990) *Collins Primary Science*. Glasgow: Collins.

Humberside Local Education Authority (1990) 'Science for special educational needs'. Unpublished Manuscript.

Johnson, D. W. and Johnson, R. T. (1986) *Revised Circles of Learning: Co-operation in the Classroom*. Minnesota: Interaction Book Company.

Joyce, B. and Showers, B. (1988) *Student Achievement Through Staff Development*. New York: Longman.

Longhorn, F. (1988) *A Sensory Curriculum for Very Special People*. London: Souvenir Press.

Mortimore, P., Sammons, P., Stoll, L., Lewis, D. and Ecob, R. (1988) *School Matters*. Wells: Open Books.

NCC (1990) *The National Curriculum: Information Pack No. 2*. York: NCC.

Nind, M. and Hewett, D. (1988) 'Interaction as curriculum', *British Journal of Special Education*, **15**:55-7.

Sebba, J. and Robson, C. (1987) 'The development of short, school-focused INSET courses in special educational needs', *Research Papers in Education*, **2**:3-30.

Showers, B. (1985) 'Teachers coaching teachers', *Educational Leadership*, **42**:43-8.

Showers, B., Joyce, B. and Bennett, B. (1987) 'Synthesis of research on staff development: A framework for future study and a state-of-the-art analysis', *Educational Leadership*, **45**:77-87.

Smith, B. (1987) (Ed.) *Interactive Approaches to the Education of Children with Severe Learning Difficulties*. Birmingham: Westhill College.

Stainback, W. and Stainback, S. (1984) 'A rationale for the merger of special and regular education', *Exceptional Children*, **51**:102-11.

Wang, M., Reynolds, M. C. and Walberg, H. (1986) 'Rethinking special education', *Educational Leadership*, **44**:26-31.

Wood, S. and Shears, B. (1986) *Teaching Children with Severe Learning Difficulties: A Radical Reappraisal*. London: Croom Helm.

CHAPTER 12

Towards Effective Schools for All: Some Problems and Possibilities

Mel Ainscow

In the first part of this concluding chapter I summarise what seem to me to be the key messages that emerge from a study of the work of the contributors to this book. These messages are undoubtedly radical in the sense of the actions that they infer. Consequently they are not simple to implement. The second part of the chapter explores some of the difficulties associated with these proposals and considers some possible ways forward.

The messages

Different orientations are evident in the accounts of the various contributors. Differences exist, for example, with respect to their perceptions of how special needs should be defined, how they occur and how they should be addressed; there are also methodological differences as to how schools should be helped to develop and what are the most effective ways to improve the skills of teachers. Overall, however, I detect a considerable degree of consensus about what should be done to provide effective schooling for all pupils. This in itself is remarkable given that the authors are from different parts of the world and represent different fields of professional interest.

No doubt readers will have made their own conclusions as to what they regard as the most important points. For myself, a series of key messages have emerged that have helped to clarify my own thinking. They are as follows:

(1) Current policies for dealing with special needs in education, based as they often are on child-deficit assumptions about causality, tend to work to the disadvantage of the pupils they are intended to serve.

(2) Progress is dependent upon a recognition that difficulties experienced by pupils come about as a result of the way schools are organised and the forms of teaching that are provided.

(3) Consequently the aim must be to reform schools in ways that will make them responsive to pupil diversity.

(4) Consideration of difficulties experienced by pupils and teachers can provide an agenda for such reforms and insights into how they might be achieved.

(5) This approach is only possible in contexts where there exists a culture of collaboration that encourages and supports problem solving.

(6) Such cultures will facilitate the learning of *all* pupils and teachers.

The implication of this set of arguments is that what we have called special education or, more recently, the field of special needs, should move from being a 'bolt on' activity to become a central element of procedures for school improvement. Consequently it has to become the concern of all those involved in the running of schools rather than the responsibility of special needs specialists.

The logic of this is not new. A number of writers have argued for the amalgamation of regular and special education (e.g. Stainback and Stainback, 1984; Wang *et al.*, 1986). In the United Kingdom there is evidence that some schools have made considerable progress towards this end (Ainscow and Florek, 1989; Ainscow and Muncey, 1989; Bell and Best, 1986; Gilbert and Hart, 1990).

Examining the arguments

Having outlined the key messages I will now explore some of the difficulties associated with them and, in so doing, look for insights as to how progress can be achieved. In this context progress must be defined in terms of steps towards establishing forms of schooling that provide success in learning for all pupils. Implicit in this goal is an aspiration that goes beyond simply providing increased opportunities for participation. In her chapter Margaret Wang emphasises the notion of 'equity'. With this in mind she states:

> Providing opportunities to receive an education without being accountable for ensuring educational outcomes simply perpetuates inequity in a more subtle form. Fundamental to this conception is the principle that standards of educational outcomes must be upheld for every child.

This then has to be our fundamental purpose – improvements in educational outcomes for all pupils. Furthermore, as Tom Skrtic notes in his chapter, 'equity is the way to excellence'.

Developments in the last few years in the special needs field have been consistent with this formulation, particularly at the level of rhetoric. For example, speaking of the situation in England and Wales, my colleague Jim Muncey and I outlined the changes in thinking that had been apparent since the publication of the Warnock Report in 1978 (Ainscow and Muncey, 1989). Pre-Warnock thinking, we suggest, was characterised by an emphasis on placing children in categories in order to provide care that tended to be given in segregated settings. This came about as a result of those within the education service accepting the following *assumptions*:

(a)   A group of children can be identified who are different from the majority.
(b)   Only this relatively small group needs special help.
(c)   The problems of these children are as a result of their disabilities or personal limitations.
(d)   Special help can best be provided when separate groups of children with common problems are taught together.
(e)   Once such a group has been provided for, the rest of the school population can be regarded as 'normal'.

Consequently, special and remedial education was geared to the identification of particular groups of children thought to have similar problems in order to provide some form of positive discrimination. For some this meant placement in a special school or unit; for many others extra help was provided by withdrawal from lessons in order to provide specialist teaching.

In the post-Warnock era, however, the style has been gradually changing, at least at the level of rhetoric. What we have seen are moves towards approaches that place emphasis on responding to children as individuals through the normal curriculum within contexts characterised by a strong sense of collaboration. This is based upon an acceptance of the Warnock argument that greater numbers of children experience difficulties in the school system than was previously recognised. It is also clear that most of these children are already in ordinary schools. Furthermore, there is a lobby for educating youngsters with more severe learning difficulties in the mainstream. The *assumptions* behind this new thinking are as follows:

(i)   Any child may experience difficulties in school at some stage in their schooling.

(ii) Help and support must be available to all pupils as necessary.

(iii) Educational difficulties result from an interaction between what the child brings to the situation and what the school has to offer.

(iv) Teachers should take responsibility for the progress of all the children in their classes.

(v) Support must be available to staff as they attempt to meet their responsibilities.

As a result, recent years have seen a reduction of emphasis on trying to find out what is wrong with children. Instead attention is focused on making the curriculum offered to all children more responsive to the needs of individuals. In other words, there has been an attempt to move away from what might be called a deficit model towards a curriculum-based model for dealing with special educational needs.

Despite attempts to move in this direction in order to achieve better educational outcomes for all pupils, progress has tended to be disappointing. Throughout this book the case has been made that one of the significant reasons for this poor progress has been the continued emphasis on explaining educational difficulties in terms of pupil-centred causes. This perspective appears to dominate the educational services of many countries and, as a result, acts as a barrier to well-intended attempts at reform. The situation is summed up by Dyson (1990a, pp. 64–5) when he states:

> ... the fact remains that the education system as a whole, and the vast majority of institutions and teachers within it, are approaching the twenty-first century with a view of special needs the same as that with which their counterparts approached the present century. That view, for all its avowed concern for the individual child, promotes injustice on a massive scale. It demands to be changed.

The argument for more resources

Associated with the deficit orientation is a tendency to conceptualise responses to special needs solely in terms of a need for additional resources. In fact, this is a complex issue. Resources are undoubtedly important and schools in many countries would benefit from increased investment. Commonsense would argue that better buildings, more equipment and books, smaller classes and teachers with good skills and high morale must be to the advantage of all pupils. However, seeing the issue of special needs as being dependent on further resources seems to have a negative impact, not least in terms of its capacity to demoralise teachers. This process has been explained with considerable insight by Roger Slee in his chapter, particularly with respect to the distinction he draws between comprehensive schooling and apprehensive schooling.

This analysis of the impact of schools arguing for more resources before they can respond positively to pupils regarded as being special is supported by evidence from a number of other countries (Fulcher, 1989).

A further outcome of the more-resources argument has been an *increase* in the numbers of pupils that become categorised in order that they can be provided with additional help. This is a paradox of policies that are established with the intention of providing integrated provision for pupils with special needs – they often seem to lead to an increase in the numbers of pupils placed in categories of exclusion. This also appears to be an international phenomenon. For example, Roger Slee refers to the introduction of what he describes as 'new integration students' in Australia. Officially these young people are referred to as students with problems in schooling. Fulcher (1989, p. 247) identifies similar trends in a number of countries, not least in England as a result of the Warnock Report and the 1981 Education Act. She notes:

> ... the report is about 20 per cent of the school population or one in five children seen as likely to have special educational needs at some stage in their school lives. While the notion of special educational needs was presented as a non-categorical approach to providing special education services the phrase retains the politics of a traditional discourse on disability and is ultimately defined as disability .... It is of course an extraordinarily political act to infer 20 per cent of the school population have an impairment but this is the political logic underlying the notion of special educational needs.

Evidence from the United States points to even greater moves to create new categories of exclusion (Anderson and Pellicer, 1990). Indeed, Ysseldyke *et al.* (1983) suggest that approximately 80 per cent of all school children can be classified as learning disabled by one or more of the procedures currently used in the USA.

I should add from my own experience that these trends are likely to have a continuing impact upon the evolution of policies in developing countries. Often, those who are influential in the construction of such policies are guided by what they see happening in Western countries (Miles, 1989).

220

The role of special educators

A further factor in the maintenance of the status quo in some contexts is the attitudes of the special education community. Special needs specialists, local authority advisers, special school staff and educational psychologists can, through their actions, encourage the continuation of traditional responses. In her account of developments in Halton, for example, Louise Stoll makes reference to the reluctance of some staff to change their approaches.

It does seem to me that the notion of the 'expert' in the special needs field has had a negative impact upon the confidence of teachers in ordinary schools to respond to pupils they perceive as being difficult. The existence of such experts reinforces the idea that what is required is specialist teaching techniques that cannot be used by most teachers. My colleague David Tweddle and I suggested another aspect of this issue in our book *Encouraging Classroom Success*:

> Many of those who have come to be regarded as experts in the special needs field (and the authors of this book are striking examples of this) have done very well out of encouraging this type of thinking. Our careers have developed very successfully as a result of the widespread belief that we are able to use techniques that are not generally available (Ainscow and Tweddle, 1988, p. 72).

Any attempts at development must, therefore, address these dilemmas. In particular they must pay attention to the following factors:

(1) The need to help all teachers, including those who have specialist roles, to move away from deficit models of thinking.
(2) The need to provide support for specialist staff as they seek to make sense of new thinking and develop the skills necessary in order that they can adopt new ways of working.
(3) The importance of managing the process of change in ways that protect the interests of those pupils who remain vulnerable to the inadequacies of the current system.

This third point is very important and creates painful dilemmas for specialist staff as they seek to encourage school-wide developments. In management terms these difficulties are part of what has been characterised as a maintenance-development dilemma that seems to be typical of contexts attempting the development of new policies (West and Ainscow, 1991). In the case of our discussion about special needs policies the issues become particularly difficult since errors of judgement may well leave children and teachers as the victims.

Root and branch developments

John Clarke's use of the metaphor of root and branch to explain the nature of the changes that are necessary in order to make more schools effective for all pupils is, I think, particularly illuminating. Allowing the metaphor to guide us we can see many attempts to provide positive discrimination for pupils with special needs as branch changes. Their limited success can be explained by the fact that they have little or no impact upon the root culture of the schools in which they are introduced. Indeed at times they may run counter to the school's overall culture, thus leading to conflict and tension between members of staff. Somehow we have to find ways of redirecting the energies of the special needs community in ways that give attention to the root culture, including a school's organisation, curriculum, methods of teaching and procedures for assessment. In this respect the suggestions made by Jacqueline Thousand and Richard Villa in their chapter about dropping professional labels and redefining professional roles in order to establish collaborative teams are particularly relevant. Further evidence of schools that have made progress in this direction is available in the literature (e.g. Ainscow and Florek, 1989; Ainscow and Muncey, 1989; Bell and Best, 1986; Dyson, 1990b; Gilbert and Hart, 1990; Redpath, 1989) and we would be wise to learn from these successes.

The need for an emphasis on increased collaboration as a basis for more effective schools for all is central to many of the recommendations made in this book. In Chapter 1, I indicate some of the difficulties associated with attempts to establish such a culture in schools, particularly in communities where there is a strong belief that increased competition is the way to improve educational standards.

Andy Hargreaves (cited in Fullan, 1990) suggests the following typology for considering school cultures: fragmented individualism, Balkanisation, contrived collegiality and true collaboration. Too often schools are characterised by the first two of these styles: fragmented individualism, whereby teachers work in isolation, or, in larger schools, Balkanisation in which sub-groups of staff may be in competition when major decisions or actions are necessary. However, Hargreaves also points to the potential dangers of contrived collegiality that may involve a proliferation of unwanted contacts among teachers that consume scarce time with little to show for it. Rather, what we should seek are true collaborative cultures that are 'deep, personal and enduring'. They are not, he argues, 'mounted just for specific projects or events. They are not strings of one-shot deals.

Cultures of collaboration rather are, constitutive of, absolutely central to, teachers' daily work'.

A further worry about moves towards increased collaboration in schools concerns the notion of 'groupthink', as defined by Janis (1982). This involves a 'psychological drive for consensus at any cost that suppresses disagreement and prevents the appraisal of alternatives in cohesive decision-making groups'. Janis suggests that groupthink can lead members to overestimate the power and morality of the group, closed-mindedness, and pressure towards uniformity. More specifically, this may involve decision-making processes that are characterised by the following symptoms:

- incomplete survey of alternatives
- incomplete survey of objectives
- failure to examine risks of preferred choice
- failure to reappraise initially rejected alternatives
- poor information search
- selective bias in processing information at hand
- failure to work out contingency plans.

Clearly such features would be inconsistent with the idea of schools as problem-solving organisations that encourage reflective thinking amongst teachers and pupils in a school. They indicate, therefore, the need to develop forms of collaboration that respect the need for independent thought and creativity.

The aim, therefore, is the radical reform of schooling, but reform undertaken in ways that minimise the risks to both pupils and teachers. The extensive research evidence with respect to attempts at change in education indicates that things seem to go wrong quite often during attempts to introduce changes in educational contexts, particularly during the early stages (e.g. Fullan, 1982, 1985; Holly, 1986; Huberman and Miles, 1984; Miles and Louis, 1990). This literature also indicates that successful innovations tend to be sophisticated in terms of their attention to the processes of introduction, implementation, support and evaluation, and that this has to be sustained over considerable periods of time. The nature of this argument is well illustrated in this book by the work of Stoll, Reynolds, Wang, Thousand and Villa, and Joyce and his colleagues.

An indication of the sorts of problems experienced by change projects is provided by Pink (cited in Fullan, 1990). His review of a number of initiatives found that the following barriers to innovation were common to them all:

(1) An inadequate theory of implementation, including too little time for teachers to plan for and learn new skills and practices.
(2) District tendencies toward faddism and quick-fix solutions.
(3) Lack of sustained central office support and follow-through.
(4) Underfunding the project, or trying to do too much with too little support.
(5) Attempting to manage the projects from the central office instead of developing school leadership and capacity.
(6) Lack of technical assistance and other forms of intensive staff development.
(7) Lack of awareness of the limitations of teacher and school administrator knowledge about how to implement the project.
(8) The turnover of teachers in each school.
(9) Too many competing demands or overload.
(10) Failure to address the incompatibility between project requirements and existing organisational policies and structures.
(11) Failure to understand and take into account site-specific differences among schools.
(12) Failure to clarify and negotiate the role relationships and partnerships involving the district and local university – who in each case had a role, albeit unclarified, in the project.

The list will, I suspect, sound familiar to those readers who have experienced school improvement initiatives that have got into difficulty. It points to the wide range of factors that have a bearing on schools and teachers as they attempt change in a context where day-to-day duties have to be given priority. Consequently, we must not underestimate the difficulties that face attempts at school reform. In seeking to change school cultures we are proposing what is probably the most difficult challenge of all. Often it will require changes in thinking and practice at all levels within a school and, perhaps, at all levels within a school system. Fulcher (1989, p. 265) explains the importance of recognising that policy is created at different levels within a system in her account of how policies for integration have been introduced in a number of countries. She concludes:

> The observation that schools, including teachers, make their own policy practices, and that teachers are highly powerful policy makers . . . accords with commonsense knowledge and observation. But of course that happens.

This being the case we must not fall into the trap of minimising the potential for *individuals* within a school to lead, inspire, encourage or support policies for improvement. Indeed, this is a further argument for collaborative cultures that do not restrict individual enterprise.

224

Changing school cultures

What, then, is the best way forward? How can we act positively to change school culture without creating further damage for pupils and teachers? In a recent paper Joyce (1990) suggests that there are a number of possible 'doors' into the culture of a school. He suggests these are as follows:

(1) *Building synergy in the faculty community*: developing cohesive and professional relationships within school faculties.
(2) *Presenting research*: helping school faculties study research findings about effective schooling practices or instructional alternatives.
(3) *Generating site specific information*: helping faculties collect and analyse data about their schools and the progress of their students.
(4) *Initiating curricular and technological change*: introducing curricula within curriculum areas or, as in the case of the computer, across the curriculum areas.
(5) *Inducing the study of instruction*: organising teachers to study teaching skills and strategies.

He notes that the 'doors open onto interlocking passageways within the culture of the school and starting at one place does not prevent effect on the others and is, in fact, hoped for'. My own view is that an emphasis on staff development of certain kinds may well be the best door in many instances. If I reflect on the more successful projects I have been involved in they share a strong element of staff development (Ainscow, 1991). In this context I am using the term 'staff development' to include a range of processes and activities by which teachers can be helped and can help one another to develop their practice.

Looking back at my own experience I note a number of common features of those initiatives where staff development has had positive effects on the practice of teachers and the progress of pupils. These are:

(1) The emphasis has been on developments in the context of particular schools and including classroom-based staff development activities.
(2) They have been conducted in ways that have encouraged collaboration between colleagues.
(3) At various stages particular individuals adopted key roles of leadership and coordination.
(4) Timing was important in the sense that changes in practice always seem to take longer than anticipated.
(5) Continued support for individuals is crucial as they wrestle with new ideas and attempt to develop their classroom practice.

In other words the evidence from my experience is that staff development is only successful when it begins to intrude into the deeper culture of a school.

In a very helpful paper Fullan (1990) has recently examined the role of staff development as it relates to innovation and institutional development. He suggests that staff development can be seen in one of three ways and these are:

- as a strategy for the implementation of innovations
- as an innovation in its own right
- as institutional development.

He concludes that whilst the first two perspectives are useful for certain limited purposes, only the third approach has the potential to make continuing staff development and improvement a way of life in a school. It is through this third perspective that true collaborative cultures of the sort argued for by the contributors to this book can be developed.

Fullan and his colleagues have developed this idea further by linking together ideas and evidence from a number of fields into a framework for analysis and action (Fullan *et al.*, 1989). He sees this as a metaphor that involves a series of interconnected cogs that have the capacity to turn one another around and, in so doing, create the conditions for school and classroom improvement.

The first set of cogs is concerned with *school improvement*. For schools to improve, Fullan and his colleagues argue, they need to have the following cogs at work:

(1) A shared purpose.
(2) Norms of collegiality.
(3) Norms of continuous improvement.
(4) Structure that represents the necessary conditions for significant improvement.

The second set of cogs relate to *classroom improvement*. They consist of:

(1) Content.
(2) Classroom management.
(3) Instructional skills.
(4) Instructional strategies.

When these four cogs function in partnership the capacity to provide classroom environments that promote learning is significantly increased.

Linking these two sets of cogs is the idea of *teachers as learners*. Once again this idea has four aspects that need to be seen in combination since each has an important contribution to make. These are:

(1)   Mastery of *technical skills* that increase instructional certainty.
(2)   *Reflective practice* that enhances clarity, meaning and coherence.
(3)   *Inquiry* in order to foster investigation and explanation.
(4)   *Collaboration* in order to receive and give ideas and assistance.

Fullan suggests that the driving factors for this complex framework should be student engagement and learning as a pervasive pre-occupation, and leadership and mobilisation. He notes that 'Leadership can, does, and must come from a variety of different sources in different situations (and different sources in the same situation over time)' (Fullan, 1990).

I find this explanation to be helpful, exciting and, at the same time, daunting. For me it links together so many proposals outlined by the contributors to this book. It maps out the broad territory that needs to be addressed if the collaborative culture necessary for improvement in a school is to be achieved. It also illustrates graphically the inadequacy of the traditional agenda of special education, with its emphasis on the progress of individual pupils without reference to the wider context within which the pupil exists.

The message is clear, therefore. Those of us who have spent our careers trapped in the narrow alleyway of special education have to become part of the wider educational environment and allow the perspectives of those in that environment to inform our thinking and practice.

In this context we have potentially important roles to play. Our experience and expertise can contribute to the improvement of schooling for all pupils. Indeed our focus on the development of individual pupils can provide understandings that can help facilitate such improvements. There is a rich literature that indicates the value of using observation of pupils in classrooms as the basis for improving policy and practice: Rowland's (1984) observation of classroom processes in a primary school; Hull's (1985) examination of the problems of communication experienced by pupils in secondary schools; Mongon and Hart's (1989) approach to problem behaviour as a basis for improving curriculum and organisation; and Hanko's (1989) idea of joint problem-solving, are all excellent accounts of how reflecting on the difficulties experienced in classrooms can lead to significant improvement. Accounts by practitioners adopting this perspective are also provided in Ainscow (1989) and Booth *et al.* (1987).

Conclusion

The suggestions made in this book provide a rich source of ideas that can be used to develop more effective forms of schooling that will be of benefit to all pupils and teachers. Much of the evidence that supports reforms along these lines is not new and the arguments are well established. They point to the need for urgent actions by all those who are interested in the future of schools and believe in the value of education. More particularly, they indicate the need for those of us who have made our careers in the special needs field to reconsider our perspectives once more and act accordingly.

References

Ainscow, M. (1989) (Ed.) *Special Education in Change*. London: David Fulton Publishers.
Ainscow, M. (1991) 'Becoming a reflective teacher', in Booth, T. *et al.* (Eds) *Learning for All* (Vol. 1). Milton Keynes: Open University.
Ainscow, M. and Florek, A. (1989) (Eds) *Special Educational Needs: Towards a Whole School Approach*. London: David Fulton Publishers.
Ainscow, M. and Muncey, J. (1989) *Meeting Individual Needs in the Primary School*. London: David Fulton Publishers.
Ainscow, M. and Tweddle, D. A. (1988) *Encouraging Classroom Success*. London: David Fulton Publishers.
Anderson, L. W. and Pellicer, L. O. (1990) 'Synthesis of research on compensatory and remedial education', *Educational Leadership*, **48**,1:10–16.
Bell, P. and Best, R. (1986) *Supportive Education*. Oxford: Blackwell.
Booth, T., Potts, P. and Swan, W. (1987) (Eds) *Preventing Difficulties in Learning: Curricula for All*. Oxford: Blackwell.
Dyson, A. (1990a) 'Special educational needs and the concept of change', *Oxford Review of Education*, **16**,1:55–66.
Dyson, A. (1990b) 'Effective learning consultancy: A future role for special needs coordinators,' *Support for Learning*, **5**,3:116–27.
Fulcher, G. (1989) *Disabling Policies? A Comparative Approach to Education Policy and Disability*. London: Falmer Press.
Fullan, M. (1982) *The Meaning of Educational Change*. New York: Teachers College Press.
Fullan, M. (1985) 'Change processes and strategies at the local level', *The Elementary School Journal*, **85**,3:391–420.
Fullan, M. (1990) 'Staff development, innovation and institutional development,' in Joyce, B. (Ed.) *Changing School Culture Through Staff Development*. Alexander, VA: Association for Supervision and Curriculum Development Yearbook.
Fullan, M., Bennett, B. and Rolheiser-Bennett, C. (1990) 'Linking classroom and school improvement', *Educational Leadership*, **47**,8:13–19.
Gilbert, C. and Hart, M. (1990) *Towards Integration: Special Needs in an Ordinary School*. London: Kogan Page.

228

Hanko, G. (1989) 'After Elton – how to "manage" disruption', *British Journal of Special Education*, **16**,4:140–43.

Holly, P. (1986) '"Soaring like turkeys" – the impossible dream?', *School Organisation*, **6**, 3:346–64.

Huberman, A. M. and Miles, M. B. (1984) *Innovation Up Close: How School Improvement Works*. New York: Plenum.

Hull, R. (1985) *The Language Gap*. London: Methuen.

Janis, I. L. (1982) *Groupthink: Psychological Studies of Policy Decisions and Fiascoes*. Boston: Houghton Mifflin.

Joyce, B. (1990) 'The structures of restructuring: The doors to school improvement'. Booksend Laboratories, Aptos, California. Unpublished paper.

Miles, M. (1989) 'The role of special education in information based rehabilitation', *International Journal of Special Education*, **4**,2:111–18.

Miles, M. B. and Louis, K. S. (1990) 'Mustering the will and skill for change', *Educational Leadership*, **47**,8:57–61.

Mongon, D. and Hart, S. (1989) *Improving Classroom Behaviour*. London: Cassell.

Redpath, A. (1989) 'How to help the ship along: An evaluation of effective support teaching', in Ainscow, M. (Ed.) *Special Education in Change*. London: David Fulton Publishers.

Rowland, S. (1984) *The Enquiring Classroom*. London: Falmer Press.

Stainback, W. and Stainback, S. (1984) 'A rationale for the merger of special and regular education', *Exceptional Children*, **51**:102–11.

Wang, M. C., Reynolds, M. C. and Walberg, H. J. (1986) 'Rethinking special education', *Educational Leadership*, **44**:26–31.

Ysseldyke, J. E., Thurlow, M., Graden, J., Wesson, C., Deno, S. and Algozzine, B. (1983) 'Generalisations from five years of research on assessment and decision making', *Exceptional Educational Quarterly*, **4**,1:75–93.

West, M. and Ainscow, M. (1991) *Managing School Development: A Practical Guide*. London: David Fulton Publishers.

Index